HOW WE COMPETE

THE MIT INDUSTRIAL PERFORMANCE CENTER RESEARCH TEAM

Akintunde (Tayo) Akinwande, *Professor of Electrical Engineering and Computer Science*

Marcos Ancelovici

Suzanne Berger, *Raphael Dorman–Helen Starbuck Professor of Political Science*

Dan Breznitz

Edward Cunningham

Douglas B. Fuller

Richard K. Lester, *Professor of Nuclear Engineering and Director, Industrial Performance Center*

Teresa Lynch

Sara Jane McCaffrey

Charles G. Sodini, *Professor of Electrical Engineering and Computer Science*

Edward S. Steinfeld, *Associate Professor of Political Science*

Timothy J. Sturgeon, *Research Associate, Industrial Performance Center*

Eric Thun, *Assistant Professor of Politics, Princeton University*

HOW WE COMPETE

WHAT COMPANIES AROUND THE WORLD ARE DOING TO MAKE IT IN TODAY'S GLOBAL ECONOMY

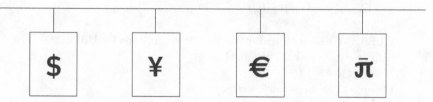

SUZANNE BERGER

AND THE MIT INDUSTRIAL PERFORMANCE CENTER

CURRENCY

DOUBLEDAY

New York   London   Toronto   Sydney   Auckland

A CURRENCY BOOK
PUBLISHED BY DOUBLEDAY
a division of Random House, Inc.

CURRENCY is a trademark of Random House, Inc., and DOUBLEDAY is a
registered trademark of Random House, Inc.

Copyright 2005 by Suzanne Berger

Cataloging-in-Publication Data is on file with the Library of Congress.
ISBN: 0-385-51359-3

Book design by Tina Henderson

All Rights Reserved

PRINTED IN THE UNITED STATES OF AMERICA

First Edition: January 2006
All trademarks are the property of their respective companies.

SPECIAL SALES
Currency Books are available at special discounts for bulk purchases for sales
promotions or premiums. Special editions, including personalized covers,
excerpts of existing books, and corporate imprints, can be created in large
quantities for special needs. For more information, write to Special Markets,
Currency Books, specialmarkets@randomhouse.com.
10 9 8 7 6 5 4 3 2 1

In memory of our colleague Michael L. Dertouzos
1936–2001

His leadership in *Made in America* continues to bear fruit.
His vision of technology joined to social well-being
continues to inspire.

Contents

Acknowledgments   ix

A Reader's Guide to a Few Unfamiliar Terms   xiii

PART ONE: A World of Opportunity and Danger   1

CHAPTER 1: Who's Afraid of Globalization?   3

CHAPTER 2: A Preview of the MIT Globalization Study   29

PART TWO: The "Lego" Model of Production   57

CHAPTER 3: Breaking Up the Corporation   59

CHAPTER 4: The New American Model   73

PART THREE: Made All Over   91

CHAPTER 5: The Dilemma: Should You Stay or
Should You Go?   93

CHAPTER 6: Making It Cheaper   113

PART FOUR: Competing in a Modular World   137

CHAPTER 7: Tracking Strategies from the Grass Roots Up   139

CHAPTER 8: Brand-Name Firms, No-Name Manufacturers,
and Everything in Between   **165**

PART FIVE: Make It at Home? Or Offshore?   **199**
CHAPTER 9: Made in America?   **201**
CHAPTER 10: Building on a Legacy at Home   **229**

PART SIX: How to Succeed in the Global Economy   **249**
CHAPTER 11: Lessons from the Field   **251**
CHAPTER 12: Beyond the Company   **278**

Notes   **299**
Index   **325**

Acknowledgments

How We Compete draws on research that thirteen of us at the Industrial Performance Center at MIT carried out in 1999–2004. Thirteen names cannot fit on a book cover, but we are together the authors of these ideas and conclusions. At the end, though, one of us had the task of converting the research and the insights we had accumulated over the life of the project into this book, and I am responsible for it, as well as for any mistakes. Along the way, many others were generous colleagues on our five-year journey into the global economy. In addition to those MIT students listed as team members, we also benefited from the help of Thomas Becker, Shiri Breznitz, Zachary Cahn, Jean Charroin, John-Paul Ferguson, Brian Hanson, Llewelyn Hughes, and Georgeta Vidican. Brad Buschur's ingenuity and intelligence as a research assistant demonstrated that almost any fact worth knowing can be extracted from the Web. Through good times and bad, Anita Kafka shepherded the researchers, their declining resources, and their rising mountain of data. This was the dream team.

We thank MIT colleagues Frank Levy, Richard Locke, and Michael Piore for help throughout the study. No act of kindness matters more to a writer than a friendly reader's detailed, idea-by-idea critique. For this, I am grateful to Arnaldo Camuffo (University of Padova), Peter Gourevitch (University of California, San Diego), and Richard Samuels (MIT), who offered penetrating suggestions and encouragement. The team is indebted to colleagues outside the United States for much we have learned in collaborative projects running in parallel with the Globalization Study: to Volker Wittke, Uli Voskamp, and Michael Faust at the Soziologisches Forschungsinstitut (SOFI) in Goettingen, Germany, with whom we are collaborating in joint research supported by the Volkswagen Foundation; to Jun Kurihara, Kennedy School, Harvard University, for research supported by the Fujitsu Research Institute; to Christel Lane, Simon Learmount, and Jocelyn Probert at the University of Cambridge, in joint research supported by the Cambridge-MIT Institute (CMI); and to Zhao Chunjun, dean of the School of Economics and Management, Tsinghua University, Beijing, People's Republic of China, who introduced us to the dynamic Chinese companies in Zhejiang Province. In addition to the institutions that backed the international collaborations, the Alfred P. Sloan Foundation, the Taiwan Ministry of Economic Affairs, and the Chinese National Federation of Industries (Taiwan) were generous funders of the Industrial Performance Center Globalization Study.

Finally, the book owes everything to the hundreds of busy executives who agreed to interviews that took hours of their time. Some—like John Glidden at L. W. Packard and Chikara Hayashi at Ulvac—met with us repeatedly over the years of the research. They showed us their factories, introduced us to their managers and suppliers, and patiently walked us through the details of the thousands of day-to-day decisions that add up to a strategy for globalization. When I asked for permission to name names and use direct quotes, most of them saw why an unvarnished account that describes failures as well as successes is useful—and they agreed.

This report on globalization in the trenches is itself a product of the very same processes it studies. The manuscript was acquired by Roger Scholl, editorial director of Currency Doubleday, an imprint within an American division of Random House, located in New York City, and owned by Bertelsmann, whose headquarters are in Guetersloh, Germany. Sarah Rainone of Currency Doubleday edited the manuscript, which was then contracted out to Chris Fortunato of Fortunato Book Packaging (Pearl River, New York), who was responsible for coordinating the design, copyediting, typesetting, proofreading and indexing. Tina Henderson of Metairie, Louisiana, was the designer and compositor of the book. The book was copyedited by Peter Grennen, who lives in Bow, New Hampshire, and the index was created by Charlee Trantino, who lives in Harvey's Lake, Pennsylvania. The text was printed and bound by Berryville Graphics in Berryville, Virginia; the book's jacket was designed by Michael Windsor of Doubleday, and printed by Coral Graphics of Hicksville, New York. Prior to its delivery to booksellers throughout the United States, the book will be stored in the Random House Warehouse in Westminster, Maryland. But I cannot tell who sold you the book. Let me know—so we can reconstruct the last link in the value chain that stretched from the glimmer in the mind of MIT researchers into your hands: http://www.howwecompete.com. You will also find more facts and figures about the Globalization Study on this Web site, along with working papers from the project and information about the ongoing research.

A Reader's Guide
to a Few Unfamiliar Terms

CM: contract manufacturer; a company (like an ODM or OEM or EMS, see below definitions) that manufactures on order for a lead or brand firm but has no brands of its own.

EMS: electronics manufacturing services contract manufacturers.

DRAM: semiconductor memory. Dynamic random access memory.

Fab: short for fabrication factory; a silicon-wafer-manufacturing plant that makes semiconductor chips out of raw silicon wafers.

Global supplier: large specialist contract manufacturer—for example, Flextronics.

IC: integrated circuit. An electronic circuit containing various electronic devices such as transistors, resistors, and capacitors fabricated on a single semiconductor substrate. They are often called chips. Printed circuit boards (PCBs) are generally made of layers of epoxy (not silicon) with metal wires embedded to create circuits. So they are "circuit boards" but not ICs. ICs and other chips are mounted on PCBs.

IDM: integrated device manufacturer; companies that make integrated circuits—for example, Intel.

Manufacturer: in most industries, the company that does physical production of goods. In apparel, though, manufacturer has come to mean the company that designs and markets clothes—frequently also the owner of a brand, and sometimes the owner of the goods being processed (fabric, trim).

Maquiladora: companies in Mexico that process or assemble inputs shipped from the United States (usually) and exported (usually) to the United States.

MNC: multinational corporation; one that owns and operates facilities in more than one country.

Modularity: a term used here to describe the technological and organizational possibilities for breaking apart a production system that might once have been contained within a vertically integrated company and having independent companies carry out these functions.

ODM: original design manufacturer; a company that does designs and manufacturing for brand-name firms. An ODM does not have its own brand. The ODMs are doing more and more design (in contrast to the OEMs).

OEM: original equipment manufacturer; a company that makes products on order or for sale to brand-name firms. An OEM does not have its own brand or develop new designs. OEMs are also called contract manufacturers.

PC: personal computer.

Pure play: a business carrying out one function with no brand name. It's used mainly to describe pure-play semiconductor foundries, which make silicon chips for multiple customers but do not design the chips or make products using them.

Vertical integration: a vertically integrated company is one that brings together under its ownership and management a wide range of different functions, such as the idea for a product, design, development, manufacturing, distribution, sales, and after-sales services—for example, Samsung.

PART ONE

A World of Opportunity and Danger

CHAPTER 1

Who's Afraid of Globalization?

Globalization means a world of opportunity and a world of danger. We rush to Wal-Mart for the basics, but we know that many of them are made in China or some other low-wage country. We want low prices at Best Buy and Circuit City on digital cameras and flat-panel TVs, but we fear that our good fortune as consumers costs jobs at home. We like to be able to place orders on the telephone twenty-four hours a day, but when we hear strange accents on the other end of the line, we wonder where on earth the operator sits. We realize when we think about it that the rise out of poverty of more than 2 billion Chinese and Indians must be good for the world; we question whether it's good for us. We celebrate the fact that American success is built on innovation and rising productivity, but we wonder whether the new technologies and products will create enough jobs and if our children will live as well as we do. Surveys in the United States and Europe find very mixed opinions about globalization, often reflecting these conflicting feelings within individuals themselves, rather than simply the rifts between supporters and opponents of globalization. A majority of Americans and Europeans think globalization raises their standard of living; a majority also believe that it is bad for employment and job security.[1]

For the questions about who wins and who loses in the new global economy and the uncertainties about whether the opportunities are worth the risks, there is no one right answer. People disagree about definitions of globalization, its causes, and its consequences. Many simply wonder whether any job in America is safe. By mid-2004, about 1,000 stories a month on outsourcing and offshoring were appearing in the U.S. print media, with such titles as "Is Your Job Going Abroad?"(*Time*, March 1, 2004), "Is Your Job Next?"(*BusinessWeek*, February 3, 2003), and "Is Your Job Coming to India? Get Used to It" (William Pesek Jr., Bloomberg.com, October 5, 2004).[2] One consulting firm predicted in September 2003 that 1.4 million American jobs would move overseas over the next twelve years, and that the real wages of 80 percent of the population would fall.[3] But a McKinsey study conducted a month earlier concluded that offshoring jobs was a "win-win" for both the United States and developing countries like India, as many low-skilled jobs would move overseas, raising incomes there, and U.S. firms would become more productive and profitable and better able to expand higher value-added operations at home.[4] Despite their optimism, however, McKinsey researchers did acknowledge that 55 percent of those reemployed after losing a job because of import competition or offshoring end up earning less than 85 percent of their old wages in the new job. Many take even bigger pay and benefit cuts.

Other studies claim that outsourcing low-end jobs leads to more job creation at home. Matthew Slaughter, an economist at Dartmouth, analyzed government data on U.S. multinational corporations and found that for every job offshored, a company created almost two in the United States.[5] Catherine Mann at The Brookings Institution showed that by lowering the cost of information hardware, production abroad has raised U.S. productivity and generated $230 billion of additional GDP between 1995 and 2002. Furthermore, an open economy in which U.S. companies can create jobs abroad is also one in which foreign companies can create jobs in the United States. Between 1986 and 2001, the number of jobs that foreign businesses established in the United States actually doubled, while the number that moved offshore grew only by 56 percent. The private services work (like legal services, programming, banking, and consulting) that the United States sells to foreigners exceeds by over $50 billion the services Americans buy from foreign companies.[6] Similar findings are reported for Europe. Oxford University researchers found that while U.K. companies are buying more services from firms abroad, U.K. exports of business services have grown even faster.[7]

Mainstream economists like Alan Greenspan, the chairman of the Federal Reserve Board, and N. Gregory Mankiw, former chairman of the Council of Economic Advisors, assure the public that outsourcing work raises productivity and the standard of living in the United States. Free trade, they argue, ultimately creates more and better jobs in the United States than it destroys. Historically, Mankiw explained, innovation has always generated good new employment opportunities:

> It is hard to predict what changes American ingenuity will bring to the U.S. economy. For example, over the past half century, new technology has led to great advances in farm productivity. As a result, the number of Americans working on farms has declined from almost 20 percent of the workforce in 1940 to about 2 percent today. In 1940, no one could have predicted that some of the grandchildren of farmers would become website designers and CAT scan operators. But they did, and at much higher wages and incomes.[8]

The economists base their optimism about globalization and jobs on standard trade theories of comparative advantage. These theories predict that as developing countries with large populations move into activities that use a lot of unskilled and semiskilled labor, the United States and other advanced countries will gain advantage in activities requiring more intensive use of capital and well-educated workers. Some of these neo-classical economists now, however, are having second thoughts. Paul Samuelson, Nobel Prize-winning economist at MIT known for his contributions to modern trade theory, published an article in fall 2004 in which he shows how even skilled workers in the advanced countries could lose out as China upgrades its economy.[9] Globalization *should* increase the world's total income and its average standard of living, but there's no reason to think that any particular country or region's advances will outweigh its losses. As Samuelson points out, worldwide gains will only be "cold comfort" for losers.

Some think that in an open global economy, government can no longer regulate or buffer citizens against strong economic tides of change. In *The Borderless World* (1990), one of the first books on globalization, Kenichi Ohmae, a well-known management consultant, claimed that "[the global economy] is becoming so powerful that it has swallowed most consumers and corporations, made traditional national borders almost disappear, and pushed bureaucrats, politicians, and the military toward the status of declining industries."[10] Thomas Friedman, the *New York Times* op-ed writer, describes globalization as a race of Formula One cars.[11] If you're worried about drivers smashing into the walls, you can give them driving lessons and improve the skills of the ambulance technicians. But, says Friedman, you can't put bales of straw around the walls of the racetrack to buffer the accidents without ruining the race. "If you don't want to do all these things, then you should forget about Formula One racing and become a jogger. But be careful, because as a jogger in this world you will be run over by a Formula One Car."

Ohmae and Friedman are enthusiastic about globalization's impact in shrinking the role of government in the economy, thereby allowing people to develop their talents without hindrance from the bureaucracy. Critics of globalization, though, see a world "running out of control toward some sort of abyss."[12] They regard the World Trade Organization, the International Monetary Fund, the World Bank, the G8 summits, and the Davos World Economic Forum as arms of multinational capitalism: institutions bound on destroying the safety nets that once cushioned economies, rather than organizations working to moderate and regulate the international system. Starting with the huge demonstrations against the World Trade Organization in Seattle in 1999, massive protests against globalization have been mounted at virtually every important international meeting. At Seattle, the "turtle and Teamster" alliance of environmentalists and union members showed the glimmerings of a new politics building on anxieties about the global economy.

In countries around the world today, political movements are organizing around these issues. Politicians have climbed on the bandwagon, too. In the U.S. 2004 presidential election campaign, Democrats accused managers who offshore jobs of being "Benedict Arnold CEOs," while Republicans claimed that savings from outsourcing created more jobs than were lost. But are the new jobs in the economy as good as the ones that are disappearing? The Democrats proposed to remove tax loopholes for companies who invest abroad. But are tax breaks really a major factor driving offshoring? To these and other basic questions about the impact of globalization, the politicians provided little in the way of convincing evidence to back up their positions.

The contradictory claims about globalization and its effects led a group of us who are researchers at the Industrial Performance Center (IPC) at the Massachusetts Institute of Technology to launch a systematic investigation into the large-scale changes in the international economy that have occurred over the past twenty years and their effects on the organization of economic life. Globalization may be the single most important change in our lifetime, yet virtually everything people think they know about its consequences comes either from opinions, anecdotes, or very general economic theories. Analyses based on hard evidence from the experience of societies dealing with these pressures are few and far between. While facts alone will not necessarily force anyone to reach one conclusion or another about the effects of globalization, they can provide an anchor and a point of reference in the hot debates being fought out everywhere from factory floors and corporate boardrooms to political campaigns.

Every day, managers and workers grapple with the question of whether their companies and jobs can survive in the New Economy and what to do about it. They do what we all tend to do when we face new problems: reach into an old tool kit filled with explanations and beliefs from previous experiences and try to use them to understand the new situation.[13] The concepts we have been using to decipher globalization are a jumble of old theories about cheap labor, competition, comparative advantage, convergence, and the inevitable triumph of the market. These ideas are all around us, and they seem to make sense.

At the start of the research, though, our group was convinced that we needed to reconsider many of the standard ideas about globalization. Instead of beginning with general theories about trade and growth and looking for evidence to confirm or reject them, we began with a bottom-up analysis of the actual experiences of 500 companies in North America, Asia, and Europe as they responded to globalization. After observing a large number of different approaches and successful or failed outcomes, we became skeptical about the notion that globalization forces any one set of strategies or sets up an inevitable race to the bottom in wages, working conditions, and environmental standards. When we discovered that there were different solutions to the same economic challenges, and found that a number of these solutions are about equally likely to produce success in the marketplace, we realized we could no longer fall back on "globalization" as an all-purpose explanation for why a company chooses one strategy over another and for why it does or does not work. Dell, the American computer company that focuses its own organization on distribution and outsources all the manufacturing of components overseas, is a rapidly growing, profitable business—but so is Samsung, a vertically integrated electronics company that makes almost everything under its own roof. GM is struggling to survive in economies with high-wage labor; Toyota, which keeps much of its production at home or in other advanced countries, is thriving. Most American apparel retailers outsource all their production, but the fastest-growing retailer in rich countries is Zara, a Spanish company that makes more than half its clothing at home.

When we observed companies whose approaches to competing in the global economy succeeded in keeping good jobs in high-wage countries, we began to wonder what it would take for *more* companies in advanced industrial societies to follow their lead. In this book, I retrace the pathway of our team's research: from an analysis of the big forces that have been changing the international economy over the past twenty years (in Parts One, Two, and Three); through an examination of the responses of many of the 500 companies we interviewed about their practices and strategies (in Parts Four and Five); to the lessons we've drawn about the wide range of choices available to businesses (Part Six).

A Short History of Globalization

Globalization is a word that has been used to describe, explain, and forecast just about every major change in society in the last few decades. To make this term a useful one, it needs to be pared down to the core idea, which is the emergence of a single world market for labor, capital, goods, and services. By globalization, I mean the changes in the international economy and in domestic economies that are moving toward creating one world market.[14] If the world really had a single global market, wages for the same work would be the same around the earth; interest rates, allowing for different levels of risk, would be the same; and the price of a product or a service would be identical no matter where it was purchased. By any test that might be applied, however, the world is still far from such a situation, and likely such an endpoint will never be reached.[15] A more concrete definition of globalization, then, is the acceleration of the processes in the international economy and in domestic economies that operate toward unifying world markets.

This is not the first time that the world has seen borders between the major economies open up enough for the prices of labor and capital in poorer parts of the globe to put tremendous pressures on wages and interest rates in more prosperous countries. Between 1870 and 1914, levels of capital mobility, trade, and immigration among the countries of the North Atlantic region were by some measures even higher than those we experience today. These factors led to a narrowing of the gap between wages and prices in different countries.[16] The major drivers of this "first globalization" were technological innovations, which drastically speeded up transportation and communication and reduced costs. At the time of the American Revolution, it took Benjamin Franklin forty-two days to travel to France. By 1912, he could have made the trip in five and a half days. In 1815, the English branch of the Rothschild bankers used carrier pigeons to learn the outcome of the Battle of Waterloo, an information coup that allowed them to earn a fortune on English markets. Before the laying of the transatlantic cable in the 1860s, stock market prices took three weeks to travel between London and New York City, but by 1914, telegraph and telephone linked the major financial centers of the world, making communication almost as fast as it is in our Internet Age. These advances rapidly reduced the spread in interest rates on the two sides of the Atlantic. Today, of course, satellites, the Internet, and broadband connections make information transfers and financial transactions virtually instantaneous.

The most dramatic effect of the new technologies in the nineteenth century was a massive wave of migration.[17] Falling transportation prices and open frontiers made it possible for 55 million Europeans to move to the New World. Countries like Ireland and Sweden lost about 10 percent of their populations per decade in the half-century before World War I. The effect of the mass entry of these immigrants into the labor markets of the United States, Canada, and Australia was a fall in wages in these countries and rising wages in the places the migrants abandoned. The prices of commodities like wheat and steel began to converge in markets on both sides of the Atlantic. Wheat, for example, which had been 58 percent more expensive in Liverpool, England, than in Chicago in 1870, was only 16 percent higher by 1913, and the same narrowing occurred across a broad range of products.[18]

During the first globalization, as today, there was widespread fear that open borders and the "disappearance of distance" were putting jobs, wages, and the basic foundations of society into jeopardy. Even though there were very limited possibilities then of breaking up production and sending various parts of a product to be made in different countries, as off-shoring makes possible today, the arrival of millions of immigrants hungry for work led to the lowering of wages. The result was a major backlash against immigration in the United States and laws that limited the numbers who could enter. And at the end of the nineteenth century, pressure grew to increase tariff barriers between industrial countries. All the same, levels of trade and investment across borders rose. As goods moved more rapidly and cheaply between Asia and the West, Westerners began to feel the first pangs of anxiety about bringing Chinese production into their markets. In a passage that could have been written today (assuming a greater effort at political correctness in ethnic labeling), a popular French economist, Edmond Théry, wrote in 1901:

> Our only protection is distance, that is transportation costs, but we should not forget that under free trade electricity and steam power have almost eliminated these costs, especially for the Far East, with the Suez Canal, fast steamships, and freight competition. . . .
>
> The yellow peril which threatens Europe can thus be defined as a violent break in the international equilibrium on which the social systems of the major industrial powers has been established, a break provoked by the sudden, abnormal, and unlimited competition of a vast new country [the Japanese in China].[19]

The generations of the first globalization believed that the changes in the international economy were irreversible. These assumptions were shattered by the outbreak of World War I. Practically overnight the walls went up around national territories, and trade, investment, and migration were drastically reduced. A British financial journalist wrote about the halt in trading:

> It came upon us like a thunderbolt from a clear sky. At the end of July, 1914, any citizen of London who was asked what a moratorium meant

would probably have answered that there was not such a word. Possibly he might have said that it was a large extinct woolly beast with big tusks. If he was exceptionally well-informed in matters of finance he would have replied that it was some sort of device used in economically backward countries for blurring the distinction between meum *and* tuum. *On the second of August we had a moratorium on bills of exchange. On the sixth of August we had a general moratorium. . . .*

The machinery of credit broke down in both hemispheres, and London, as its centre, had to be given time to arrange matters under the new conditions. After all, you cannot have credit without civilization, and at the beginning of last August civilization went into the hands of a Receiver, the God of Battles, who will, in due course, bring forth his scheme of reconstruction. When the five chief nations of Europe turn their attention from production to destruction, it is idle to expect any system of credit to go unscathed. Credit depends on the assumption that goods produced will come to market and be sold and that securities that are based on the earning power of production will fetch a price on the exchanges of the world. War, on the smallest scale, weakens this assumption with respect to certain goods and certain securities; if its scale is big enough it makes the assumption so precarious that credit is shaken to its base.[20]

Even though the causes of the first globalization were rooted in new technologies that were not rolled back—no one returned to sailing ships or carrier pigeons—governments were still able to close the frontiers and rechannel economic flows within national boundaries. The walls did not come down again for seventy years.

The high-growth economic miracles of Western Europe in the 1960s and East Asia in the 1970s and 1980s took place in an international economy still bristling with three barriers that limited trade: capital controls—the national rules about how money moves in and out of a country; tariffs—taxes on goods as they enter a country; and quotas—flat limits on the numbers of a particular product that can be imported. From the outbreak of World War I on through the 1930s, these obstacles to cross-border movements continued to gain strength, and they peaked around the time of the extremely restrictive Smoot-Hawley tariff law in 1930. Governments and public opinion eventually came to see this worldwide wave of protectionism as a major factor in the Great Depression and in spawning the social conflicts that produced fascism, Nazism, and war. After World War II, the tide of protectionism began to recede. The 1944 Bretton Woods conference, which brought the victorious Allies together to draw up rules for the postwar international system and eventually led to the establishment of the World Bank and the International Monetary Fund, launched a process of lowering border-level trade barriers. It was hardly a plan for a borderless world, however, since governments and leading economists, like John Maynard Keynes (U.K.) and Harry Dexter White (U.S.), the main authors of the Bretton Woods agreement, still supported letting each government regulate how capital entered or exited its country.

It was not until the 1980s that the world economy returned to the same high levels of capital mobility, foreign direct investment, and trade of the first globalization. As for immigration, the doors that closed in 1914 have never fully reopened. Immigration remains highly controlled everywhere, and even with illegal entrants, the numbers of immigrants in Western nations are far lower than in the nineteenth century. While migration played a major role in globalization in the 1870-to-1914 period, in the twenty-first century—and this is one of the great differences from the past—the effects of globalization work mainly through changes in the organization and location of production, as Parts Two and Three describe.

Globalization today is the product of a series of political, economic, and technological shocks that came together and gathered momentum from the early 1980s, drastically altering the structure of production itself. When China began to open to the West in 1979, when the Berlin Wall fell in 1989, the mightiest political barriers to trade and capital mobility came toppling down. Part of the big push to open borders also came from political decisions by the United States and the other major world economic powers to liberalize capital markets and to remove obstacles to trade. Through successive rounds of trade negotiation carried out to implement the 1947 General Agreement on Tariffs and Trade, tariffs were lowered, quotas eliminated, and a host of nontariff obstructions to the entry of foreign goods and services dismantled. In the "Uruguay Round" negotiations (1986–1994), even deeper cuts were agreed upon, along with the 1994 decision to establish the World Trade Organization (WTO). Today floods of foreign direct investment, currency trading, and goods and services pour across national borders, and producers everywhere find themselves in global competition.

Once again, communication and transportation technologies have lowered the cost of moving information, goods, and services across distance, thereby making it ever easier and faster to operate globally. Though geographic distance continues to matter in decisions about where to produce large, bulky, and heavy items like TVs and cars, the falling price of transportation means that producers are sending more and more by air. Dell notebook computers travel by air from Penang, Malaysia, to the United States; luxurious Tse cashmere sweaters are flown from Xinjiang, China, to high-end department stores in Europe and the United States. When we interviewed Bob Zane, the senior vice president of Liz Claiborne, one of the largest American clothing companies, in 2003, he predicted that within a few years, 30 percent of their items would be flown in from China.[21] Software programming, call-center services, back-office operations, and medical transcription all move cheaply from contractors in India to Western customers because of innovation and falling costs in telecommunications. The capacity of fiber-optic lines to India has grown so rapidly that the 2004 cost of a telephone and data line under the Pacific that can transmit twelve voice calls at a time fell to one-quarter its cost two years earlier.[22]

Changes in the international financial economy have led to surges in investment abroad and rapid fluctuations in capital markets. The liberalization of national financial markets accelerated in the 1980s under pressure from the United States and from international monetary and trade organizations. This deregulation increased the fluidity and the volume of funds flowing between countries. As national controls over the movement of capital across borders disappeared, novel opportunities for both productive investment and speculation began to emerge. Large amounts of money could be transferred in and out of countries rapidly by a simple stroke on a computer keyboard of a hedge fund or a bond trader anywhere in the world. While this made capital easier to access around the world, it also generated a dangerous new volatility that national governments could do little to mitigate. Once deregulation had taken place, national governments found it difficult to protect their economies when their currencies came under attack, as they did in crises like those in Western Europe (1992), Mexico (1994), Asia (1997), Russia (1998), and Argentina (2002).[23]

Financial crises are certainly fueled by domestic weaknesses as well as by international openness. But these disasters are so contagious in open international markets that at times like the 1997 Asian financial crisis, even economies with solid foundations and deep reserves came under deadly attack. The boats that nearly capsized in 1997 were not all leaky ships with corrupt captains at the helm—the heavily indebted South Koreans and the crony capitalists of Indonesia and Thailand brought the well-managed economies of Hong Kong and Singapore into danger as well.

For any company that operates across borders, the fragility of the international monetary regime translates into greater risks and higher cost of capital. This makes companies more reluctant to sink long-term and heavy investment in brick-and-mortar facilities, particularly in cyclical industries prone to oversupply, like semiconductors, where fabrication plants ("fabs") cost around $3 billion to build. In such an environment, using outsourcing or contract manufacturing allows lead firms to reduce capital costs and risk. This has created opportunities for a vast new business of outsourcers and global suppliers who specialize in high-quality manufacturing and who thrive on managing risks by spreading the costs of their investments across a wide customer base.

The processes of change involved in globalization put punishing pressures on firms to adapt but at the same time present great opportunities for expansion. The liberalization of trade opens new zones for investment and production, as an ever-wider array of goods and services can be made in low-wage markets and exported into the markets of advanced countries. Firms are beginning to use their production bases in developing countries not only to manufacture goods to export back into rich home markets, but also to reach customers in the developing-country markets. Consumers in China and Russia and other emerging economies who once were barricaded behind political iron curtains and trade barriers have now become potential customers for Western firms.

The lure of 1.3 billion Chinese customers has a powerful appeal. A joke circulating in China has Procter & Gamble calculating its potential market as 2.6 billion armpits.[24] But converting potential customers into actual customers turns out to be very difficult, especially when they are as poor as the inland Chinese. Coca-Cola, for example, has invested over a billion dollars in China and plans to blanket the country with its products. A survey carried out in Yunnan, a southwest rural province, however, found that a peasant's spending on soft drinks and snacks is somewhere between 6 cents and 36 cents per year—yet one Coke alone costs 30 cents. Many of the investors who are pouring money into China seem to share the faith of that fictional Iowa farmer who resurrected the baseball stars of his dreams by carving a baseball diamond out of his cornfield, believing that if only you build it, they will come.[25] In China, however, most of these fields of dreams have yet to yield any harvest. Over time, with rising incomes, the Chinese consumers will undoubtedly come. For the time being, however, the reality is that the United States is importing far more from China than it is selling. The U.S. trade deficit with China rose to about $162 billion in 2004.[26]

Globalization and Jobs

Over the past fifteen years, the economy and our concerns about it have changed dramatically. In the eighties, when Americans worried about the outside world, it was Japan and other countries with advanced economies, such as Germany, that seemed to pose the biggest threats.[27] After all, the Japanese had gained a commanding position in high-technology industries like semiconductors; the top three chip producers (Toshiba, NEC, and Hitachi) selling to the market were all Japanese. As for consumer electronics, American firms had lost the market completely for some of the most successful new products, like VCRs, leaving the Japanese unchallenged. In automobiles, machine tools, textiles, and steel, as a result of a strong dollar and a U.S. manufacturing system that had failed to keep up with new consumer demands and with competition, European and Japanese manufacturers managed to capture large shares of the market previously dominated by Americans. These developments outside our borders seemed menacing for two reasons. First, the ability of the Europeans and the Japanese to develop high-quality, reasonably priced goods for a wide range of consumer markets led to a massive surge of imports into the United States. Assisted by high U.S. interest rates and a strong dollar, foreign companies made major inroads into U.S. markets in the 1980s. Predictably, the results were plant closings, job losses, and trade deficits, as the United States bought more than it sold abroad.

Our economic weaknesses seemed to spell trouble for our national security, as well. People claimed that the Japanese and Europeans were doing better than we were because they kept foreign competition out of their markets and did business with closed networks of customers and suppliers. Japanese and European companies cooperated in ways that many Americans perceived as cheating or barely disguised coercion and collusion. Tight links between banks and producers, exclusive relationships with customers, and cross-shareholding within big groups seemed to work well in Japan and some European countries, although they involved kinds of pressure and influence that in the United States would have fallen under the axe of antitrust law. Similarly, the preferences of these overseas consumers for goods made in their own country and their lack of interest in buying U.S. products were, many argued, the result of hidden protectionism aimed at keeping American goods out of these markets. If we in the West kept this open international economic system without insisting on a "level playing field," we would end up, as defenders of high-tech industry said at the time, with Japanese selling us silicon chips and Americans selling potato chips to the Japanese.[28]

No matter how much the U.S. food-processing industry might have insisted that making potato chips was a complex affair that required sophisticated capital equipment and skilled technicians, most Americans believed that any kind of international division of labor that moved information technology and electronics out of the United States was inherently dangerous. Since we thought then (and we still do) that innovation and commercialization in high-technology industries are the foundations not only of a high standard of living but also of our nation's military capabilities, we feared that the rise of the Japanese economy spelled the decline of American power in the world. One leading political scientist, Samuel Huntington, even argued in 1991 that we needed to halt the Japanese from capturing a leading position in key industries or else see a shift in the world's balance of power.[29] In 1989, the U.S. government drew up a list including more than 200 features of Japan's domestic economy and society—like *keiretsu* (Japanese conglomerate holding companies) and antisupermarket legislation—that supposedly provided Japanese business with unfair advantages. Trade negotiators threatened to block the entry of Japanese products into the United States if the Japanese did not alter their structures.

Today we are once again experiencing a time of great uncertainty and public anxiety about the fate of American workers faced with foreign competition and about the challenges to our economic preeminence in the global economy. Once again, we see the threats to our prosperity as located abroad, only now we are focusing not on Japan and Germany but on the rising capabilities of countries like China and India. Perhaps the most important of the changes under way as part of globalization is the emergence of some of the developing countries as major challengers of the advanced economies. The developing countries' share in world merchandise trade rose to 31 percent of the total in 2004.[30] In the past, poor countries exported agricultural commodities or natural resources; today, more than 70 percent of all developing-country merchandise exports are manufactured goods.[31]

After Japan, the first of the big success stories from the developing countries were the "four little dragons": South Korea, Taiwan, Hong Kong, and Singapore. Their rise took them from the edge of subsistence to the frontier of world technology. After World War II, Taiwan was a miserably poor agricultural society with a per capita income of $200 a year. Through the fifties and sixties, Taiwan developed light, labor-intensive industries and began exporting cheap consumer goods like toys, lighters, and plastics. Forty years later, as the result of a combination of education, investment, farsighted economic and industrial policies, prudent macroeconomic management, and a shift in the balance between public and private initiatives, Taiwan has emerged as a major world technology power.[32] By 2001, Taiwanese companies were manufacturing 70 percent of the world's motherboards, 55 percent of all laptops, 56 percent of liquid crystal display (LCD) monitors, and 51 percent of color display tube monitors.[33] The standard of living of the population has risen dramatically from the postwar years to a per capita income in 2003 of $12,465. Hong Kong, Singapore, and South Korea experienced similar growth and improvements in the standard of living.

In a few sectors, like textile and apparel and electronic components, the triumphant ascent of the dragons had a major effect on jobs and companies in the West. But no matter how successful the four little dragons, they were, after all, little countries, with limited manpower and land, and therefore limited possibilities for overwhelming the established hierarchies of production in the world. The biggest changes in the global economy would come from the eighties on, when China, India, and the former Soviet Union opened their borders to exchanges and to the entry of foreign direct investment. Now countries with vast populations, large numbers of well-educated workers and engineers, and rising capabilities in mastering technology would become true competitors across the board of already established industries in Europe, America, and Japan.

The deep reserves of unskilled and skilled labor of emerging economies have now become available for hire to producers from high-wage countries. Over the past twenty years, countries on the periphery of the advanced industrial world have educated large numbers of semiskilled and skilled workers, technicians, and engineers, making it possible to carry out sophisticated manufacturing processes like semiconductor fabrication just about anywhere. For example, two new semiconductor-fabrication plants (frequently called "fabs"), Semiconductor Manufacturing International Corporation (SMIC) and Grace, with near cutting-edge capabilities, were opened in China in 2001 by Taiwanese engineers operating with foreign capital and American and Japanese technology.

Today, manufacturing and services can be handed off from Western countries to workers and technicians in India, China, Romania, and elsewhere with wages that may be as low as a tenth of the wage in the more advanced country. Europeans shift production from high-wage plants in Germany or France into low-cost sites in Romania, Hungary, or Poland and then reimport the goods made there back into the European Union without any tariff duties; Americans can do the same with goods that are processed in Mexico or in the Caribbean. Software and telecom companies with a scarcity of educated workers who will work for low wages at home can open facilities in places like Bangalore, India. The global market makes it possible for firms to access resources like manufacturing, a low-cost semiskilled workforce, skilled technicians, and innovation around the world and to incorporate them in the home company in new ways.[34]

Is Any Job Safe?

Over the past three years, Americans have come to fear that no job in the United States is safe. More than two million jobs disappeared from the workforce between 2001 and 2004.[35] By one calculation, a half-million of them were in high-tech industries like electronics, components, and telecoms.[36] The layoff rate has risen, and while many of those who lose jobs get hired again fairly soon, two-thirds of the jobs they get pay less than the jobs they lost. This stands in contrast to experience in the past, when most laid-off workers could expect to be rehired for the same or higher wages — most recently, after the recession of the early nineties, when fewer than half the rehires were at lower wages. The loss of manufacturing jobs hits minority-group members especially hard, since for many of them, employment in manufacturing was a first step into the lower rungs of the middle class.[37]

Many people, like a senior economist at J. P. Morgan Chase quoted in the *New York Times*, think that the growing frequency of layoffs and falling wages are "the echo of globalization."[38] If this is the case, the "jobless recovery" from the 2001 recession may be more than a passing phenomenon. Many believe that even if we maintain high levels of innovation in our own country, globalization will result in a downward slide of wages, social welfare, and environmental practices as competition forces companies and governments to align their standards with the lowest-cost producers. The outcome we most dread is convergence in a race to the bottom, with firms competing by seeking ever-cheaper labor, land, and capital, and societies competing by deregulating and shrinking social benefits.

There are stories our team heard in our interviews that show these fears are not unfounded. Consider L. W. Packard, one of the firms we visited in October 2002. We had first interviewed John Glidden, the president and owner of the Ashland, New Hampshire, firm that spins yarns and weaves fabrics of cashmere, alpaca, and other fine wools, in the 1980s when it was a prospering enterprise.[39] In 1995, *Textile World* ranked it among the best-run mills in the country. When we returned in October 2002, we found the factory almost empty — just a day before it was to close its doors forever. The machines were being crated up and shipped off to Inner Mongolia, where Glidden had entered into a joint venture with a Chinese company to produce fabric that would be shipped to the Caribbean, made into clothing, and imported into the United States under the special lower tariff and quota rates for Caribbean Basin countries.

When the factory had been working full steam in the middle 1990s, it had employed 325 workers earning $10 an hour plus 30 percent health and retirement benefits. When Packard began to experience a drop-off in its orders, Glidden had first tried to lower costs by moving the spinning and some of the weaving to Mexico. Costs crept up there and within two or three years were almost as high as at home. That's when Glidden decided to move everything to China. At the time of our visit, there were only four workers left in the plant packing up the last rolls of fabric. A handful of workers were at work in another part of the building, now converted into a commercial laundry business whose customers were local hotels and hospitals. As Glidden pointed out, a laundry is not likely to face global competition. The few workers on the job were earning $8 an hour with no benefits. On top of that, the consequence for the town of Ashland was the loss not only of jobs but also of its second-largest taxpayer. The value of the mill property fell from $9 million in the midnineties to $1 million in 2002.

HOW WE COMPETE

We Did the Classic American Industry Thing
JOHN GLIDDEN OF L. W. PACKARD

"From the 1990s right through 1997, we were still making quite nice profits here. We did the classic American industry thing—as our low-end market was getting beat up, we crawled our way into the high end. But we really hit a brick wall in 1998–9 with NAFTA and other trade deals. Our competition now comes from imported garments, and they are really pretty good. When you visit a Kmart or Wal-Mart, you don't see the American label there. But the quality is not bad. It's good value for money, and that's what really stopped us in our tracks. Our number-one cashmere competitor is Italy. They have high wages and they make a good product, maybe at a bit less [cost], because they're able to send that fabric to—let's say Croatia—to make it into garments, then import them to the U.S. for less money than our American people could. . . . Our revenue dollars came from the expensive cashmere and camel hair, but our volume came from the wool. As we lost the wool business, we ended up with a plant capable of doing 1,200 pieces a week—and we were down to 300 pieces a week. The overhead was too high—and then we dropped below that level. It was like giving up. Even 100 pieces a week, 100 pieces of cashmere, we could run on that and make a decent living, but you couldn't go two or three weeks without that production, otherwise you had the whole place sitting there. We didn't go broke. We quit the business before we lost our money.

"And when we went to China and saw what they were making, and the quality compared to the Italians—not this year or next year but the year after, they're going to knock the socks off the Italians. We just didn't want to dump family money, which is what this company is, into something that might break even or might show a small profit when you knew darn well in a couple of years that it was all going to be gone. It just isn't going to work."

Our researchers wondered why John Glidden saw Wal-Mart and Kmart as a threat when he'd never sold his product in these kinds of stores, and we concluded that Packard's main problem wasn't low-cost competition but rather an industry-wide shift, as the number of American men who wear suits and jackets to work every day has declined in the last two decades. If Packard had picked up the signals from its customers sooner and shifted its product lines, could the company have been saved?

When we last heard from John Glidden, in January 2005, he reported that the Inner Mongolia joint venture had not worked out and that he had entered a new joint venture in Beijing. "My family has lost a huge amount of money in this Free Trade World," he wrote.

For some people thinking about globalization, dismal outcomes like L. W. Packard's appear to be the inevitable consequences of the unrestricted global mobility of factors of production. It seems to explain the fate of manufacturing in the United States—which has fallen from 30 percent of the workforce in the fifties to 11 percent today—as well as the fact that more than half the manufactured goods that Americans buy are imported.[40] If firms can compete only by relocating activities in low-wage countries, then pay and employment are bound to suffer at home. But—and here's a question that gets to the heart of the argument of this book—with different strategies could L. W. Packard, like the Italian companies that John Glidden mentions, have continued to prosper? Can, in fact, the Italians continue to do well, or, as Glidden believes, will the Chinese knock the socks off them? Will the job losses at companies like L. W. Packard be counterbalanced by the gains from myriad new products and services brought to market by new companies, as economists like Mankiw predict?

To answer these questions, we must look not only at globalization's potential for shifting work to low-wage countries, but also at the job-creating possibilities of our own economy, which has been transformed over the past ten years. Production that used to be contained within the four walls of factories in the United States can now be broken up into bits and pieces connected by value chains stretching around the world, so which pieces—if any—will remain in our own society?

We discovered in our interviews that there's no one winning formula for success. Dell, operating in the fast-tech electronics sector, outsources all the manufacturing of the components that go into its computers. But American Apparel, a slow-tech T-shirt maker, makes it all in Los Angeles. How a business competes depends on what it can do better than any other firm and where it needs to do it: For Dell, it's a distribution system and the Internet that bring it close to its customers; for American Apparel, it's the speed, style, and the cool, sweatshop-free image it's created in L.A.

What's Next?

Clearly, it is American manufacturing that has taken the most visible hit when it comes to offshoring, but this trend does make us wonder: If all manufacturing leaves, can research, design, and services be far behind? Our team found remarkable progress in high-technology fields in the Chinese firms we studied between our first visits in the nineties and the last ones in 2004. Surely the Chinese and Indians, who are certainly as clever and hardworking as we are, should be able to move up into design, R & D, and marketing. And even if the majority of jobs like product design, marketing, research and development, and all the innovative activities at which our society is supposed to excel stay in the United States, can they alone still provide a sufficient number of good jobs?

The glorious boom in the nineties raised boats all across the economy and created millions of good new jobs. But in the years since the dot-com crash, the American economy seems to have run out of steam. Even when the economy is expanding, we do not seem capable of creating enough good new jobs to absorb both the new entrants into the labor market and those workers who have lost jobs in declining industries. Stephen A. Roach, chief economist at Morgan Stanley, estimated that there are about 8 million fewer jobs than we would have expected on the basis of previous economic recoveries.[41] Beyond that, most of the new jobs seem to be ones with low wages and few benefits. Many people wonder whether these trends are the harbinger of things to come, as technological advance and rising productivity reduce the number of employees needed on the job, as work moves to low-wage countries, and as new hiring takes place abroad, not at home.

The reasons why Americans might be both hopeful and worried about the future of innovation and the economy are illustrated perfectly in the experience of one of our MIT research team members. In the 1990s, Charles Sodini, a professor of electrical engineering at MIT, developed a CMOS image-sensor chip that could be incorporated in a camera the size of a credit card.[42] He and colleagues demonstrated the concept in a prototype and in 1999 started SMaL, a company to commercialize their invention of what the *Guinness Book of World Records* listed as "the world's thinnest camera." The original innovations—the idea for the product, the image sensor, and the technology to reduce the amount of battery power needed—were Sodini's and his colleagues', but they decided not to manufacture the cameras themselves. As Sodini explained,

"Manufacturing is a high-fixed-cost, lower-margin game. There are other people who can get that done. What we have is 'product definition' and the key technological components that allow us to capture value."[43]

Instead, they sold kits incorporating SMaL's major proprietary components to brand-name firms, who then designed the final camera bodies around the SMaL kit. The first brand-name customer was FujiFilm AXIA, a Japanese company. Fuji sent the detailed plans for the camera to be worked out by engineers in Hong Kong, and the manufacturing to mainland China. All the marketing of SMaL's products would be done by brand-name firms like Fuji, Logitech, and Oregon Scientific (the brand of IDT), who were to sell the cameras. More than 2 million cameras with the SMaL kits were sold by the brands and SMaL's 2004 sales were $10.5 million. SMaL engineers have started developing new imaging products for cell phones and for automotive vision systems. In February 2005, Cypress Semiconductor Corporation bought SMaL for $42.5 million in cash, plus a performance-based sum.[44]

It's only because it was possible to separate innovation, component and industrial design, manufacturing, and marketing and then contract many of these functions out to separate companies—which already existed and had lots of other customers—that SMaL could be launched so rapidly and with relatively little investment. As Part Two will explain, it's this modularity in the production chain that stimulates the entry of newcomers and allows new products to move so quickly into the market. In a world where it's possible to buy high-quality manufacturing from contractors and no longer necessary to possess such capabilities in-house, new companies are born far more easily. They need not spring forth into the world capable of undertaking all the operations required to transform their innovations into goods and services.

Companies like Cisco Systems, which sells routers and switches for networking systems; Bird, a Chinese mobile phone operation; Uniqlo, a Japanese clothing retailer; and Zoff, a Japanese eyeglass retailer, have launched enormously successful new businesses without manufacturing their products themselves. Cisco products are mostly made by global contract manufacturers like Flextronics and Jabil; Bird buys chips and casing for its phone on the market in China; Uniqlo designs its clothing collections in Japan and has them cut and sewn in China; Zoff designs eyeglass frames that are made in China, fits them with lenses made in Korea, and sells them to customers, who receive the glasses forty minutes after they enter the shop in Japan, at less than half the old price for glasses. These are very successful companies by any measure—Cisco, for example, was founded in 1984 and twenty years later had $22 billion annual revenues and 34,000 employees; Uniqlo started in 1984 as a single shop in Hiroshima and twenty years later had more than a thousand stores in Japan and the United Kingdom, 9.2 percent net profits, and $3 billion net sales.

Distributing economic functions among many different players in a supply chain accelerates innovation and the birth of new companies. It may also create more opportunities for developing countries to get in on the act in new and expanding industries, since they need only carry out one part of the operation. In fact, it's only because the SMaL cameras were manufactured in China that they could be sold from the start for less than $100. This was a boon for consumers and indeed essential for the success of the project, because it created a market niche that had not existed before—all similar cameras had been selling for much more.

But the SMaL story may also illustrate a gloomier scenario: By 2004, SMaL had created only about fifty jobs in the United States. (How many it might have generated in Hong Kong and mainland China is unknown, but is doubtless many times this number.) From this perspective, the SMaL success seems to confirm the fears of the pessimists, who believe we may be moving into a historical phase in which even great creativity and innovativeness might not result in much job creation in advanced societies. In the past, product cycles usually started with a long period during which an innovation was manufactured and brought to market entirely within an advanced society. Only as the product matured, as its fabrication was standardized, and its price dropped did it migrate to lower-wage countries to be manufactured. Today, many new products will be made from the start in China or India or some other country with an educated lower-cost workforce.[45] These trends may be beneficial for developing countries and profitable for some highly educated and talented people in our own societies. But will the benefits be broadly distributed across the population?

CHAPTER 2

A Preview of the MIT Globalization Study

When reports about the impact of globalization start from the macro picture of pressures toward a single world market, they usually predict that companies competing under the same constraints around the world will have to imitate the successful models. If that's the case, they would end up looking much the same, as they converged on a set of common organizational patterns and best practices. But that is not at all what we discovered in our interviews. On the contrary, because we started at the micro level—from experiences we have analyzed in hundreds of companies competing in the same markets—and traced out their evolution, we found great and lasting diversity.[1] Dell, which is growing by $6 billion to $7 billion a year in North America—*Fortune* named it America's most admired company in 2005[2]—focuses on product definition and marketing and outsources all its manufacturing except for a little final assembly. Dell's supplier, Quanta, is a Taiwanese original design manufacturer (ODM) of notebook computers. ODM companies are ones that play a role in design and do the manufacturing, but they have no brand, little or no role in product definition, and no contact with the end consumers. Founded in 1988, Quanta has annual sales of more than $10 billion and is the world's largest manufacturer of

PC laptops—making one out of every four globally. In order to produce final goods, companies like Dell, Broadcom, Cisco, the Gap, and Nike need to link up with these nonbrand contract manufacturers like Quanta, Hon Hai, Solectron, Flextronics, Fang Brothers, and Pou Chen. These names are mostly unknown to the public, but they make our computers, our MP3 players, our sweatshirts, and our sneakers.

Alongside this world of fragmented companies joined in value chains stretching around the world, there are parallel worlds of production, with companies that compete in the same markets but have different organizations and strategies for responding to globalization. Firms like Intel, Motorola, Samsung, Matsushita, Fujitsu, Siemens, and Philips are giants who retain most or many of the activities needed to make their products in-house. These firms place a high premium on the gains they achieve by controlling everything from the initial product development, through manufacturing, all the way to getting the product into consumers' hands. When these integrated firms shift activities abroad, they are more likely to invest in their own plants, unlike the fragmented companies, which use subcontractors both at home and overseas.

The information technology communities in Silicon Valley or the biotech companies around MIT and Harvard, the science parks of Taiwan, and the companies around the University of Cambridge in the United Kingdom represent yet another kind of productive system: a "cluster economy" that thrives on the promoting of an intense and continuous exchange of knowledge, skills, and specialized talents among firms located in close geographic proximity. These innovative and productive industrial districts exist not only in fast-tech sectors but also in slow-tech industries, like the highly profitable eyeglass-frame makers of the Venice region, which produce 25 percent of the world's glasses, or the woolen fabric regions of northern Italy, where the counterparts of L. W. Packard continue to prosper.

How can we know if the different organizational forms our team discovered in our snapshot of the system of production are all equally viable? After all, our five-year photo has captured in frozen motion some firms as they were taking off and others as they entered into decline. It's quite possible that the next frame in time would show a vastly different picture. Can the diversity we saw in the last five years be resilient over the long term? How well will these various kinds of economic organizations fare as business grows more global? Do different industries have distinct patterns—for example, clustering in biotech and software—that will change over time? Will global competition force every firm in the same sector making the same products to converge on the same set of best practices? Or do the basic variations have to do with each firm's home country? Would a French or a Japanese firm see different possibilities in responding to new international challenges than would a U.S. firm? These are the puzzles that our team set out to solve.

Because our team was made up of both social scientists and engineers, from the start we knew it would be a long, hard slog through the field to bring together our different skills and insights. When an engineer visits a semiconductor fabrication plant, he or she assesses the capital equipment and the record of yields, watches the line work, and reviews with the managers the history of the plant's progression through ever-more-demanding chip generations. After the day's visit, the engineering researcher can evaluate what level of performance the plant has achieved compared with others in the industry. When the social scientist visits the same plant, he or she wants to figure out why they put the plant here and not in another region or another country altogether. Who put up the capital and why? Did the government provide tax breaks and free land? In the networks of suppliers and customers of this plant, who really calls the shots? How do the wages here compare with those at a similar plant in the United States? That workers' dormitory across the road: How many people are sleeping in the same room? Will the factory be a cathedral in the desert? Or can it trigger growth all around? At the end of the day, the social scientist wants to know whether the characteristics of the plant are the same as those making chips anywhere in the world, or whether its capabilities and strategies reflect the country in which it's located and the particular choices of its managers. The engineer's questions and the social scientist's questions are each pieces of the big puzzle of globaliza-tion. And so we went together to the interviews. On the long minivan rides between one Chinese industrial park and another; on the factory floors as we stood together watching printed-circuit boards or model air-planes or sweaters move down the line; and in our twice-a-month group seminars at MIT, we explained to each other what we were seeing and we tried to figure out how to piece it all together.[3]

We wanted to understand how globalization is changing our society and economy and what we can do about it. Statistics show great increases in productivity and innovation in the economies of developing and devel-oped countries over the past decade. Have they resulted in rising stan-dards of living all around, or do the gains of some inevitably mean losses for others? The world has changed in ways that make it possible to turn out most of the goods and services that used to be made in America almost anywhere on earth. Does this mean that there is now a best and a cheapest way of making things that we all need to follow or else risk falling out of the competition? Are these changes inevitable and irre-versible? Or can we choose and shape the ways we adjust to the pressures of a new global economy? What do we need to do to remain an economy that promotes innovation and productivity and that also provides oppor-tunities for people in all parts of our society to do well?

Thinking about how to tackle these questions, we drew on the expe-rience of the research team (of which I was a member) that had carried out the *Made in America* project at the end of the 1980s. At that time, too, there were great controversies over the state of the American economy and about the United States' ability to meet the challenge of powerhouse economies in Asia and Europe. There was a flood of articles and books lamenting the decline of the American economy and offering one or another sort of diagnosis and cure. MIT's *Made in America* stood out from the others, because the researchers had started not from general formulas and recipes for the economy but from hundreds of plant visits and inter-views in the United States, Japan, and Europe. *Made in America* explored from the bottom up how companies in key industries put together technology, human beings, and markets, and it came up with an explanation of why American industry was falling behind and what changes were needed in order to stimulate innovation and growth. To the great debates of the eighties, *Made in America* contributed an analysis based on ground-level realities.

When we set out five years ago to figure out how globalization is changing the face of the economy, we again chose to work from the bottom up. We began a journey through the United States, Mexico, France, Italy, the United Kingdom, Italy, Germany, Romania, China, Taiwan, Korea, Hong Kong, and Japan and carried out interviews at 500 companies. We talked with managers at firms of all shapes and sizes, from integrated-circuit design firms in Silicon Valley and Hsinchu Science Park (Taiwan), to a German company that weaves high-tech protective fabric for firefighter uniforms, to a balloon manufacturer in Minnesota, to biotech firms in Cambridge, Massachusetts, to a factory in Timisoara, Romania, that makes clothing for Harrods in London, to auto-parts makers in Mexico that supply parts to GM, to vast semiconductor-fabrication facilities in Taiwan, Korea, and mainland China. In each place, we asked the managers how they are responding to global competition and opportunities. We noted which parts of the production process they were carrying out in their own plants, which they outsourced, and why. Which parts did they offshore and which did they keep at home? We asked them to compare themselves to their toughest competition anywhere in the world.

Our choice of firms was not random. We focused on a few sectors in which the underlying technologies have been changing very rapidly—electronics and software—and on a few others where the basic technologies change more slowly: auto and auto parts and textile and apparel. We thought that the fast-tech/slow-tech distinction captures the realities of the new economy far better than high-tech/low-tech, for there is no correlation between the complexity or massiveness of capital equipment and the pace of technical advance required to stay at the frontier. New small software companies may require relatively low capital investment and a small workforce, but still, the engineers they employ must be highly educated and capable of producing a full stream of rapid and continuous innovations if the enterprise is to thrive. In contrast, in a slow-tech sector like textiles, a new spinning mill may require a capital outlay of $30 million to $50 million, but its basic technologies differ little from the previous generation and the human resources to run it are available in most countries.

Even when extremely efficient and profitable, a company is considered slow-tech if its products and production processes change only incrementally from year to year. Slow-tech sectors, like textiles, do have exceptional and transformative moments, like the invention of nylon in 1935; and fast-tech sectors like pharmaceuticals have profitable businesses that crank out the same vitamins year after year. But after taking the exceptions into account, when we look at these industries over the past fifteen years and speculate about the next five, we find that our classification into slow- and fast-tech sectors holds up well.

Our ultimate objective was to explain how globalization alters the opportunities and problems of the American economy, but we know that there is no way of evaluating what is happening or what could happen in the United States without contrasting our own situation with that of other advanced industrial countries and emerging economies. Looking abroad for comparisons is necessary because those firms are our customers, competitors, and our suppliers. What we can do and what we have to do are defined, in some measure, by those with whom we work and compete. Equally important, if we want to understand which adaptations are forced on us by hard economic realities and which pressures still leave room to maneuver, we can estimate the space for choice by comparing the different ways that companies go about competing in the same sector—only in different countries.

After all, how could we have questioned the apparel company executives in France who insisted that it's impossible to survive making clothes in high-wage economies, unless we had interviewed apparel company executives in neighboring Italy, whose companies are thriving by doing just that? If we looked only at the Gap and Liz Claiborne, we might conclude that apparel companies in high-wage countries need to outsource everything to China or Mexico or some other low-cost economy, but Zara (Spanish) and Benetton (Italian) still make most of their clothing at home with high-wage workers. U.S. firms like Hewlett-Packard and Texas Instruments send many of their chips to be made in Taiwan by powerful local semiconductor foundries like TSMC (Taiwan Semiconductor Manufacturing Company). But there are still world-class companies like Intel and ST Microelectronics that make most of their chips within their own walls. How could we challenge Dell's claim to have hit upon the single best way of organizing a PC company (by outsourcing everything except four and a half minutes of final assembly) unless we had interviewed managers in Sony and learned that Sony makes half its Vaios in its own factories in Japan? In short, by comparing companies around the world, we can move beyond the tired old management recipes that fail to make use of the wide variety of options available.

Three Models of Globalization

While they might disagree on just about everything else, advocates and critics of globalization basically agree on the big forces behind it: a great freeing up of trade and capital flows; deregulation; the shrinking cost of communication and transportation; an IT revolution that makes it possible for companies to digitize the boundaries between design, manufacturing, and marketing and to locate these functions in different places; and the availability of large numbers of workers and engineers in low-wage countries. Where all agreement stops, and sharp debates begin, is on the question of whether globalization forces everyone onto the same track. But that's not what our team found. The diversity we saw among the fragmented companies and value chains, the vertically integrated companies, and the cluster economies might be temporary—a kind of foot-dragging by societies unwilling to embrace the tough realities of the new global economy. Maybe the Japanese are still just too unwilling to lay off workers; maybe the Germans are still attached to welfare-state policies that have become too costly to maintain in a world of global competition with rivals from low-wage countries. If this is the case, we would expect these laggards to pay a hefty price for failing to adjust.

But in theory at least, our alternative conclusion seems equally plausible. The varieties of response and the different organizations we see competing in the same markets today may prove that there really are different ways of meeting the same economic challenges. Over the long haul, then, we expect to find that important differences persist. Chinese low-wage production puts all manufacturing around the world under severe pressure, but it is possible that the wool producers of northern Italy have a brighter future than John Glidden at L. W. Packard predicted for them. A wool textile district like Biella, an hour north of Milan, with a population of about 200,000, still has around 1,500 mills, more than 25,000 workers in this industry, unemployment under 5 percent, and a per capita income one-third higher than the Italian average.

The Convergence Model

The conjectures and predictions about globalization that we hear and read every day come from two very different ways of thinking about the evolution of society. Of course, every newspaper pronouncement about globalization does not come with a complete social theory attached. But when we dig down to basic assumptions, we find that two relatively coherent sets of ideas or models are shaping different expectations about the consequences of globalization: the convergence model and the national varieties of capitalism model. The convergence model derives from theories in mainstream economics, from David Ricardo in the eighteenth century to Paul Samuelson today, about the "comparative advantage" and "factor price equalization" that occur when labor and capital move freely across borders or when goods and services embodying labor and capital move freely across borders. The prediction is that wages, interest rates, and prices will even out across all the countries that trade and invest in the international economy. In fact, very much the same set of assumptions about how competition forces all societies onto the same track is at work in Karl Marx's analysis in *Capital* of capitalist economies.

The idea that globalization forces a convergence and homogenization of economies and societies around the earth is an intuitively powerful one, too. In *The Borderless World*, Kenichi Ohmae noted: "If the government tightens up the money supply, loans may gush in from abroad and make the nation's monetary policy nearly meaningless. If the central bank tries to raise the interest rate, cheaper funds flow in from elsewhere . . . On a political map, the boundaries between countries are as clear as ever. But on a competitive map, a map showing the real flows of financial and industrial activity, those boundaries have largely disappeared."[4] As a British commentator quoted in *The Economist* put it, with open borders, "[the state's] powers over the price of money . . . tax rates, industrial policy, the rate of unemployment, have been blown away."[5]

The breakdown or the negotiated surrender of national controls over the flows of capital, goods, and services across borders means that producers everywhere find themselves in competition. Capital is free to move to whichever locales provide opportunities for the highest returns. Workers, however, are still largely confined to their own home countries. Immigration controls have become stricter even as the barriers to capital mobility have fallen, so even where there are eager candidates for migration, they are often blocked at the frontier.

* As globalization shrinks the resources under national control for shaping economic and social outcomes, so, too, the convergence theorists argue, does it shrink the legitimacy of different national cultures and institutions. The effects of the internationalization of the media, the marketing and export of American popular culture, and the deregulation of information all combine to weaken national values and traditions. The prediction is not only that Big Macs drive out the French *croque-monsieur*, but that the culture portrayed on American television comes to be the standard of the good life presented to audiences around the world. In short, in addition to economic change, it is also cultural change driven by globalization that shifts the ground on which domestic politics plays

out. If national values are undermined, political leaders may have less power to define a common public interest. In this widely held view of the coming world order, the eclipse of the national state would be one of the major consequences. This vision of globalization is held not only by those who are optimistic about the effects of these developments for societal well-being, like Ohmae, but also by people who find these changes threatening—for example, the antiglobalization protesters at the G8 meetings.

Most of the convergence theorists see globalization as a strong and irreversible trend. They have somewhat different stories about what caused globalization and about how quickly it is advancing. Some see the origins in the liberalization of financial markets and deregulation of public utilities. These might be explained by the triumph of neoliberal ideas of political leaders like Margaret Thatcher and Ronald Reagan, as well as by the pressure of powerful interests like Wall Street investment bankers who seized upon moments of opportunity to make new gains from cross-border exchange. Changes in rules or technologies that reduce barriers to international exchange or increase the gains associated with such trade create new opportunities for some groups within society to gain from buying and selling across national boundaries. For example, once U.S. trade negotiators in the Structural Impediment Initiative talks (1989–1990) had convinced the Japanese to allow big supermarkets to open and to let foreigners invest in them, Toys "R" Us was free to establish stores in Japan. A rule change like the end of textile and clothing quota systems that went into effect in January 2005 (discussed in Parts Three and Five) translated into immediate gains for Chinese exporters and losses for U.S. domestic producers. In this perspective, no matter who or what initiates liberalization, the process gains momentum as people realize the possibilities for using their resources more profitably in more open markets.

The effects of globalization can sometimes be achieved without moving anything across borders. To lower wages in the United States, for example, the factory owner does not need to bring in Mexican workers or move his factories to Mexico. He simply needs to be *able* to do it or threaten to do it. The possibility of substituting foreign workers and production for domestic workers and production reduces labor's bargaining power by making the demand for domestic labor more elastic.[6] In an opening international economy, then, increases in trade and foreign direct investment that are small relative to the size of the domestic economy may trigger large effects on factory and product prices.[7] Globalization can have major effects on domestic economies and politics even where—as in the United States—most investment is national and where goods and services made and sold in the domestic market dominate imports and exports.

Whatever the different explanations about the causes and mechanisms that produce the globalized economy, the most common prediction is the convergence of systems of production and distribution. As firms making the same products compete with each other around the world, they advance along common technological trajectories. They are driven to move along faster and faster by shorter product cycles, new rivals in emerging countries, and by the disappearance of safe markets. For example, the differences that once existed between the ways Japanese and American auto assemblers organized production are bound to disappear, convergence thinkers anticipate, once the capital markets they draw on are the same. Once American and Japanese cars can be freely sold all around the world, once they both start making their cars in Brazil, Mexico, China, or the Czech Republic instead of in their home societies, once they both start using the same global suppliers, the differences between GM and Toyota are predicted to vanish. But will they?

The National Varieties of Capitalism Model

The second major model of globalization's effects on society starts from variations in the ways economic systems operate in different nations and emphasizes that globalization will have different effects on different societies. The idea of national models of capitalism was first launched in a 1991 French bestseller, *Capitalism vs. Capitalism* by Michel Albert.[8]

Albert argued that there are two basic variants of capitalism: a German-Japanese model and an Anglo-American model. At the time, it looked as if German and Japanese firms were doing better than American, and Albert offered several explanations for this: the long time horizons of German and Japanese managers and investors—unlike U.S. and U.K. investors, who focus on quarterly returns and short-term gains; the highly skilled and committed workers in those countries; their cooperative labor-capital relations; and their ability to make high-quality and diversified goods, instead of the standardized products of American mass production lines. The cement binding the German-Japanese-type economic systems together are norms of social solidarity that make for trusting and long-term relationships. Layoffs are rare—in Germany because of strong unions; in Japan because of lifetime employment in big companies. In these countries, employees typically spend their whole careers in the same company. This creates powerful feelings of loyalty and belonging to the firms.

In the United States and United Kingdom, in contrast, Albert saw markets and the relationships people arranged through contracts as the central organizing institutions of the economy. In Anglo-American-type economies, there are short time horizons for investors and managers; a flexible labor market, with lots of turnover in jobs; an education and training system that is poorly meshed with work opportunities; a rather inflexible production system that works best when making longer series and larger batches, rather than customized products; equities markets and venture capital that do well at channeling resources to new activities; and societies with great inequalities. These are countries that excel in innovation and have considerable public acceptance of disruptive change.

There are, of course, almost an infinite number of differences among countries, and possible sources of these differences, like culture, historical traditions, legal systems, and political choices. Many of these probably have some kind of influence on economic activities. But like Albert's, most theories of national varieties of capitalism end up with a limited number of basic classifications. The reasoning here is that there are a limited number of basic coordination problems involved in running a capitalist economy and only a few limited efficient institutional solutions to these problems. All advanced economies need to figure out how to allocate resources among workers, managers, and investors; how to organize production, research, and development; how to educate a workforce; how to encourage innovation; and how to finance investment.

Working in the same vein as Albert, Peter Hall and David Soskice, professors of political economy at Harvard and Duke, describe two basic approaches to these tasks: *liberal market economies*, like Britain's and the United States', in which allocation and coordination of resources take place mainly through markets; and *coordinated market economies*, like Germany's and Japan's, in which negotiation, long-term relationships, and other nonmarket mechanisms are used to resolve the major issues.[9] Hall and Soskice describe how these liberal and coordinated market economies produce companies with very different strengths and weaknesses. A German firm such as Siemens or BMW is born into an environment with certain built-in features: institutions that provide a big role for labor in the governance of companies; good labor-capital relationships that are seen as very important for the firm's strategies and operations; financial institutions that have historically provided corporate funding through banks rather than through stock markets, and hence are under less pressure for producing short-term returns on investment; vocational education that turns out a highly skilled workforce through collaboration of companies and schools.

An American company comes into a world where capital is likely to come from venture-capital investors and then the stock market; where workers are educated and trained by schools, not by the company; where new skills are acquired by hiring new employees, not by retraining the old ones; and where labor-management relations are often tense. Because different institutions provide incentives for different kinds of behavior, a German firm and an American firm are likely to organize business in disssimilar ways, even when they are operating in the same sectors, with the same technologies, and making the same products.

Hall and Soskice predict that firms from liberal and coordinated market economies will not react in the same ways to the challenges of globalization. The institutions in each country generate different kinds of behavior at the micro level of the firm because of different resources and competitive capabilities. As firms from various countries enter into competition in an open international economy, according to the national varieties model, they try to capitalize on their special strengths. If they need to acquire capabilities that they cannot generate well within their own systems, they can buy them abroad by outsourcing or foreign direct investment. So, for example, if German pharmaceutical companies excel at process innovations but not at basic research, or if German legislation limits biotech research on genetic modifications, Germans can decide to locate laboratories in the United States, and thus get access to resources that they are not able to generate within their own society. From the perspective of this national varieties model, globalization leads to competition in which national differences are preserved and even reinforced. Far from pushing the German company along the same trajectory of change as its American counterpart, as the convergence model would predict, the national varieties model anticipates that globalization will increase the premium on specialization in those technologies and productive activities in which German firms excel. Globalization should maintain and even increase divergence as companies scramble to build on their special strengths.

To continue with the predictions of the national varieties model about German and Japanese companies: Because they originate in countries with coordinated-market capitalism, they draw many of their resources from relationships with labor, government, and banks in their own home base. Training, research and development, negotiated relations with workers, and bank-based finance are all products of their national home bases. Since the home-base resources cannot be found abroad, firms in these coordinated-market economies are likely to be more reluctant to move abroad. When they do, they may need to substitute for the missing institutions by creating organizations overseas that are quite different from the ones at home. So Toyota, accustomed in Japan to promoting only managers who worked their way up the ranks, in the United States has had to learn to hire senior employees in the labor market. In contrast, American and British companies have always been accustomed to buying their resources in the market: hiring people with new skills, rather than retraining old workers; seeking new finance in the market, rather than working through old relationships with banks; and using the venture-capital market to support innovation, rather than developing new products and processes in-house. Less dependent on relationships in their home country for vital assets, more confident about using the market to buy the necessary resources, companies from liberal market economies are primed for the world of fragmentation and outsourcing.

Dynamic Legacies Model

As our MIT project began, we debated which of the two models—convergence or the national varieties of capitalism—would best explain our findings. To make it a tougher test, we focused on those fast-tech and slow-tech industries, like electronics, autos and auto suppliers, textiles, and garments, that were feeling intense competitive pressures—and could break off parts of the parent company and send them overseas relatively easily. By stacking the deck this way, we tried to ensure that we gave the convergence model a fair run. In each of the countries in which we interviewed, we made a special effort to identify companies and sectors with track records of success—in order to give the national varieties model a fair chance. Even our team members disagreed about what we were likely to discover, and each model had its defenders in the group. But, as the cases of the electronics and of textile and clothing industries that we present in detail in Parts Four and Five show, what we found was very different from the predictions of either the convergence or the national varieties of capitalism model. For companies in the same sectors, making more or less the same products, outcomes were all over the board. The convergence model did get it right in pinpointing the competitive pressures in our economies, and we did find at least some shift toward modularity almost everywhere. The national varieties model did correctly predict that these pressures would produce different outcomes in different countries, and that even common trends would generate dissimilar reactions and strategies. But beyond these generalities, the fit between the models and the findings in our interviews was poor.

I will spell out the reasons for the divergence between the models and our findings in the companies in the chapters to come. But the basic explanation of the poorness of fit of both the convergence and the national varieties models is that they start from the macro level in analyzing how economies function and change. They deduce how individuals and firms are likely to react under common pressures—rather than studying the evidence of how they actually respond. Deductive thinking does usually focus on similarities in the way individuals of any particular type react under the same stresses. This is hardly surprising, because in such models the actors are only very thinly described—companies, for example, are seen as only and everywhere out to maximize profit. If we start with these stripped-down assumptions about individuals and companies, then most of the action in the globalization story is likely to take place in the international markets, as world prices for goods and services, capital, and labor force companies and even whole countries to adjust their domestic arrangements to global levels.

In How We Compete, I lay out a different way of understanding globalization, based on what our team witnessed on the front lines of business. We call our approach "dynamic legacies," because it starts from a company and its reservoir, or legacy, of resources that have been shaped by the past.[10] By resources, I mean a stock of experiences, skills, human talents, organizational capabilities, and institutional memory—not only material resources. After all, a firm's experiences are not only the product of the institutions and values in the country in which the company was born, but also the product of learning over time from different customers, suppliers, or rivals, and as a result of acquiring skills and solving problems of survival, renewal, and growth. The history of the business shapes the way the owners and managers structure their organizations. Their strategies and the way they implement them reflect the stamp of their origins, of previous successes and failures, of relationships over time with suppliers and customers, and of particular capabilities they have nurtured in their workforce. Some legacies are specific to an enterprise and have their origins in accidents of history. The personality and basic beliefs of a company founder like Henry Ford, for example, can make a lasting difference. Our group looked at these legacies both as resources and lenses—resources that can be put together in new combinations to form new strategies; and lenses that bring into sharp focus what's familiar and what's new in a situation. How well the firm mobilizes and reorganizes its legacy in an open economy is what we believe will separate the winners and the losers.

The early experiences of a company with its first customers and products can be decisive. Hong Kong garment companies, for example, began their expansion in the sixties by selling to either U.S. or Western European customers. The U.S. buyers wanted larger volumes, lower prices, and less input on fabric and design from the Hong Kong side than did the Western European buyers, who sold to smaller and more demanding markets that were willing to pay more for higher quality, and who had fewer employees in the field to supervise the Hong Kong manufacturers. The requirements were so different that Hong Kong companies usually felt they had to choose between working with Americans or with Europeans. At the start, whether a Hong Kong firm worked with Americans or with Europeans was largely a matter of chance. But as these partnerships matured, each Hong Kong firm developed specific capabilities to satisfy the requirements of the different buyers. The firms working with the Americans became good at producing to exact schedules and specifications; the firms working with the Europeans began to offer design services to their customers and to move toward higher-priced garments. Over time, the experience of working with the initial customers created different firm legacies in the form of organizational resources that influenced future choices about strategy and implementation.

Continuities that derive from the way the impact of an initial condition or event limits the range of subsequent events are usually called "path dependencies." The classic example is the QWERTY keyboard—its awkward combinations of keys was originally designed to prevent typists from speeding up and jamming up keys on typewriters.[11] Once generations of typists had been trained on the QWERTY keyboards, even the invention of improved typewriters and computers with no danger of sticky keys did not cause people to make or buy keyboards with keys arranged in more convenient configurations. Here the resources (typists trained on QWERTY keyboards) created by the initial event limited the future path of innovation (by making customers resistant to buying machines that required unlearning old habits). In the QWERTY example, as in many other cases of continuities that are accounted for by path dependency, the idea is of the reproduction over time of an original pattern.

Our notion of "legacy" borrows from these insights, but in our definition legacies are composed of rather disparate elements and support at least a few different scenarios. To return to the example of the Hong Kong apparel firms, if the only element in their repertoire had been experiences with U.S. or European brands and retailers, then firms would probably have kept working with only Americans or Europeans, and nothing short of a situation like the collapse of one of these markets would have altered the pattern. But, in fact, each of the Hong Kong firms also had a legacy tied to mainland China. Because some of the owners still had networks of family and business there, they could quite easily start small-scale operations in China and make products there for their American or European customers, or they could use the Chinese market to move out from under the thumb of their American or European buyers. Other Hong Kong businessmen had very negative personal experiences with or convictions about Communists in China, and therefore hesitated about moving production to China. They were more likely to try to continue manufacturing in Hong Kong by making higher-end products, or else to shift production into South Asia—both choices that left them still tightly linked to their American and European buyers. In other words, the different elements within the legacy (in this example, a relationship with foreign buyers coupled with an aversion to working in mainland China) have a dynamic relation to one another as well as to changes in the external environment (such as the opening of China), and no simple reproduction of the starting conditions can be expected. The legacies are dynamic in a second sense as well, for elements are added over time.

Just as important as the particularities of a firm's own founding and past experiences are the characteristics imprinted in the firm's DNA by virtue of birth in a given society. Here there is a lot to be learned from the national varieties approach and from spelling out the impact of national patterns on incentives for companies to pursue one pathway rather than another. When I compare the different strategies of Dell, Sony, Matsushita, and Fujitsu in Parts Four and Five, the strong impact of home-country institutions will become apparent. But institutions and practices are more loosely joined than these models suggest. Within a given country we find a range of variation of types, of linkages, and of ideas about how things ought to be run. In the United States, we find successful companies like Liz Claiborne, which outsources just about everything, alongside ones like American Apparel, which does just about everything in-house. There are certainly family resemblances across the institutions and ideas in a given country. But some of these similarities look less like chips off the same block than like permanent family quarrels. Such diversity has been discovered even in the countries, such as Japan and the United States, that provide the basic models for the "varieties of capitalism" literature. But whether conceived as a tightly soldered institutional frame or as a more loosely connected set of practices and norms prevalent in a given country, the home society has a critical shaping and conditioning impact on the legacies of companies. Like the individual experiences of a firm, these societal patterns nourish specific resources and capabilities.

Our team sees globalization as an outcome in the making through the tens of millions of decisions about moving capabilities and assets across the borders and about acquiring capabilities and assets that are produced outside a home society. Our focus is on companies rather than on migrants or on investors—though they are all border crossers in an open international economy. What we wanted to know is how and why they determine which activities to keep within their own company walls, which they outsource to other firms, which they keep within their own home countries, and which they locate outside their borders. Each company's globalization strategy, we believe, can be thought of simply as a combination of choices about reorganization and relocation.

It's no revelation that a firm's main goal is to make profits.[12] Managers may either calculate profits with short time horizons in mind, if their companies are listed on a stock exchange and make quarterly earnings reports; or with long time horizons, if they are privately held and bank-financed. Leaders may be more or less focused on capturing market share, and all kinds of other considerations, from prestige and power to family control and reputation, may enter into the reckoning. But at the end of the day, every company needs strategies for making profits. Managers have to choose among different ways of using the resources and capabilities of their own organizations to sell goods and services that customers value. They compete with rivals on price or by making a product that's difficult for others to copy. Brand names, intellectual property, higher quality, and bundling services together with hardware are all strategies that slow the advent of challengers, and that also provide some shelter against competition based purely on a never-ending search for lower costs.

Globalization is the result of managers' everyday decisions about how they distribute their activities among various sites of innovation, design, production, and sales. They can shift functions they once carried out within their own brick-and-mortar walls into supply chains that link many independent enterprises and identify new customers, partners, and competition around the world. These choices about reorganization and relocation of the firm's basic activities became the main focus of our research. By comparing the paths of firms making the same products in the same sectors in various countries, we hoped to discover which combinations of organization and location are possible—that is, which allow a firm to do well.

The cases that exemplify the puzzle are ones like the contrast between Sony, which makes half the Vaio laptops in its own factories in Japan, and Apple, which outsources all its laptops to Taiwanese original design manufacturing (ODM) firms, or between Zara, which makes a large proportion of its garments in its own factories in Spain, and the Gap, which outsources all of its production, mostly outside the United States. We started from these intriguing differences in choices about locating functions because they open up under scrutiny to reveal the main fact about globalization and the main argument of this book: that the range of possibilities is broad. We see the pathways before these firms as wide open—that is, there are different possible ways for firms to do well under the constraint of the great new pressures to adapt rapidly to international markets. We agree that the pressures the convergence theorists identify are real ones, but our research suggests that they do not dictate a single best strategy for surviving and growing, even for firms in the same industries.

Who's doing well? We are skeptical about using metrics to declare winners and losers. No one measure sums up all dimensions of performance, and the figures can change fast. Wal-Mart towers over the retail industry in the United States and its power has driven down prices across the economy. Its market valuation is more than $200 billion, its sales have been growing 11 percent a year, and it ranks in the top ten of the *Forbes* list of the world's 200 leading companies. Yet its stocks are not doing particularly well; total returns over the past three years (2002–2005) are down 15 percent.[13] Whether we see good numbers depends a lot on the year we choose to examine, as a company's fortunes can vary widely from year to year. The iPod, a blockbuster digital music player, drove Apple's sales and profits off the chart. In the last three months of 2004, Apple sold 4.6 million iPods and Apple's quarterly revenue rose to $3.5 billion— a record for the company.[14] Its share price appreciated 201 percent in 2004. Samsung, which had barely survived the 1997 Asian financial crisis, earned $10 billion net profits in 2004. If Sony, which has been struggling with falling profitability and sales, has a hit with the PlayStation

Portable or with a stream of products that use its new Cell microprocessor chip, it too could have a big bounce back. In short, even when I use these metrics of performance in this book to describe the status of the companies we have interviewed, I am reluctant to put too much stock in them. Our team looked at the main contenders and their rivals, at long-term track records as well as recent history, and we tried to keep an open mind.

A final caveat: Although I focus on opportunities and the openness of options for companies under globalization, I realize that by now some of them have very limited possibilities. The French clothing manufacturer who specializes in children's sleepwear delivered to Mom and Pop retail shops, who has no brand and no designers to fashion a distinctive look, and whose workers are paid the French minimum wage, has virtually no chance of survival once large discounters and supermarkets start importing children's pajamas made at Chinese wages. But in the same industry we found others who will continue to do well, companies with brand names that trade on adult fashion design or technical features (like flame retardants, or "pure organic green fabric," or stretch fibers like spandex), companies that are expanding their overall businesses by moving some of the manufacturing to low-wage countries, while increasing their staff of designers, technicians, logistics experts, and marketing specialists at home.

Since what we really wanted to know were the options for any particular activity a company might decide to carry out, we needed to start not by deducing the firm's future from the overall situation of its industry, but by looking at the different kinds of resources available to the firm and the ways in which the firm developed and deployed these resources. The fate of the hypothetical pajama manufacturer depends not on the overall state of the French apparel industry (although that can help or hurt), but on its past choices determining market niche, hiring designers, developing a brand, working with retailers, outsourcing some parts of the manufacturing, and putting all these resources together.

A Preview of Our Argument

In *How We Compete*, I report on what our team learned about constraints and strategic choices in the global economy. As far as I know, this is the first large-scale analysis of globalization that starts with a view from the trenches—the people under great pressure to respond to new challenges in hundreds of companies around the world. Using this bottom-up approach, we have tried to understand what is happening and why. From thousands of decisions made by people facing more or less the same challenges but with very different capabilities made available to them by their own past experiences, we have tried to figure out how much choice remains in a world under globalization.

Out of a complicated and variegated picture of different routes to success, we have come to four general conclusions about the processes of globalization that we present in this book.

Match the Best or Outsource to the Best

To start, in sectors like electronics and textiles that have been the most heavily affected by globalization, changes have taken place via a fragmentation of production that makes it possible to break apart stages of research, development, design, manufacturing, and marketing and move them to different companies and locations around the world. Where fragmentation of production is technically possible, companies need to keep within their own walls *only* those activities in which they can compete with the best in the world. In fact, they have to be able to match their performance with best-in-class across each of their functions. If, for example, Sony is to continue to make many of its own laptops in-house and compete with Apple, which outsources the manufacturing of its laptops to Taiwanese firms and benefits from both Taiwan's world-class manufacturing skills and lower wages, then Sony had better have equally strong manufacturing capabilities.

If a firm can buy services like manufacturing from others who are lower-cost producers, should it? Outsourcing is among the most difficult of the decisions facing a company, and the fate of manufacturing on any large scale in advanced economies hangs on it. As manufacturing in many industries has become a commodity that can be purchased from outside and, increasingly, offshore vendors, many American companies have gone down this route. But can the advantages of keeping all the pieces of the production process in one set of controlling hands *ever* outweigh the costs of hanging on to activities that are being outperformed by others? We think so.

There may still be reasons to keep manufacturing in-house, or at least so think many large Japanese corporations. Companies such as Matsushita and Samsung continue to bet heavily on the possibilities for capturing benefits from integration that overwhelm the costs of keeping manufacturing in a high-wage society. Are many Japanese, Korean, and European firms remaining more-integrated companies just because it is so hard to lay off workers in their societies? Or are there advantages here? Our research tracked closely the decisions on outsourcing and offshoring of Americans, Asians, and Europeans in order to unravel this puzzle. As we hope to show in the cases of the electronics and the textile and apparel companies discussed in Parts Four and Five, no one model wins all the time.

The organization that works best in a period of stable underlying technologies may not be the same as the one that wins in a period of radical innovation. Over the past twenty years in electronics, the fragmentation of production has facilitated a division of labor between lead brands, contract manufacturers, design firms, and component and product companies—each of which may carry out only a limited part of operations on a product. (I'll discuss this trend in detail in Part Two.) But suppose that technologies in the industry shift, and suddenly require that designers and manufacturing engineers collaborate closely throughout the life of the product. Would the integrated companies of Japan and Europe that still employ design and manufacturing specialists within their own four walls do better than the American companies that had outsourced all their manufacturing?

Grow Out of a Legacy

Companies' best practices will vary—even in the same sector, even for the same product—depending on each firm's history, the way each has built up particular human and technical resources, and the differences between the societies in which firms grow up. Take, for example, the differences between American and Japanese firms I outlined earlier in the chapter, when describing the national varieties of capitalism model. The shift to a global economy based on modularization and supply chains and market-based transactions plays to the American strengths. In contrast, Japanese firms, which operate in a world of tight, long-term human relationships, do especially well when close day-to-day cooperation is needed. It's not surprising that today these historical differences in "DNA" produce American and Japanese firms with very different capabilities.

Nationality is not destiny, however. The legacies on which firms draw are composites, with capabilities, talents, and aspirations shaped by very diverse experiences as well as national "imprinting." It's this multiplicity of available resources that makes leadership and strategic choice so important. It is also why we see legacies as dynamic, rather than as repetitive patterns.

Low-Wage Strategies Lose

Contrary to the widely held belief of many managers, we conclude that solutions that depend on driving down costs by reducing wages and social benefits—in advanced countries or in emerging economies—are always dead ends. As I will argue in Part Two, wages are only a small part of total costs. Even in very labor-intensive industries like garments, many other costs and risks overwhelm the advantage of low wages. No matter how cheap labor and land might be in North Korea, no firms are likely to set up shop there, nor are investors breaking down the doors to outsource to low-wage societies like Haiti or Sierra Leone. For now, many of the poorest countries on earth lie beyond the pale of globalization. In the end, what matters are unit labor costs, and these may be very high in low-wage economies where workers are inexperienced, need close supervision, work on old or poorly maintained equipment, and move frequently between jobs.

Strategies based on exploiting low-wage labor end up in competitive jungles, where victories are vanishingly thin and each day brings a new competitor—today from the coastal regions of China; tomorrow from the interior of China, or from Vietnam and Indonesia; next year from India or Burma or Swaziland. As low-end firms that compete on price move from one overcrowded segment of the market to the next, there is virtually no chance of gaining any durable advantage. The activities that succeed over time are, in contrast, those that build on continuous learning and innovation. These allow companies to build capabilities—brand name, long-term working relations with suppliers and customers, intellectual property, specialized skills, reputation—all of which are out of reach to companies whose only assets are their access to cheap labor.

To Win, Choose

Finally, we conclude that the pressures of globalization force virtually all economic actors to transform their activities—but they do not dictate a single best way to do it. In our choice of interviews, we loaded the dice by selecting sectors and companies under tremendous competitive pressure, with technologies that have great potential for modularity, and with organizations that are relatively easy to transfer to new locales. We reasoned that if even in electronics, with its great advances in codification and modularity, we found a real diversity of successful approaches to decisions about outsourcing and peeling off manufacturing, we would know that alternative responses to globalization were possible. If, even in sectors like clothing and eyeglasses, we found companies with a high-wage labor force enjoying profits and relatively stable levels of employment—as we did in northern Italy—we would have to question whether globalization inevitably condemns any particular activity in our own country.

PART TWO

The "Lego" Model of Production

We need to give manufacturing a more important role in company affairs. We've undervalued manufacturing in the mix of things we need to do as managers to compete in world markets.
—John Young, CEO, Hewlett-Packard, 1987[1]

Manufacturing is just not a source of competitiveness!
—European electronics firm senior executive, 2002

Basically, anything that can be done by an hourly employee can be outsourced.
—interview with manager of American telecom equipment company, 2002

CHAPTER 3

Breaking Up
the Corporation

Globalization is not something that just "happened" but the product of millions of choices: choices made by corporations about what to do within the four walls of a company, choices about what to buy from others, and choices about where to locate all these activities. At the core of these choices are two key decisions about reorganization and relocation. By reorganization, I mean the strategy for selecting which of the steps, from defining a product to delivering it to a customer, should remain in-house versus the functions that will be outsourced—that is, purchased from other firms. Relocation (or offshoring) involves moving activities out of one's own home country. A company might outsource to another U.S. business—in fact, most outsourcing is domestic. An offshoring decision, on the other hand, involves a transfer of production overseas, either to affiliate firms of a multinational corporation, or else to independent contractors.

I am using the terms *reorganization* and *relocation* on purpose, for these are decisions that most companies today do not make one time and for all. They are revisited and revised over and over again, as competition heats up, as contract manufacturers improve their capabilities, as foreign workers develop new skills, or as new technologies change the game. Strategies of reorganization and relocation translate into layoffs and hires, opportunities for the emergence of new enterprises, and the creation of good new jobs at home and abroad. Of course, macro conditions of supply and demand domestically and in the global economy play a fundamental role in aggregate levels of employment and investment. But so, too, do these strategic choices at the grassroots level about how to organize a company and where to put its activities. These basic decisions about production form the ground floor of the economy.

For managers today, the practical problem of globalization is how to combine resources and capabilities from within their own organizations with those they find outside their walls, whether at home or abroad. Over the past twenty years, new pieces, new players, and new sites for production have changed the game, and they make it possible to build companies that are very different from the great corporations of the 1980s.

Think of the products of the companies of the 1980s as a model airplane kit. Each of the pieces in an airplane kit attaches neatly to the next because each was designed to fit in just one place. The pieces fit together in a unique way, and none could be reused in other configurations to make other airplanes. Similarly, the structures of companies in the 1980s also had to be tightly integrated in order to turn out uniquely matched-up parts and processes. These were likely to be made in the same plant, so that veterans of the previous generation of production could share their experiences and knowledge. In the automobile industry even today, production has this kind of "integral and closed architecture."

HOW WE COMPETE

Toyota Maintains the Integrity of a Product Through Integration
TAKAHIRO FUJIMOTO, UNIVERSITY OF TOKYO PROFESSOR AND LEADING EXPERT ON TOYOTA, EXPLAINS WHY TOYOTA MAINTAINS IN-HOUSE CONTROL OVER EVERY STAGE OF THE PRODUCTION PROCESS.

"Take the example of three functional elements (handling, ride, fuel efficiency) and three structural elements (body, chassis, power train of an automobile).

Engineers know that the characteristics of the product's handling are determined by a subtle orchestration of body, chassis, and power-train designs, and likewise in the cases of ride and fuel efficiency. . . . Each component is functionally incomplete and interdependent with other components functionally and/or structurally. . . . Mix and match is difficult, and so is the use of many common components without sacrificing functionality and the integrity of the total product."[1]

The Facts: Toyota is the world's largest automaker by market value. While GM reported a $1.1 billion loss in March 2005, and Ford was struggling to sell off inventory; Toyota had its best-ever quarter, with sales increasing in all key markets. Toyota's operating margin for nine months ending December 31, 2004, was 9.4 percent—despite a high yen/dollar exchange. Toyota employed 246,410 workers in 2004, slightly higher than the previous year, even after deep cost-cutting measures.[2]

In contrast, for many industries, the changes of the past twenty years mean that organizing production has become more like playing with a set of Legos than building a model airplane or a car. In other words, it's now possible to create many different models using the same pieces. New components can be added on to old foundations; elements from old structures can be reused in new configurations; parts can be shared by many players with different construction plans in mind. As this chapter will describe, the myriad possibilities of organizing a company have grown out of new digital technologies that create countless opportunities for using resources, organizations, and customers all over the world to build businesses that did not even exist ten years ago. This chapter tracks the history of this modular approach to business, when and how it came into being, and how it has changed the ways managers can pick and choose in reorganizing and relocating their operations.

How best to use the many options made possible by modularity raises fundamental questions of strategy. To take one problem, if managers use only the Lego pieces available to everyone, they risk making products like everyone else's and plunging into a competition based only on price. The hazards of losing product distinctiveness by sharing components and platforms come up even within single companies. When VW, for example, used the same basic platform architecture for making its German Golfs and its Czech Škoda, sales of the cheaper Škoda started to eat into sales of the Golf.[3] If, however, managers try to differentiate their products by using *only* proprietary technologies and components, they risk finding themselves back in the model-airplane game, required to produce everything in-house and unable to benefit from external capabilities.

Sony's difficulties in developing a digital music player that can compete with Apple's iPod illustrate the trap of trying to go it alone. By making a player loaded with Sony components and one that works only with music downloaded with its own proprietary compression standard, Sony ended up with a high-cost product with limited appeal to music fans who wanted MP3 downloads. The same issue arose with Sony's digital cameras, because the company wanted customers to have to use Sony Memory Sticks with the cameras. Commenting on Sony's problems, James Surowiecki, a *New Yorker* columnist, wrote: "Companies are a little like nations. In an era of globalization, a healthy economy relies on a steady flow of ideas, resources, and capital from outside. So it goes for a big company, in an era of open innovation."[4] Part Four lays out a wide range of different solutions that the companies our team interviewed have developed for dealing with the dilemmas that arise from trying to balance the benefits of using capabilities that can be shared and the potential windfalls of creating unique and highly valued products. This is only one of the many trade-offs businesses must make.

In our interviews with managers in Asia, North America, and Europe, our research team found not one best solution but diverse successes, each combining different elements of old legacies and new resources. But before we can appreciate the puzzles the companies are trying to solve now, we need to see where they come from and what is involved in transforming the old model-airplane businesses into innovative Lego constructions.

Lining Up the Lego Pieces

Each of the managers we spoke to has had to resolve a few basic problems about what to make and where to do it. Production is a sequence of functions that stretches from an innovation or idea for a product to manufacturing it and delivering it to a customer, sometimes also providing after-sales service. Some of the tasks along the chain include making and transforming tangible goods; other stages involve services and intangible exchanges of information. Most valuable goods in the world today— whether cell phone service or $500 designer jeans—combine physical production and services. However different industries may be, if we step back from the details we can see similar patterns in the sequence of functions involved in making a product and in the links that join one function to the next. Whether we're looking at a desktop computer or a car, we can identify a common set of tasks that must take place between product definition and sale to the customer.

FIGURE 1: FROM IDEAS TO CUSTOMERS

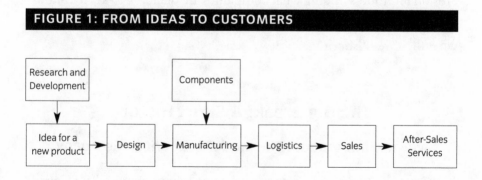

When IBM made a personal computer twenty years ago, virtually all of the functions up to retail sales took place within the four walls of the company. Some, though not all, of the components (chips, keyboards, monitors, entry device) that IBM used in making the machine were also fabricated in-house, the rest by U.S. suppliers. Similarly, up until 2002, a pair of Levi's blue jeans would be defined, designed, and manufactured in Levi Strauss plants, shipped by Levi's, and often sold in Levi's stores. The "components"—mainly the denim fabric, zipper, and thread—were purchased by Levi's from suppliers. The links between the functions in the sequence of production at IBM and at Levi's—as in hundreds of thousands of other companies around the world at the time—were ownership links. In other words, the functions were coordinated by managers in the same company, reporting to common bosses.

In the years between the 1980s and today, one after another of these functions have been outsourced by brand-name companies like Levi's and IBM. The links of common ownership over the production process have been replaced by contracts between independent enterprises. (Each of the components used—whether denim or memory chips—also moves through a sequence of tasks from conception to sale. These operations can all take place in-house under common owners, or in separate companies linked by outsourcing contracts.) Why and how this breakup of ownership took place and where the new pieces and the new actors came from are the subject of Chapters 3 and 4. This is indispensable background for understanding what companies are deciding to keep in-house today and what they are outsourcing, what they are keeping at home and what they are offshoring.

The Big Break: A Short History

Vertical Integration: The Model T American Company

It's surprising to discover that our world of fragmented and specialized companies resembles in many ways the American economy of the early and mid-nineteenth century, before giant multi-unit, vertically integrated corporations like DuPont, Singer Sewing Machine, G. F. Swift & Company, and Ford Motor started to develop.[5] Before the triumph of the vertically integrated companies, businesses had to contract with many

providers of goods and services for inputs that were vital to their operations, and they commonly used others for logistics and distribution.
Change came rapidly from the mid-nineteenth century on, when railroads, canals, and steamships lowered transportation costs and made it
feasible to sell in a vast national market. Advances in production created
new economies of scale. Companies began to expand their boundaries,
and the first of the huge modern corporations began to take shape. Alfred
D. Chandler, Jr., the great historian of the rise of American corporations,
explained how these vertically integrated, multi-unit, manager-run companies overwhelmed and devastated the competition.[6] These businesses
were remarkably resilient, so that still in the mid-1970s, many of the companies dominating their industries, like DuPont, Ford, and General
Motors, were the same ones that had been at the top a half-century earlier.[7] In fact, many of these companies are still doing well. On the *Forbes*
list of the ten top companies in the world in 2004, only Wal-Mart was
founded within the past forty years, as Niall Ferguson, professor of history
at Harvard, has pointed out.[8]

The big success stories of the end of the nineteenth century were
businesses that integrated a wide array of functions, from defining a product to delivering it into the hands of a customer. The classic stories are
those of companies like Singer Sewing Machine and G. F. Swift & Company.[9] Singer realized that consumers were more likely to buy sewing
machines if they could be taught to use them and could count on reliable
repair services; so beginning in the late 1850s, Singer extended its business into distribution and provided repairs and instruction in its stores.
Then, as demand grew, Singer transformed its manufacturing processes
to use more automated special-purpose equipment in order to reduce the
need for skilled workers.

The vertically integrated corporations drew on the enormous new
potential of a national market unified by railroads and the telegraph. No
example illustrates the exploitation of these possibilities better than the
meatpacking company Gustavus Swift built in the 1870s to integrate all
stages in the process of making meat—from the ranch to the retail

butcher—into a single enterprise. In so doing, he eliminated a host of local and regional intermediaries that had once controlled each one of these steps. Gary Fields's illuminating history of G. F. Swift & Company compares its transformation of logistics in its time with Dell Computer's revolutionary use of the Internet in the 1990s. Where Dell, however, would use suppliers from around the world to provide every component needed to make a personal computer and focus Dell's organization on customizing products to order and on distribution, Swift created an organization that brought under one ownership a broad range of functions that independent companies had previously carried out. As Fields concludes: "A formerly disaggregated, locally oriented, and small-scale activity had given way to an industry controlled by vertically integrated, large-scale enterprises. As the first vertically integrated meat-packing firm, Swift was the forerunner of large-scale nationally oriented business organizations."[10]

The larger the scale of these corporations, the less they could afford to let valuable capital equipment sit idle if delivery of some vital component was delayed, or if the quality of some purchased input was below par. This led, as the Singer and Swift examples illustrate, to an extension of ownership and control over an ever-expanding range of adjacent activities. By incorporating these upstream and downstream functions, the companies reduced their vulnerability to the erratic performance of suppliers. For example, by 1949 the Ford Motor Company (founded in 1903) had acquired extensive iron and coal mines and timberlands in Michigan, West Virginia, and Kentucky; railroads; a rubber plantation of 2.3 million acres in Brazil; and its own ships to transport parts that would be assembled into cars in Ford factories abroad. According to the admiring 1949 *Encyclopaedia Britannica* entry, Ford had "its own lighting, heat and power plant; its fire department; paper mill; its foundries, hot and cold sheet mill; hot roll bar mill; tire plant; sintering plant; coke ovens; tool and die shop; press shop; cement plant; body plant; open hearth furnaces; box factory; blast furnaces; telephone and telegraphy exchanges;

machine shop; paint factory; artificial leather plant; freight and express offices; hospitals; laboratories; and a trade school for boys."[11]

In the boom years of mass consumption after the Second World War, the vertically integrated companies flexed all their muscles. Giants like RCA, IBM, Levi Strauss, and Volkswagen coordinated all the functions from R & D to distribution within their own control in the company. They still used subcontracting for some components and for balancing production in peak times, but they dominated the suppliers and dictated prices and terms. Long, stable production runs and long product cycles lowered costs. For the first time in history, a great number of complex manufactured goods—like automobiles, refrigerators, canned foods, bicycles, and radios and television sets—became affordable for people with ordinary earnings. The broad mass market and steady demand stimulated heavy investment in specialized capital equipment and plant facilities.

Fordism Did Not Win Out Everywhere

Yet even in the heyday of the big vertically integrated company, there were other ways of coordinating production functions.[12] In retrospect, two of them—Italian industrial districts and Japanese manufacturers—look like important deviations from the American norm. They were living proof that even in the three decades after World War II, at the peak of mass production in large-scale manufacturing facilities, there were alternative ways of organizing economic activities that were profitable, innovative, and sustainable. The DNA of the organizational models that the Italians and the Japanese developed in the postwar years today continues to generate successful and prosperous companies, as I'll discuss in later chapters.

The Italian industrial districts of the 1970s and 1980s were communities of very flexible small and medium-scale producers specializing in consumer goods like textiles, shoes, clothing, furniture, and eyeglasses.[13] Originally, these were businesses with obscure names that made products for brands like Ferragamo, Gucci, and Armani. They excelled in producing high-quality goods with a great array of styles and colors and fashions. Today, although many of these small and medium firms still operate as suppliers and manufacturers, many of them have expanded and made their own brands that now have large international reputations. Businesses like Benetton, Sàfilo, Max Mara, Luxottica, Geox, Tie Rack, and Ermenegildo Zegna are world-class companies whose production base remains in the districts. Ermenegildo Zegna, for example, is a textile manufacturer that also makes menswear and owns about 400 retail shops around the world. It has about $785 million turnover a year.

Amazingly, these district firms turn out about a quarter of Italy's exports. Each firm specializes in only a few stages of production—sometimes only one—and in order to fill orders, they combine their efforts. The role played by managers in big, vertically integrated firms is substituted here by cooperation between businesses and by the market. If Italian district firms can coordinate in this way, it is in part because of norms of trust built up through repeated experiences of collaboration. Local institutions like trade associations, vocational institutes, and unions have also contributed, by providing training, design expertise, information on foreign markets and exporting, trade fairs, showrooms, and other services that were too expensive for individual small firms to do by themselves.

The districts are located mainly in the north and center of Italy, near the cities of Venice, Biella, Bergamo, Modena, Bologna, Reggio Emilia, and Prato—in regions with little or no unemployment. Although the districts make goods like clothing and furniture that are under heavy competition from low-cost producers in developing countries, the wages in the district companies remain high. Firm performance is also excellent. Studies by the Bank of Italy found that firms in the industrial districts were more profitable than Italian "nondistrict" firms with the same size and technology in the same product markets (the Bank's research results covered the years 1982–1995).[14] As we will see in Parts Four and Five, the Italian district firms today continue to move along a trajectory very different from the one that firms in the same industries in the United States have been following. Leaping ahead to preview some of our findings on these Italian firms that will be analyzed later in this book, we saw that though there has been a certain decline in these labor-intensive traditional activities even in the Italian districts, it is far from the collapse that has taken place in the U.S. or U.K. clothing, shoe, and furniture sectors. When the Italian district firms invest in China or in Central Eastern Europe, they do not transfer everything to them; rather, they mainly use the plants in these low-wage economies as the bases for new businesses and expansion and keep their businesses in the district working on higher-end products.

In the boom times of mass standardized production in America in the 1960s and 1970s, when vertically integrated companies dominated the scene, the Italian districts seemed like interesting but quaint holdovers from traditional industry. By the 1980s, however, consumers in advanced countries were more prosperous than they had been in the fifties and sixties, and they were no longer satisfied with the standard products that the big companies were turning out. It's true that big companies like Ford and GM presented more options than Henry Ford had proposed at the turn of the century when he supposedly offered customers a car in "any color they want so long as it's black," but much of this variety was cosmetic. Not compact cars, but different colors. Tail fins. Air-conditioning. But American companies continued to depend on long production runs and long design cycles, and this rigidity characterized industries as diverse as automobiles, steel, textiles, and machine tools.[15] Consumers started demanding more choice and higher quality. Product cycles shortened and the cost of capital rose. By the late eighties, the Italian experiences began to look more relevant, and articles about districts and policies to create them in other countries became fashionable. Districts were a proof of concept that high levels of productivity and quality could be achieved by coordinating companies carrying out only a few core functions in tightly linked networks, rather than in factories controlled by a single set of owners and managers.

Just in Time: Made in Japan

But the Italian industrial districts were hardly likely to provide realistic inspiration to large American companies who found themselves in trouble in the 1980s and 1990s because of intense competition from European and Japanese firms. Instead, these companies looked to another model—the Japanese firms, which by the 1980s were gaining market share and dominance across a range of industries, like autos, consumer electronics, semiconductors, textiles, and machine tools, that had previously been American turf. The Japanese, too, had an industrial economy with large, vertically integrated enterprises. This company model was born during Meiji Japan's rapid industrialization in the last quarter of the nineteenth century, as Japan tried to catch up with the West. The broad encompassing structures (vertically or horizontally integrated *keiretsu* businesses) of Japanese companies were built on tight links to banks and cross-shareholdings with suppliers and affiliated businesses. Some of the *keiretsu* companies (Mitsubishi, Mitsui, Sumitomo, Yasuda) survived more or less intact the trust-busting efforts of American occupation authorities and went on to become postwar giants. New companies like Matsushita and Hitachi were constructed along similar lines.

In these firms, there were important differences from large-scale American companies. Where Americans relied on steep pyramids of managerial authority for coordinating activities, the Japanese had much "flatter" organizations, with fewer levels of bosses and supervisors between the top and the bottom, so people could communicate more directly across the workplace. The web of human informal relationships that linked the lifelong careers of Japanese workers and managers to a single company generated high loyalty and trust. These precious resources allowed the organization to get high levels of commitment and performance, not only from its own workforce but also from suppliers and customers. The premium set on learning across all levels of the company went hand in hand with an emphasis on quality control, continuous improvement, and "just-in-time" production. As a result, Japanese companies did not need buffers like fat inventories and multiple suppliers that were built into the American system. The Japanese "lean manufacturing system" was far more flexible than the American Fordist mass production system in swiftly turning out a stream of varied new products of high quality and at reasonable prices.[16]

The lessons of Japanese success were spelled out in a flood of books in the 1980s and 1990s, like James Womack et al.'s *The Machine That Changed the World*, on the car industry, or Ronald Dore's *British Factory, Japanese Factory*, which compares Hitachi and British Electric.[17] When applied to the American situation, the overall thrust of these lessons was to reform the vertically integrated company model to make it more efficient, more flexible, and more capable of driving innovation into production and into the marketplace. The Japanese example was used to demonstrate that even tighter integration between product design, manufacturing, and marketing was needed to improve outcomes. In addition to gleaning guidance from these texts, American managers themselves devoted a great deal of attention to observing the Japanese in action—both in Japan and in the Japanese "transplant" plants in the United States like NUMMI, the GM-Toyota joint venture in California.

When MIT researchers on the *Made in America* project conducted interviews across the United States in 1987 and 1988, we learned about senior corporate executive delegations making visit after visit to Japanese plants to fathom the secrets of Japanese success. Even in the Deep South, in an old-line textile business like Milliken (located in Spartanburg, South Carolina), we were told tales of days spent on Japanese factory floors and heard Japanese terms like *kanban* (implementation of just-in-time production) and *kaizen* (continuous improvement) used as everyday language. These efforts made a real difference in the performance of

American companies such as Motorola, which built its famous "Six Sigma" quality system on the Japanese model. The Japanese impact was also visible in the reform and recovery of the U.S. car industry. But the truly revolutionary changes in the structure of American companies would come from an entirely different direction.

CHAPTER 4

The New American Model[1]

The technological advances that changed the menu of options for large, vertically integrated companies had been in the making for a long time, but they would come together in a burst in the mid-nineties. While the technology did not force companies to adopt new organizational forms, it made such transformations possible. New digital technologies allowed smooth and rapid coordination of stages in the production process, even when these phases were located in independent enterprises situated all around the world. The reasons why firms leapt on these possibilities for fragmentation require other explanations, ones that I have already laid out in Chapter 1, like the increase in the cost of capital and of new plants and equipment that in the eighties and nineties made producers more hesitant about pouring heavy new investments into brick and mortar. The cost of starting up a new semiconductor fabrication plant, for example, rose from about $1 billion in 1980 to $2 billion in 2000 and around $3 billion in 2005.[2] Rising costs and the volatility of demand made companies in many industries—from fast-tech sectors like electronics to slow-tech sectors like clothing—ever more willing to explore subcontracting solutions that would shift the burden of capital investment and the risk of overproduction onto others.

Tough competition from new players like the Koreans and Southeast Asians made companies more sensitive to labor costs as well as to the cost of capital. Companies started looking for ways to hive off the labor-intensive parts of their operations. These new competitive pressures in the international economy were the drivers of the shift toward a modular system in which companies would carry out fewer and fewer of the functions in the production process within their own walls.

What made this transformation possible in a wide range of industries across the economy were the new digital technologies coming on line in the 1990s. In other words, these new information technologies, involving both design and production, are the enablers of modularity.[3] The point of departure from vertical integration to modularity, as Harvard Business School professors Carliss Y. Baldwin and Kim B. Clark explain in their pioneering study of the origins of design modularity at IBM, was the development of products with integral architectures that had to be made by teams working in close collaboration in-house. (Recall the airplane kit model of organization.)

In the 1950s, virtually all computers had instructions sets that were literally hardwired into their control logic and arithmetic units. This high degree of interdependence also characterized input/output design, the processor-memory linkages, and all hardware and software interactions. Because the design parameters were so interdependent, each new system had to be designed from scratch; hence every market niche had a different whole system matched to it.[4]

As the information systems built into products like computers based on integrated circuits had become more complex, however, it became more expensive and difficult for a single designer or team of designers to create a whole new system every time a new computer was developed.[5] In the fall of 1961, IBM began searching for ways to enable different teams to work on the same project together. The idea was to break design problems into separable blocks of tasks, or modules.[6] The engineers looked for natural break points—that is, points along the production sequence where it was either unnecessary to transfer large amounts of information across the border between one activity and the next, or points where it was possible to specify in advance complete rules for how the two adjacent clusters of activities should connect. Sometimes designers could find these natural break points in the processes already under way. Sometimes they had to engineer them in by reorganizing processes so that teams could operate in relative independence on either side of the "break."[7] The efforts to create modularity in design had a first big triumph with IBM's System/360 computers in the 1960s. As a result, "between 1970 and 1996, the industry changed from being a virtual [IBM] monopoly into a large 'modular cluster,' which today comprises more than a thousand publicly traded firms and many more hopeful startups."[8]

For the separate components that each team designs to fit together at the end of the design work, the engineers had to agree at the outset on what each subsystem would have to do and the parameters within which it would operate. These rules of the game operated like standards—specifications that many different independent companies all take as the starting points for creating new products designed to work together with those already on the market. Standards sometimes are the result of the enormous success of a single company's dominance of a market, as with the Microsoft Windows standard. In other cases, companies agree on standards, as in the RosettaNet nonprofit consortium created in 1998 by companies like American Express, Microsoft, and IBM to codify business transactions over the Internet and cut response time and cost out of the supply chain.[9] As fragmentation of the production system exploded, companies now deal with more suppliers and customers. For example, in 2001 contract manufacturer Solectron was buying components from more than 7,000 suppliers, was producing in 60 manufacturing plants, and was selling to more than 300 big customers. This kind of business generates the need for common ways of designating objects and transactions and talking about them over the Internet.

Modularity in the production system does not, however, require design rules across the board that specify in advance how to create new products and components that can work together. If I can plug my personal digital assistant Palm Pilot into my Mac Powerbook and "hot sync" my calendar appointments, it's because Palm Pilot engineers knew enough about PC and Apple requirements to be able to design a PDA that works with either of them. This makes it possible to launch a vast number of new businesses making components, subsystems, and software that are compatible with existing products and can just be "plugged in" without any need for IBM (or Apple or Intel or Microsoft) collaboration.

Modular production in electronics started to take off in the 1990s. New software made it possible to provide digital instructions ("codification") so that companies could give suppliers exact information on how to carry out parts of production.[10] In the past, companies drew on the tacit knowledge and experience of engineers to link one phase of the production process to the next. But as soon as engineers learned to write digital code specifying how to translate designs into production specifications, the "hand-off" between one function and the next no longer required having the designers and the production people in the same facility working out problems together. Now the engineer who lays out the circuit-board design can write specifications in software that tell the technicians making the board or the chip exactly what to do.

Even today, negotiation between people on the two sides of the hand-off may still be needed to work out problems—as we learned, for example, from the experience of Hewlett-Packard and the Taiwan ODM companies.[11] Handling negotiations across the frontiers of different companies is usually the responsibility of an engineer in the brand firms, though increasingly, contract manufacturers are also taking on this new role of "supply-chain integrator." To do it well takes technical expertise and experience and the ability to manage in situations with complicated differences in language and culture.[12] This new role also prompts critical questions about the future of high-level engineering jobs in advanced economies. Where can such skilled people be found and how can they be trained in the United States once manufacturing moves out of the lead firms? Digitization thus far has squeezed tacit knowledge out of the system, so fewer people are required to bridge the interface between different stages of production. But radical innovation could once again increase the demand for engineers capable of working "across the functions" as integrators.[13]

In Part Six, I will return to this question of what the United States has to do to generate the human capital needed for high levels of innovation and change.

The Multiplier Effect

The breakup of functions allows innovation to flourish by making it possible to pull together new combinations of "Legos" that were invented for altogether different purposes. Take a hit product like the Apple iPod, first put on the market in 2001. By the end of 2004, Apple iPods had 70 percent of the market for portable digital music players, and income from their sales amounted to almost a quarter of Apple's total revenues.[14] The enormous success of this slim device has a lot to do with an elegant design and with software that helps the user work the device easily and connect it seamlessly to other boxes and software.[15] It's impossible to figure out how much of the cachet and value of the iPod comes from design—which was partly done in-house and partly outsourced; how much from the connection to the Apple iTunes music database; and how much from sophisticated hardware. Here, as with many of the most valuable products today, services and manufacturing are tightly woven together.

Because Apple conceived a product that combines components that were already being made by others, the iPod could move from concept to market in less than a year. The vital parts of the iPod include a tiny Toshiba hard disk, a Nidec disk-drive spindle, an ARM core processor, a Texas Instruments firewire controller, a USB interface chip from Cypress, and flash memory from Sharp.[16] Final assembly is done by Inventec, a Taiwanese contract manufacturer with more than $2 billion sales a year. (The cost of all the components and services that Apple buys amounts to about half the retail cost of the iPod.) Could Apple have developed such a product so rapidly and at an acceptable price if it had had to develop its own hard disk, memory chips, and so forth? The iPod example is one of thousands that illustrate how modularity has contributed to an explosion of new products and new entrepreneurship, unleashed from many of the heavy old constraints of time and capital investment.

How Modularity Transformed Semiconductor Making

From the commercialization of the transistor in the 1950s through the 1980s, semiconductor production had been carried out in vertically integrated firms. Companies like IBM, Hewlett-Packard, Motorola, Siemens, Toshiba, Sony, NEC, Fujitsu, and Matsushita had done everything within their own four walls, from designing, fabricating, assembling, testing, and selling integrated circuits (ICs) to designing, manufacturing, and marketing many of the products in which ICs were used—products like televisions, Walkmen, computers, and printers. From the 1980s on, a combination of U.S. government support for new technologies and private initiative began to create opportunities to break apart functions that had always been bundled together.[17] The U.S. Department of Defense Research Agency (DARPA) financed the CalTech Interchange Format project to develop a standard that would allow computer exchange of the data between chip designers and the foundries that fabricate chips. This standard, called the MOSIS foundry system, took about a decade to work out. Finally, by the early 1990s, two companies, Cadence and Mentor Graphics, were able to provide software that allowed designers to send specifications directly to the foundries.

On the other side of the Pacific, in Taiwan, the government from the 1970s on had been trying to build a local semiconductor industry. It financed the acquisition of technologies and, most important of all, encouraged Taiwanese engineers who had emigrated to the United States and risen through the ranks of American electronics companies to return to Taiwan to help build high-technology industry in what was still a very poor developing society.[18] A Taiwanese government agency, Industrial Technology Research Institute (ITRI), launched a joint venture with Philips in 1987 to create Taiwan Semiconductor Manufacturing Company (TSMC). TSMC would grow into the world's leading semiconductor foundry producer, with 2004 net revenues of $2.76 billion. TSMC's founding president was Dr. Morris Chang, a Taiwanese with MIT and Stanford degrees who had worked for years in the U.S. semiconductor industry at Texas Instruments and General Instruments, and was persuaded to come back to Taiwan to head ITRI. Dr. Chang's radical new idea was to create a "pure play" silicon foundry that would manufacture chips for a variety of different customers but would not develop its own designs and products. By the time the new codification technologies appeared on the scene in the nineties from companies like Cadence and Mentor Graphics, design firms like Broadcom could send instructions as digital files by Internet or on a diskette, and TSMC had had enough foundry experience to be able to seize the opportunity.

The pure-play foundry was an organizational innovation that transformed the electronics industry, for it allows the sequence of functions in the making of components to fragment. Manufacturing at lead firms can be broken off and transferred to chip-manufacturing specialists at these foundries. New firms can be created (and old ones transformed) to carry out only one, two, or several functions, in place of the formerly integrated companies like Texas Instruments, Philips, or IBM that once made both electronic products and components. Modularity also changed the "integrated device makers" (IDMs), companies like Intel, Analog Devices, and ST Microelectronics that make chips, not products. They, too, started sending some of their work to foundries.

Pure-play foundries like TSMC and others that were founded in the wake of TSMC's great success—like United Microelectronics Corporation (UMC) in Taiwan; Chartered in Singapore; Dongbu-Anam in Korea; and now Grace and Semiconductor Manufacturing International Corporation (SMIC) in China—perform only one function in the component value chain—wafer fabrication. (This involves etching circuits onto silicon wafers, which are then broken down into individual silicon chips.) This division of labor makes it possible for firms to pick what they do best, whether designing integrated circuits (ICs), manufacturing them, or marketing them. The wafer-fabrication foundries (usually called "fabs") use much the same equipment to process a variety of design files for customers in different businesses.

A fab turning out chips for computers, telecoms, digital cameras, cell phones, and automotives is less vulnerable to the cyclical ups and downs of any particular industry than is a company making chips mainly for its own use, as companies like IBM and Burroughs did in the 1980s, or for a single sector. Of course, when the dot-com bubble burst in 2001 and almost all the customers were in trouble, the fabs were in trouble, too, but like TSMC, they mostly weathered the storm and bounced back. A wide and diversified customer base also makes it possible to bear the huge capital investment of building a new fab—around U.S. $3 billion today. Often the fabs get major investments from several big customers in exchange for commitments of a certain amount of capacity—which reassures the lead firms that they will be able to ramp up quickly when they have new products.

The resources that the fabs depend on in order to woo the business of the old vertically integrated companies and the new fabless IC design houses are complex. They depend not only on the skills of their own engineers but the availability of production equipment with increasingly sophisticated built-in capabilities. As the big companies shifted production to the foundries, they cut back on their R & D for wafer fabrication. Today it's the equipment makers who have to do much of the R & D that used to take place in the vertically integrated companies. Over the last ten years, semiconductor equipment manufacturers like the U.S. firm Applied Materials, the giant in the sector, and Ulvac, a very successful but much smaller Japanese competitor, embed in the machines they sell to the fabs many of the skills and knowledge that used to reside in the heads of the engineers in the semiconductor divisions and laboratories of the big electronics companies.[19]

As important as any of these technical capabilities, the fab has to convince its customers that it can protect their intellectual property (IP). The fab cannot compete with its own customers and survive. It has to manage the business in a way that prevents the leakage of one customer's IP to the others. The files created by the chip designer and sent to the fab contain information on the positioning of the microcomponents. If this leaked out, the designs could be copied and made into counterfeits, and rivals could learn each other's secrets. Since customers of TSMC include fabless firms like Nvidia and ATI, which compete in graphics chips, this concern is very serious.[20] It is a mark of the extraordinary achievement of the Taiwanese pure-play foundries that even in a society still plagued with severe problems about the protection of intellectual property, the fabs have succeeded in obtaining the confidence on this score of so many of the world's most important electronics companies. In the many interviews in which we explored this issue, no example was cited of a violation of this trust.

The development of the foundries was the catalyst for the emergence of new "fabless" integrated-circuit (IC) design companies. Before the pure-play foundries, life was very difficult for such firms. Crystal Semiconductor, one of the early American fabless design houses, found itself juggling production among the fabs of seven different large integrated electronics companies and worrying about dependence on them for key products. Once the pure-play foundries came into the picture, they provided production capacity to design houses, companies like Crystal, Broadcom (U.S.), Silicon Labs (U.S.), Cambridge Silicon Radio (U.K.), and VIA (Taiwan)—all of which sell ICs to many different customers— and to product companies like Sun, which design chips for proprietary products like Sun servers. Broadcom, for example, specializes in component definition and IC design for broadband markets, including wireless networks, cable/satellite set-top boxes, cable modems, and digital subscriber lines (DSL). TSMC acquired customers like Broadcom, along with a number of the old integrated device makers like Texas Instruments, which were starting to shed some of their manufacturing. By 1997,

TSMC was doing so well it became the first Taiwanese company on the New York Stock Exchange. By 2002, fifteen years after its founding in a still poor and technologically backward society, TSMC was the world's tenth-largest semiconductor producer.

Exit Manufacturing

The digital technologies that transformed semiconductors had an explosive fragmenting impact across the board in electronics. As modularity made it possible to build new businesses, it also transformed old ones. Perhaps the most important change was the movement of large chunks of manufacturing out of brand-name electronics firms and into contract manufacturers. In giants like Hewlett-Packard, IBM, and Texas Instruments—all of which made components and final products—manufacturing had once been a central function. When these businesses came under severe competitive pressure from the Japanese in the seventies and eighties, they tended to respond first by tightening up the integration of manufacturing with other functions.

The recommendations for improving productivity and profitability in U.S. corporations in the eighties emphasized joint decision-making at all stages of a product's development—an idea that has been called "simultaneous engineering," "concurrent engineering," or "multifunctional teams." By whatever name, the notion was that tighter integration of functions was needed in order to increase efficiency and quality, and to bring innovation to the marketplace quickly. When IBM's profits fell nearly 27 percent in 1986, it followed with Japanese-like campaigns to improve quality, listen to the customer, and become "leaner, more competitive, more responsive," as an IBM mission statement put it.[21]

Ten years later, after such declarations of devotion to improving manufacturing, the world had revolved 180 degrees. From the mid-nineties on, technical advances in modularity made it possible to take a radically different approach. Modular solutions shifted companies' attention from fixing manufacturing and integrating it more closely with design and marketing to getting rid of manufacturing altogether. As of 1996, IBM was spinning off its high-end computing manufacturing as a separate business unit (Celestica) and selling off factories to contract manufacturers. Hewlett-Packard (HP) had shed most of its manufacturing plants and engineering-detailed design activities, having closed down or sold off its plants and laid off production workers. Jobs that once were carried out within HP are now performed by contract manufacturers, mostly in Asia. As Geoffrey Parker and Edward Anderson, management experts who studied HP, discovered, the results for the company have been dramatic. In the notebook computer division, for example, where HP now outsources all of its products to Taiwanese original design manufacturers, revenues grew by about tenfold and return on assets improved. The results were equally striking on the employment side: The number of HP jobs in the notebook division fell from 400 to 50.[22]

Today much of manufacturing has turned into a commodity like any other service or good; many different vendors offer manufacturing services to a number of customers without providing much—if any—customization based on the needs of the particular buyers. If it ever becomes a true commodity, then there will be no differentiation at all, and one supplier could easily replace another. While electronics contract manufacturing has not reached this point, it has become possible to purchase on the market manufacturing functions that used to be carried out in-house. In a growing number of industries, managers of brand-name firms no longer run manufacturing, but buy it from contract manufacturers that have been able to capture significant parts of the production system. Top-quality performance in many complex manufacturing operations used to require carrying out all important functions either in-house or else in the plants of closely controlled "captive" suppliers. Today the same level of performance can be achieved through coordination of a supply chain with multiple autonomous firms located along the links between product definition and sale to the final customer. Given the availability of new technology options and the whip of severe economic pressures, most large multinational corporations have transformed themselves into organizations focused on a smaller set of core competencies.

If IBM was the poster child of success in the eighties, today's symbol is Dell, one of the world's biggest and most profitable information technology companies.[23] Dell sells computers with an innovative system that allows customers to customize their orders online and to receive their machines rapidly. But the only manufacturing Dell does in-house is final assembly; it outsources the rest to suppliers like Intel, who build the microprocessors, and to contract manufacturers located in Asia, who build the rest of the computer's components, including the motherboards, the LCD displays, the mouse, and the hard drives. Many of these businesses did not even exist twenty-five years ago.

In the electronics industry, three types of contractors have emerged: original equipment manufacturers (OEMs), original design manufacturers (ODMs), and global suppliers. Confusingly, these labels are used in different ways in various parts of the world. In this book, OEM refers to companies that manufacture products on order from brand-name firms but do not themselves develop brands or new designs.[24] ODMs are companies like the Taiwanese laptop makers (Quanta, Compal, ASUSTeK) that do design and manufacturing on orders from brand-name companies (like Dell or Hewlett-Packard) and do not develop their own brands. Global suppliers are a group of very large specialist contract manufacturers (Sanmina-SCI, Solectron, Flextronics, Jabil, Celestica are the biggest) that mainly focus on manufacturing and have production sites around the world. Flextronics, for example, had 2004 revenues of $14.5 billion.[25] Its top ten customers account for 64 percent of its business—with Sony-Ericsson (cell phones) and Siemens as its largest accounts.

Subcontracting is as old as industry itself, but these new OEMs and ODMs are something quite different. In the past, companies used subcontractors for specialized items that were beyond the main firm's capabilities—for example, automakers buying floor carpeting. Or they looked to subcontractors when they wanted to expand production without adding on workers or new facilities in a period of peak demand. This traditional kind of subcontracting still goes on. But the new OEMs and ODMs carry out functions that used to be carried out in-house by vertically integrated companies. They are likely to do all of a firm's manufacturing or detailed design or logistics—and not just the overflow during periods of heavy demand. As Timothy Sturgeon has pointed out, what is new in production systems today is that outsourcing need not involve sale of a single component or process (e.g., disk drives or metal machining), but can be the entire manufacturing process, bundled, made generic, and applied to a range of related industries, such as when contract manufacturers serve various electronics subsectors.[26]

These OEM, ODM, and global suppliers are no longer the weak, dependent, captive subcontractors of the past.[27] They are major powerhouses able to negotiate from positions of autonomy and strength with the brand-name companies. The research found a similar division of labor emerging in apparel between brand companies like Liz Claiborne and New Balance and contractors like Fang Brothers and Pou Chen and in autos and auto parts between assemblers like GM and Ford and suppliers like Bosch and Delphi. The rise of these contract manufacturers in many industries stands out as one of the most important developments in the new global economy.

Reorganizing the Auto Industry

The push for modularity and fragmentation has been strongest in industries like electronics, where codification enabled the hand-offs at technologically defined frontiers and in the clothing industry, where there were already natural break points between design and manufacturing. But in the 1990s, modularity also made big advances in many other industries where few natural break points existed. Our team looked closely at the auto industry, one in which modular design is very difficult to implement.[28] Products and processes with modular and open structures are ones in which "each element (i.e, component, module, or subassembly) is functionally complete."[29] This means that each element can be separately designed; elements can be reused for new purposes; and it is possible to put the same pieces of the "Lego" together in different ways to make a variety of different products. Much of the electronics industry has this open, modular character. In carmaking this is not (or not yet) a full-blown reality.

In practice, the more closed, integral architecture of vehicles as products means that car assemblers have to work in constant close contact with suppliers. That way the parts makers can provide components that fit exactly into the models the brand-name firms are designing. They cannot, like the electronics suppliers, make parts that will just "plug and play" in every car model. Because suppliers need to provide parts and subassemblies (like a dashboard put together by a supplier from multiple parts) specific to a particular brand's model, they usually cannot reuse the same components and processes to gain economies of scale, as the electronics contract manufacturers do. In part this has to do with the way cars work. But also, in order to give a distinctive look and feel to each car brand, the companies design in features that require parts suppliers to make very different components, even for the same task. When car companies do try to use "common platforms" for a range of models in order to reduce costs, there is the risk of producing cars that look alike to consumers and blur the differences between their top-of-the-line and their cheaper models.

The more the brand tries to maximize its distinctiveness and quality, the harder it is to hand over whole modules or subassemblies to suppliers without losing control of the overall design and identity of the car. American carmakers have been trying to shift more of the responsibility for module design and assembly to their "first-tier suppliers"—large global companies like Lear Corporation, Magna, Bosch, Denso, and TRW, and the result has been bland-looking cars that do not excite consumers.[30] One of the German parts suppliers we talked to predicted that if European carmakers went the same route as the Americans in handing over larger and larger parts of the car to be made by suppliers, "it would only be a matter of time before European assemblers have as little control over design as North American assemblers do today."[31] For high-priced cars like BMW and Lexus, losing distinctiveness is a showstopper. So brand-name firms still bump up against real limits to "reusing" elements, as electronics firms do. They require suppliers to produce different parts for the same function. As one parts maker told us, even if they are designing a simple joint, they cannot come up with one that both VW and Toyota would buy, because Toyota has different durability specifications than VW. If they made the joint to Toyota's standards, VW "would be penalized on cost and paying for a more durable joint than they specified."

For all these reasons, assemblers cannot just "hand over" a blueprint to suppliers, but need to work with them throughout the design process of the car. This creates a premium on having suppliers locate close to the automakers' design centers in Detroit, Turin, Guyancourt, and Toyota City. A manager of a tier-two supplier of parts of fuel tanks to BMW in South Carolina explained to us that proximity and "face time" with the assemblers are competitive advantages for suppliers. They reduce product development time and avoid costly misunderstandings.[32] But if suppliers need to be near automakers' design centers, they need to hire people in specific locales. They cannot seek out engineering talents and workers around the world. The automakers operate on the principle of "build where you sell," and since the design centers are located in first-world, high-wage labor markets, that's where the suppliers are going to have to be, too. Some of the most labor-intensive parts, like wire harnesses, may move to low-cost labor markets, like Romania, that are quite distant from the assemblers, but in general, auto suppliers have less freedom to scan the world for low-cost labor sites than do the electronics contractors.

Another major reason for locating close to assemblers is to deliver parts "just in time" for sequencing their insertion at the right moment into cars rolling along the assembly lines. This is hard to do—if not impossible—when suppliers are distant from assembly plants, even when excellent infrastructure and transportation are available. When Ford set up its new "flexible assembly" factory in Chicago in 2004, it convinced its major suppliers to locate nearby.[33] The idea was to be able to produce eight models on two chassis in the same plant. By having the suppliers next door, inventories could be cut, and Ford engineers could work more closely with the suppliers on the new models. Lear, one of the Ford suppliers, which used to transport its assembled interior ceilings from 350 miles away, will now be only half a mile away.

DaimlerChrysler has moved its suppliers even closer: right into the plant.[34] In a $1.2 billion expansion announced in 2004 for an Ohio Jeep factory, DaimlerChrysler got suppliers to finance and run parts of the plant that do welding, assembly, painting, and chassis modules. The components that Ford and DaimlerChrysler are demanding to have made next door are clearly not likely to move to China or any other low-wage country anytime soon, except of course as the assemblers themselves start making cars in China, as we will see shortly.[35]

Despite all these real barriers to modularity in autos, competition and overcapacity were so severe in the nineties that companies tried to hive off as many functions as possible in order to lower costs. The firms rebundled processes in ways that allowed them to break off divisions and "deverticalize" the company, even though the hand-off was rarely as clean and distinct as in electronics. GM and Ford spun off internal divisions that became independent suppliers Delphi and Visteon. When we asked one of the managers why Ford had broken off Visteon, he explained bitterly that they want a "Dell model—with no assets." In other words, the idea is to shift workers and fixed capital off Ford's books and onto the suppliers'. Ford did indeed move 78,000 employees off its payroll, and revenues per employee went up.

Assemblers like Ford and GM outsourced more and more of the car to fewer suppliers. Companies like Lear, Johnson Controls, Siemens Automotive, Valeo, Bosch, Magna, and TRW grew and swallowed up the smaller fish.[36] Even as the brand-name firms were shedding functions in order to save on labor costs and investment in their own facilities, the suppliers had to add on functions in order to satisfy the assemblers' demands for buying modules and systems, and not single parts. Increasingly, the carmakers asked their suppliers to provide whole subassemblies, like dashboards with all the switches and displays, or air-conditioning units, or drive trains with engines, transmissions, and axles. The modules handed over to the suppliers became bigger and bigger. Dana (an automotive supplier started 100 years ago in New Jersey) offers chassis system modules—which involve about 30 percent of the value of the car. Magna, a Canadian supplier, can produce "the ultimate module, a complete car system plus final assembly," and it makes whole cars in niche markets, like the Jeep Cherokee in Europe.

Workers in the "big three" are mostly unionized, with high wages and good health and pension benefits, while workers at the suppliers are more weakly organized, so shifting the workforce from assemblers to suppliers is likely to lower wages. From the mid-seventies on, the wage gap has widened between workers at the assemblers and those in the suppliers' plants. Hourly wages at suppliers were slightly lower than hourly wages at the assemblers in the early seventies, but by 2000 the former were only 74 percent of wages earned at U.S. automakers.[37] At 1,010,000 in 1999, overall employment in the U.S. auto industry was as high as it had been in the mid-seventies, having rebounded from a low of about 700,000 in the early eighties. Twenty-five years ago, though, there had been about equal numbers of American workers employed at the assemblers and at the suppliers. Today, about two-thirds of the workers are at the suppliers. So the revival of the industry has not produced the same kind of bounce in earnings and benefits for workers as it would have if the two parts of the industry had grown at the same rate.[38] In all likelihood, the shift toward the suppliers will continue. It's a sign of the times that when DaimlerChrysler announced its plans to hire new workers for the new Ohio Jeep without the same contracts as today's workers, union leaders conceded, "We have to recognize the enemy is not in the same room; the enemy is the competition somewhere else."[39]

What to Do with the New Legos?

The consequences of the changes in the production system are still unfolding, but some of them already contrast sharply with previous industrial practice. First of all, in many industries it is now possible to create a successful company based on a single function or a very few functions. This makes it easier for newcomers to get into the game, since they no longer have to reinvent the whole wheel, but only one part of it. At the same time, the move toward modularity raises a challenge to more integrated firms. They can do well only if each of the functions they keep in-house can compete with the best-in-class of the "single function" companies. This is the reasoning that lay behind IBM's decision to sell its loss-making personal computer (PC) division to Lenovo, a Chinese computer company, in 2004. As I describe in more detail in Part Four, IBM came to see PC manufacturing as a high-volume commodity business—and not a function at which it could excel.

Additionally, the modular revolution has created a greater equality between companies located at different points in the production process. In the past, brand-name companies were in the driver's seat, and the suppliers and subcontractors had to follow their lead. Today, there are powerful companies that stand on virtually every function along the sequence of production. In times when demand is high for chips, fabs—subcontractors though they may be—call the shots. When laptops were in high demand, brandless ODM companies like Quanta and ASUSTeK were able to command a high return for their manufacturing and design services.

Finally, the breakup of the production system leads not only to hiving off activities and moving them to outsourcers. It also means that these operations can be moved abroad. The next chapter examines how dramatic political changes (the opening of China in 1979, the fall of the Iron Curtain in 1989) and the transformation of the rules of the international economy opened possibilities that would allow the modular production system to expand on a global scale.

PART THREE

Made All Over

CHAPTER 5

The Dilemma: Should You Stay or Should You Go?

n January 2000, our team met with Ah-Ping Lin, founder and president of Lee Chi Enterprises, a very successful bicycle-component company based in Taichung, Taiwan. At the time, Lin was facing some tough choices.[1] He fell into the bicycle business by accident in the seventies when he was looking for a way to invest some savings and at the same time a friend needed help keeping his small, floundering brake-component company alive. Knowing nothing about the business, Lin copied Japanese bike models and got designs from foreign buyers and trading companies. Originally, Lee Chi bought the brake parts and just assembled them. As the company developed experience, they started making the key components themselves.

By 1995, however, the world had changed and many of the bicycle assemblers began moving to mainland China for cheap labor. Lin said he had to follow them because "you need to be in the network; you need the cluster. You need to get firms together. It's easier to communicate with Taiwanese businessmen. So we go together with them to China. It's a matter of survival! You can't stay away!" His first customers in China were big exporters like Giant and Merida. Gradually, Lee Chi developed domestic Chinese customers as well.

In 2000, Lee Chi had captured the largest world market share in bicycle brake systems, with products for both low- and high-end models, and had gone public on the Taipei exchange. It had a plant in Shanghai with 1,000 workers and 20 Taiwanese managers making low-end products to sell in China. It had 600 workers in Taiwan and employed 80 graduate engineers. All of Lee Chi's 300 subcontractors were Taiwanese, most of them located near Lee Chi's plants. The move to China helped business. But it also meant a loss of Taiwanese jobs. By the end of 2004, Lee Chi was down to 480 workers in Taiwan and up to over 2,000 in China.

In the future, Lin wondered, should he expand the production for the Chinese domestic market and leave the high-end part of the business in Taiwan? That would reduce the risk in his relationships with demanding Western customers who wanted high quality and knew they could get it from Taiwan-made products. Or should he move everything to China? If he did, would he be one step ahead of the competition, or one step too far out on a branch that might not yet be strong enough to support precision and quality manufacturing? And how many of his subcontractors could he get to move with him to China? Would he have to start making some of the parts he currently bought from them?

For almost every company we studied, from giants like Dell, Hewlett-Packard, and Sony to small "multinationals" like Lee Chi and L. W. Packard, the question of where to locate different parts of the business has become a critical one—and it's one that comes up again and again. Every time another trade barrier falls, or more-skilled labor becomes available abroad, or competition intensifies at home, or new consumers appear on the horizon, companies revisit their policy. Twenty years ago, the issue was virtually absent from discussions about industrial performance. Why and how have relocation choices become so important for companies today?

The new "Lego" model of production does not in principle require geographic relocation. The fragmentation and reconstruction of U.S. production could have taken place strictly within U.S. borders. In fact, most outsourcing does happen at home (though U.S. government statistics offices do not collect the numbers we would need to nail these facts down definitively). Outsourcing increasingly involves services, and many of the most sophisticated product-design and -development services are likely to be carried out by teams in the United States or other advanced economies.[2] For example, IBM's Engineering and Technology Services group, a "hypergrowth" area for the company, does chip designing for the Sony PlayStation 3, and the IBM team works in the United States. Companies sell U.S. factories to Solectron, Flextronics, and other contract manufacturers who run the plants under new management but may keep them in the United States. Businesses outsource IT services and, increasingly, business-process operations, like corporate human resources offices, finance, and accounting and other back-office operations, to American firms like IBM, Accenture, Hewlett-Packard, or EDS, or, in Europe, companies like Siemens in Germany and Cap Gemini in France.[3] In 2004, European firms won the largest share of new contracts for outsourcing services (49 percent); U.S. companies garnered 42 percent; and firms outside of the United States and Europe got less than 10 percent. So most of this activity takes place among companies within the advanced industrial world.[4]

If all outsourcing were domestic, the new production system's impact on employment might be minimal.[5] As the economy became more efficient and specialized, costs would fall. Innovation and new businesses might find a more rapid entry into the market. While productivity increases due to technologies that replace labor do have a big impact on employment, changes that shift workers from one employer to another do not necessarily have such an effect. If a product-development engineer works for IBM rather than Honeywell, her wages are likely to be about the same, and it is not clear that IBM will need fewer such people for a project than Honeywell would have employed. If all the work stayed in the United States, outsourcing might not greatly affect jobs or wages. But this is not what is happening. In reality, once modularity makes it possible to break up production, firms have many more choices about where to locate the pieces. When industries can move factories abroad and freely bring the products they are making there back home, or when they can easily import what they used to make domestically, jobs and wages at home become vulnerable.

Relocation abroad requires governments to remove legal obstacles to the free flow of capital, goods, and services across borders. Since the mid-1980s, international trade agreements in the GATT (General Agreement on Tariffs and Trade) and in its successor, the WTO (World Trade Organization), have progressively liberalized the movement of foreign direct investment and trade in goods and services among the world's major economies. In a wholly unanticipated turn of history, the Iron Curtain around the Soviet-dominated countries of Eastern Europe came down in 1989. Ten years earlier, the Chinese leaders had decided to open China to the West. With China's entry into the WTO on November 11, 2001, many of the remaining barriers between the Chinese economy and the global economy have been leveled. A vast new space has been opened, allowing for the reconstruction of the international economic system into networks linking production sites around the globe.

It's the combination of modularity and the breakup of the production system, together with the opening of the international economy, that delivers the real punch of globalization. The two processes of reorganization and relocation go hand in hand—creating new opportunities for some producers in both the advanced rich countries and in emerging economies and new threats to jobs and income for others.

About three-quarters of the jobs, capital investment, and production of American multinational corporations (MNCs) take place in the United States, according to surveys conducted by the U.S. Bureau of Economic Analysis. These proportions have been quite stable over the past twenty-five years.[6] When American multinational corporations produce abroad, it is mostly in other rich, high-wage countries like Japan, Canada, and Western European societies, so the motivations for offshoring are something other than simple cost reduction.[7] What these reasons might be we discuss later—but as a first cut, it's clear that multinational companies' investments in other affluent countries do not represent the threat to wages and working conditions that people fear in globalization.[8]

The principal new danger, if there is one, is that jobs are being shifted from or created outside the multinational corporations through outsourcing and offshoring in countries with low-wage economies, like China and India. As a 2004 study by the U.S. Government Accountability Office (GAO) admits, we do not have reliable information on exactly how much outsourcing and offshoring are taking place.[9] The value of the goods and services that U.S. multinationals buy from suppliers has risen from under 60 percent of sales in the 1980s to over 70 percent of sales in 2001 — so there is more outsourcing, but we do not know if these are domestic or foreign suppliers.[10] Nor do we have solid data on how outsourcing and offshoring are affecting jobs at home. To start with, the United States has about 140 million jobs. The Department of Labor's surveys on layoffs due to locating overseas show a rise from 1999 to 2003, yet the numbers are still very small — only 13,000, or less than one percent, of all big layoffs in 2003 were a result of moving abroad.[11] Most of the job losses in manufacturing result from productivity gains, as new technology introduced at home makes it possible to reduce the number of employees.

In the first three months of 2004, the numbers of jobs lost in big layoffs because of overseas relocation went up to about 2 percent of the total, according to the Bureau of Labor Statistics — still not a very big number.[12] But some researchers claim that the government's statistics are incomplete and greatly underestimate the shifts. The government collects data only on plants with fifty or more employees who lay off at least fifty workers in a five-week period. Moreover, employers do not like to report that they are shifting production overseas. Using different methods of tracking layoffs — scrutinizing local and regional newspapers for stories of plant closings — Kate Bronfenbrenner and Stephanie Luce, professors at Cornell and at the University of Massachusetts (Amherst), concluded that about 406,000 jobs a year are ended by offshoring.[13] Since their final numbers are estimations — they think media tracking captures only two-thirds of the shift to Mexico and a third of the shift elsewhere — their methodologies may inflate the numbers. But the bottom line is that the numbers in each study are so different that it's impossible today to draw any clear picture. As matters stand now, the title of the Government Accountability Office (GAO) study says it all: "Current Government Data Provide Limited Insight into Offshoring of Services."

Some jobs—gardeners, miners, schoolteachers, policemen—are securely stuck to home territory. But they are not necessarily the well-paying, good ones. Thirty years ago, it did seem that only low-skilled work was in danger of transfer to countries with lower wage costs. Politicians' response to that prospect was legislation that funded education for displaced workers so they could move up into more-skilled occupations that were likely to remain in the United States. The 1974 Trade Act contained provisions for aiding workers whose jobs had been eliminated by imports or overseas relocation, and subsequent trade legislation has added to the benefits provided for "trade adjustment assistance" (TAA). These benefits came in the form of retraining courses, income supplements, and job search help.[14] But they are far from covering all laid-off workers. When companies do not admit that they are shifting production abroad, employees can fall through the cracks. Furthermore, service employees are not eligible for TAA. Bronfenbrenner and Luce estimate that only about a third of the workers who lose jobs because of trade or offshoring file TAA petitions for support.[15] Even when they do, the quality of the retraining they receive is spotty. The evidence on these retraining courses does not provide much room for optimism about reeducating out-of-work, middle-aged people whose initial school experiences may never have been very positive and who are not likely to have received continuing education on the job.[16]

Over the past few years, an even bleaker question has come up: If we could provide good retraining for displaced workers, what would we educate them to do? Service work? As you read this book, many white-collar jobs in software, banking, insurance, medical services, and back-office operations are moving out of advanced industrial countries into offices in India, the Philippines, and elsewhere in the developing world. These shifts are eliminating the jobs in the United States once held by employees with high school and even college diplomas.[17] True, in 2004, it did not seem that very large numbers were involved: perhaps only 60,000–80,000 business, professional, and technical (BPT) services jobs a year in the United States' vast labor market, in which some 13 million jobs disappear every year and some 14 to 15 million new jobs are created.[18] Imports of computing and business services were low, only 0.4 percent of GDP in 2003, though double what they had been in 1993.[19]

The numbers as they stand today seem relatively small. But management consulting firms anticipate sharp increases in the future. Forrester Research predicted that 3.3 million service jobs would go offshore by 2015.[20] The Boston Consulting Group urged businesses to offshore sooner rather than later: "The largest competitive advantage will lie with those companies that move soonest. Companies that wait will be caught in a vicious cycle of uncompetitive costs, lost business, underutilized capacity, and the irreversible destruction of value."[21] It concluded: "Companies that continue to hesitate do so at their peril." With dire warnings like this about services employment, what kind of retraining should we offer to laid-off workers?

It's not clear how much education or what kind of education anyone needs or could get that would put him beyond the danger that his or her job may be outsourced. These are questions I return to in Part Six. Here my point is that most workers who are laid off when their employers close down or move abroad are not likely to find jobs as good as the ones they lost. All things equal, these people would be better off if their jobs continued. But all things equal for society must mean that keeping these jobs does not handicap productivity growth in a company, an industry, or the economy as a whole. It's productivity growth that allows a nation to provide better standards of living than poor countries do. It makes it possible, for example, for a bus driver in Germany to have thirteen times the purchasing power of a bus driver in Kenya, even one with about the same skills.[22] So our question should be: Which jobs should disappear in order to build an innovative, competitive economy? Which ones can remain as vital parts of prosperous and dynamic enterprises in our own society?

The best way to approach this is to look at the experience of various companies producing more or less the same goods or services. If we find that all the firms that are doing well in advanced countries are getting rid of the same functions and jobs, we can reasonably conclude that these jobs do not have much of a future in high-wage societies. Competition as a result of technological change or trade liberalization—or both—would explain why these activities are disappearing from advanced economies. But if we find some successful companies keeping jobs in-house while others move the same ones offshore, then we must conclude that something other than economic inevitability and the invisible hand of the market are at work. We then need to figure out why companies have different strategies, whether they are equally sustainable, and what the consequences are for the future of the business, its workers, and society.

To sharpen up our comparisons, our team decided to look at companies in textile and apparel companies as well as electronics. In electronics, wages play a small role in total product costs; in textile and clothing, wages make up a much larger fraction of overall costs. Moreover, most of the manufacturing jobs in textiles and apparel are rather low-skill, so they should be the easiest ones to teach to new workers in the developing countries. Because of high labor content and low skills, we expected to see the trend toward offshoring most strongly in industries like textiles and clothing, and we did.

In the United States, the number of manufacturing jobs in electronics fell from 1994 to 2004 by about a fifth, from about 2.2 million workers to 1.8 million. Over the same period, employment plummeted by 60 percent in textiles and clothing, from about 1.5 million workers in 1994 to 576,000 in 2004—50 percent fewer textile workers and 66 percent fewer apparel workers.[23] Three factors might explain this decline in jobs: new technologies that make labor more productive so that fewer workers are needed to make the same bag of goods, imports that replace domestic products, and movement of the jobs and the factories abroad. Economists disagree sharply about how much responsibility to assign either to technology or globalization. This is an important issue and one I will revisit, because the right policies for encouraging the creation of good jobs in the United States depend on the diagnosis of the problem.

In electronics the causes of job loss are especially difficult to disentangle, because of the revolutionary technological shifts, including digitization and offshoring. In textiles and clothing, on the other hand, technological change has been very slow and not particularly labor-saving. It would seem, then, that for the textile and clothing industries, job losses are a result of globalization—from competition with imports in our markets and outsourcing abroad. In this labor-intensive sector, competing seems to require moving the industry to countries with cheap labor. The IPC team expected these pressures to be equally strong in all high-wage countries.

But even in textiles and apparel, we found that matters are not so simple. By looking at textile and clothing companies in other advanced industrial societies, we discovered quite a different picture from country to country. In the European Union between 1991 and 2001, for example, with countries that compete in a single market, employment in textile and apparel combined fell overall by 46.2 percent: in the United Kingdom by 41 percent, in Germany by 59 percent, but in Italy only by 18.8 percent. In this same period, the United States' decline was 39.1 percent.[24] It's not that Italy has lower wages than the United States or France or the United Kingdom. On the contrary: Italy has higher wages, and the currently strong euro and weak dollar make exporting out of Italy even harder than before. So how can we explain why a country like Italy could do so much better than others in maintaining employment in sectors under heavy competition from low-wage producers abroad? Can Italy teach us something about how to better maintain and upgrade traditional manufacturing jobs? Should we even try to learn? Or would it be better to look at textile and garment manufacturing as a sunset industry that ought to die out in advanced economies? These are all questions I will return to in Part Six.

The Location Imperative:
Make It Where You Sell It—or Else

Getting a Foot in the Door

The movement of production abroad started long before the current wave of globalization. During the first globalization (1870–1914), there were many examples of foreign direct investment and of firms setting up operations outside their home countries in order to tap foreign markets. World War I spelled calamity for many of these investments. French investors, for example, by 1918 had lost two-thirds of their 1914 foreign holdings. One such case was the French company Gratry Enterprises, which had established a textile business in Russia in 1899 to capture the almost "unlimited" Russian consumer market.[25] There was no danger of overproduction there, they promised shareholders. But each year, there was a new problem: An unruly workforce plagued by alcoholism refused to work on the new looms, and a wildcat strike broke out in 1905; fuel costs rose in 1906, after revolutionaries blew up the Baku refineries; problems with tax authorities kept coming up; and finally, with the 1917 Bolshevik Revolution, the company disappeared.

Foreign direct investment in North America, Australia, and Western Europe, however, fared far better than movement to the countries on the periphery of the industrialized world. In the years before World War I, American and European multinational companies (MNCs) had already established important beachheads outside their home countries, and this movement continued ever more strongly in the postwar period.[26] Within a year of their founding, both Ford (1903) and General Motors (1908), for example, had set up plants in Europe. The reason for foreign direct investment in the years before trade liberalization was simple. To sell a product in a foreign market, it usually had to be manufactured there, or else quotas, tariffs, and transportation costs would make the price prohibitively high. In a world of high tariffs, quotas, and strong governments determined to keep out imported goods, setting up production sites within the walls of protection was and remains one of the only ways around the barriers to markets.

The investment in the United States in 1910 by the British synthetic fiber producer Courtaulds illustrates the logic of many multinationals over the twentieth century.[27] In 1908, just as the company was on the verge of setting up sales offices in the United States to distribute its London-made rayon, Congress voted new tariff legislation raising the duties on "artificial silk" to 40 cents a pound. Courtaulds' U.S. agent proposed banding together with American braidmakers and other consumers of this synthetic fiber to oppose the new duties on rayon yarn, but the London office saw that "arguments from foreign manufacturers in favour of reducing or placing limits on duty are likely to be regarded rather as reasons for interference."[28] It seemed Congress might increase the duties further.

Courtaulds realized it would have to produce in the United States in order to sell there. It bought out an existing manufacturer with a small operation in synthetics. The plant was in Pennsylvania, a state that did not allow foreign corporations to own real estate, so Courtaulds' New York lawyers became the owners on paper, in a shaky legal maneuver.[29] Courtaulds thus became an "American" company, and went on to capture a dominant role in the U.S. market. Now American tariffs protected *its* products. From this point, Courtaulds became one of the industry leaders in lobbying Congress to protect an "infant industry" against the "invasion" of the U.S. market by "pirate" imports from other European countries.[30]

In recent times, many companies have similar stories. In 1963, the Mexican government decreed that 60 percent of the value of cars sold in Mexico be produced there, which led to a boom in suppliers setting up plants in that country. The Chinese government required foreign automakers like Jeep, General Motors, and Volkswagen to set up joint ventures with the Chinese and invest in China if they wanted to sell cars in China.[31] The government also demanded that multinationals transfer technology to assemblers and suppliers in China as a condition of operating in their market. In return, the Chinese officials offered assurances that they would allow only limited competition in the industry from other foreign rivals or even from domestic challengers. Like Courtaulds, foreign car companies could count on reaping the rewards of operating in a protected market.

The Chinese were not the only ones demanding that automakers produce cars in-country if they wanted to sell them. The United States and the European Economic Community also set up restrictive policies. As Japanese cars started gaining a large market share in the United States in the 1980s, menacing threats about trade sanctions from the U.S. government first forced the Japanese government to accept "voluntary export restraints" and then led to Japanese companies like Toyota, Honda, and Nissan setting up the "transplant" assembly plants within the United States. By 1995, two-thirds of the Japanese cars sold in the United States were manufactured locally.

In the nineties, as governments in developing countries like China required the auto assemblers to manufacture where they wanted to sell, the assemblers insisted that their suppliers follow them if they wanted to keep contracts in the lucrative home markets. So auto-parts makers like Bosch, Benteler, Visteon, Delphi, Autoliv, and others set up plants in China, Mexico, and Eastern Europe. Many of the suppliers told us in interviews that their experiences in developing countries were little short of disaster. All of the auto-parts suppliers we interviewed reported operating expenses to be higher in countries like Mexico and China because so much has to be imported—special steel, aluminum, paint—and transportation is so expensive. These costs canceled out the savings on labor— that is, when there were savings on labor costs.

According to one contractor, during its first years in Mexico his company could not find enough qualified technicians and engineers and had to bring them at great expense from Germany. With a workforce that was 40 percent German, "our approach was like the occupation of a country," the manager remembered. And yet the supplier felt he had to succeed in Mexico or else lose profitable business with VW in Europe. In another case, we heard of a plant in Mexico where resentment of the foreign managers (Japanese this time) was so high that the workers dropped their tools and walked out. GM had to take over management of the plant, find a Mexican to put in charge, and offer the workers six times their normal wages to get them back.

The problems of suppliers sometimes translate into poor quality. Our team was told that taxi drivers in Ningbo, China, went out on strike in 2001 because of defects in their VW Santanas. The assembly plant had to close while managers worked on fixing the problems in the suppliers. In all these cases and many others we found, what is driving production overseas is *not* the lure of lower costs. On the contrary: Companies are willing to accept enormous hassles and high-cost production abroad because *being there* is required in order to sell there. And they want to sell abroad in order to capture new markets with consumers already rich enough to buy—as Ford and GM were able to do in Western Europe— or because they see a vast "field of dreams" of potential consumers, who may materialize one day if only jobs, incomes, and opportunities come.

Why the Jacket Has Zip-off Sleeves

On January 1, 2005, a great natural experiment started to play out with the disappearance of textile and clothing quotas, as agreed upon by the members of the WTO. Tariff duties still remain, but quotas—absolute limits on the entry of foreign goods—have fallen. A massive relocation of the world's clothing production—which employs about 40 million people—has been set in motion. Except for agriculture—the last remaining holdout in trade liberalization—no sector in the world has received so much protection for such a long period. Even as the world's trade liberalized after World War II, international trade agreements granted one special exemption after another to textile and apparel industries in advanced countries, under pressure from their owners and workers. In the 1950s, there were bilateral agreements between the United States and various European countries with Japan, India, and Pakistan that limited their exports, like the 1957 "voluntary" restraints that President

Eisenhower extracted from the Japanese.[32] Then, within the General Agreement on Tariffs and Trade (GATT) negotiations in 1962, Americans and Europeans pushed through the Long Term Agreement Regarding International Trade in Cotton Textiles (LTA) to regulate exports from developing countries. This was replaced in 1974 by the Multi-fibre Arrangement (MFA), which lasted until 1994 and extended protection to many more types of natural and man-made fibers. When the WTO came into existence in 1995, the MFA was changed into the Agreement on Textiles and Clothing, and was finally phased out on January 1, 2005.

During the half-century that these supposedly "temporary" conventions operated, trade rules were the most important factor determining where goods were made. Take the case of Hong Kong, which in the early 1990s was the world's largest exporter of clothing and second-largest exporter of textiles (after Germany).[33] Hong Kong had been lucky in getting rather large quotas for their exports into the United States and Europe, because it already had a big industry in 1974 when the quota system started and because it was a British colony perched strategically on the edge of Communist China. The Hong Kong manufacturers were so dynamic that by the seventies they were using up their quotas, and they started looking for places around the globe with unused quota where Hong Kong could locate some of its production capacity. They had to go well beyond the Chinese-speaking world. Even when mainland China opened to foreign investors in 1978, it had relatively little quota—for reasons exactly the opposite of Hong Kong's: It was a latecomer to the postwar trading system and a Communist country for whom the United States and Western Europe were not disposed to make generous accommodation.

Among the countries that the Hong Kong apparel and textile manufacturers discovered in their search for quota was Mauritius, a poor mountainous island in the Indian Ocean off the coast of Madagascar. However unpromising as an industrial base, Mauritius did have one great advantage. It had been colonized first by the French, then by the British, and so under the 1975 Lomé Convention that countries in the European Common Market had negotiated on behalf of their former colonies, Mauritius could sell goods to Europe without tariffs or quotas.[34] With the foreign direct investment that Hong Kong poured into Mauritius, the island became one of the world's major exporters of knitwear, wool garments, and T-shirts, and one of the most prosperous African economies. Today, about 15 percent of the Mauritius labor force works in this sector. This island may have been one of the least likely of the countries that Hong Kong investment promoted into the big leagues of textile/apparel production. But in Thailand, Malaysia, the Philippines, Indonesia, and mainland China, too, one of the unintended outcomes of the quota system was to make Hong Kong the agent of economic development far beyond its borders.

Trade rules not only changed the geography of production. They also shaped the content of the product. To continue with the example of Hong Kong: In the 1980s, as its manufacturers found their quotas on cotton and linen clothing filling up, someone thought of ramie, a natural fiber similar to linen, but coarser and even more wrinkly.[35] This obscure fiber had been left out of the Multi-fibre Arrangement and so there were no quotas for it. Hong Kong manufacturing rushed into the breach, and suddenly floods of ramie clothing appeared in the American market. Similarly, under the quota system, the number of jackets that Hong Kong could export to the United States and Europe was limited, so an entrepreneur designed jackets with sleeves that could be zipped off and on. These "vests" entered the U.S. market in an underused quota category, while the sleeves were shipped in separate containers. Garments that might never have seen the light of day were created to circumvent trade barriers.

Hong Kong textile and apparel manufacturing peaked in 1980, and after that employment fell off as the companies started moving production to Southeast Asia and, as mainland China opened, to Guangdong Province in southern China, adjacent to Hong Kong. With little quota available in China, Hong Kong clothing makers had to split up their operations between Hong Kong proper and the mainland. In order to use Hong Kong quota to sell goods that were mostly made in China, manufacturers kept in Hong Kong functions that legally defined place of origin—so fabric would be cut in Hong Kong, trucked over the border to be mostly sewn in China, and trucked back to Hong Kong for final finishing touches.

With equal innovativeness and flexibility, when in 1984 U.S. legislators and trade officials, under pressure to stem the flood of Asian imports, changed the rules of origin to require that knitted goods destined for the U.S. market under the Hong Kong quota must actually be knitted (instead of only assembled) in Hong Kong, Hong Kong businesses rapidly built up their knitting capacities. They took back much of the knitting they had moved into mainland China in order to be able to sell it under the Hong Kong quota. As Hong Kong rapidly restructured, the boom in purchases of highly automated knitting equipment made the fortune of Shimaseiki, a Japanese company that had formerly been on the verge of bankruptcy. Shimaseiki today is the world leader in computerized knitting machinery—basically as a result of how U.S. customs rules changed Hong Kong production capabilities. In the microcosm of Hong Kong's clothing and textile businesses we see at work the tremendous impact of international trade rules and how they shaped location. This is the world that officially came to an end on January 1, 2005, with the end of quota.

Still, let's not underestimate what a government can do even under current WTO rules. Governments can no longer legally require that goods be produced in a country in order to be sold in its domestic markets. But there are some products whose characteristics make it likely that they will be made where they are sold. In some of these cases, governments are major consumers or backers, as in infrastructure projects—like construction, electricity, and water supply—all of which now involve multinational players operating in multiple countries. Uniforms and protective clothing worn by police and firefighters are made to national specifications, and it is very difficult—often impossible—for foreigners to get in. Telecommunications equipment requires government licenses. Very heavy products, like television sets and trucks, and perishable goods (food that spoils, fashion that's likely to go out of style quickly) all need to be provided near customers. Given transportation costs of household appliances like refrigerators, it was not so surprising that Haier, a big Chinese firm, invested $40 million in a factory in Camden, South Carolina, and hired 200 workers to get its refrigerators to American retailers quickly and cheaply. Wages in the South Carolina plant are ten times higher than those in the Qingdao factory, but Haier seems to believe that getting the goods to market quickly and establishing an American presence outweigh the added labor costs.[36] In 2005, Haier made a bid to buy Maytag, again showing its willingness to take on higher costs in the United States in order to get brand recognition and closeness to customers.

There is also a big advantage in locating design or product definition near future consumers: It allows managers to identify local needs and taste and style. The cell phone shapes that appeal to Americans feel clunky and awkward to people in Hong Kong. Japanese teenagers want messaging services on their cell phones that leave the French cold. Working in a country helps a company catch consumer preferences and trends quickly and bring them to market.

By bolstering these economic factors, governments still can leverage what gets sold domestically. For example, for years after the North American Free Trade Agreement (NAFTA) passed in 1994, U.S. safety requirements were applied to Mexican truckers so rigorously that virtually no Mexican trucks could cross the border, thus protecting U.S. trucking and also adding to the cost of bringing goods from Mexico. Even a slowdown at the customs inspections on the Mexican border can serve the same end. A U.S. company that makes party favors both in the United States and in Mexico told us in despair about how its trucks, loaded with Thanksgiving turkey decorations, were stalled for weeks in long traffic jams at the border as the holiday approached.

And governments still find ways of using the same old methods to restrict markets to outsiders. For example, agreements negotiated by the United States and the European Union for China's entry into the WTO included "safeguard" provisions for reinstating limits in case a huge increase in exports causes "market disruption" or "threatens to impede the orderly development of trade." It's the importing country that gets to determine when these emergency conditions exist, so when bra imports from China more than tripled after bra quotas were removed in 2002, protests from apparel manufacturers brought Washington's decision to invoke the emergency provisions.[37] (It's worth noting that there are virtually no bras made in the United States. Most major American bra manufacturers are in fact located in Mexico and the Caribbean.) And again, after January 2005, there was a tremendous surge across the board in Chinese garment exports into the United States and Europe—cotton trousers, for example, went up by 1,521 percent. Predictably, American and European producers mobilized, and by July 2005, both the U.S. and the E.U. governments had agreed to decree new restrictions. These "temporary safeguards" are supposed to disappear by the end of December 2008, but given the history here, it's hard to imagine that the role of governments in shaping this industry is at an end.

Tariffs and quotas are far from the only weapons governments have for keeping foreign goods out and for providing incentives for foreigners to set up within their markets as producers, rather than outside as exporters. Regulations about domestic content, government procurements, health and safety standards, and labor and environmental practices are exploited for the purpose. Agricultural trade provides a large pool of examples. To take a few at random: The European Union bars U.S. agricultural products with genetically modified organisms on grounds that they may constitute serious health hazards (although thus far no such effects have been detected). The United States halted sales of Canadian cattle to the United States after one animal in Washington state was detected with mad cow disease and found to have had Canadian origins. The Japanese banned beef imports from the United States because of the same one animal (and their claims about the inadequacy of U.S. inspection procedures).

But all these explanations do not wholly solve the puzzle of why locally made goods usually do so much better than the same foreign-produced goods. There are some exceptions to this rule, mainly in developing countries, where consumers often seem to think that foreign-made goods are superior. A customer browsing in the television section of the Beijing department store on Wang Fu Jing Street in the center of downtown Beijing finds television sets decked out with signs describing not only their features but also where they were made. The set made by a Japanese company (presumed to be run by Japanese managers) in China sells at a higher price than a set made by a Chinese company; the price of a set made by Japanese in Malaysia is higher than the price of the Japanese set made in China; and the price of the Japanese set made in Japan is highest of all. But in most markets, consumers prefer home-made products. In China, too, things may be changing to the advantage of local products, as the recent successes of Bird cell phones and Haier washing machines show.

The overall preference for domestic products means that boundaries still matter. Even when governments allow free access, even when there is strong economic interdependence between societies like the United States and Canada or within the European Union, even when there are strong cultural similarities, as between Americans and Canadians, there are still powerful border effects. Border effects are a measure of the negative impact of national boundaries on the volume of trade between two localities situated in different countries. They mean that two localities in different countries trade less (by some factor) than two localities with similar economic profiles that are situated within the same country—after controlling for size, distance, and income.

The predictions about how much trade is likely between different places are derived from gravity trade models.[38] Using such models, economists have shown significant shortfalls between predicted and actual levels of trade even between countries like the United States and Canada, with common language, low border-level barriers, and strong economic interdependence. These shortfalls, or border effects, are large: as much as 10 to 20 times less trade between two localities if they are on opposite sides of the United States-Canada border than if they are on the same side of the border—everything else being equal.[39] Crossing a border within the European Union—even though all trade barriers have been officially eliminated—has a downward effect on sales equivalent to multiplying transportation costs by four or like having a tariff of about 37 percent.[40]

Why borders should matter even when trade barriers go down remains a mystery. Perhaps businesses feel safer buying and selling in their own home country, where they understand from experience what to do when things go wrong. Most economists see borders' effects on sales as some kind of lag, but many companies believe that boundaries will always matter. Whatever the reasons, and there are a variety, the fact remains that if companies want to sell abroad they cannot simply export all their products from their own home societies. They need to produce abroad as well.

CHAPTER 6

Making It Cheaper

I f some companies go abroad because they have to in order to sell there, many more businesses are moving for other reasons. Sometimes seeing others do it gets a company to invest outside of its own country.[1] And there's a multiplier effect here, as well, since if a lead firm goes to China thinking it's the wave of the future, the lead firm will bring along its suppliers, too. In the absence of good information or solid results, imitations and fads may carry the day. But mainly, companies establish facilities overseas or outsource to foreign businesses in order to get access to resources they cannot find in their own home countries or to lower the cost of production. In our interviews, many managers explained that the possibilities for expansion at home were exhausted. In small, congested societies like Taiwan, Hong Kong, and the industrial districts of Italy, this reasoning seems literally true. Morris Chang, the president of Taiwan Semiconductor Manufacturing Company, pointed out to us how little land suitable for semiconductor foundries remains in Taiwan. He reported that the Chinese were willing to lease him four times the amount of land he now occupies for less than the amount he currently pays in Taiwan. In small countries, it seems possible to run out of not only land but also workers. Taiwanese managers explained to us that their companies are building new semiconductor foundries in China instead of Taiwan because it is too difficult to find enough qualified engineers in Taiwan, while there are vast pools of qualified technicians who could be recruited in China.

In the United States, it is not only repetitive, low-pay jobs like sewing where it may be hard to recruit good workers. Engineers and skilled technicians were also in short supply in the boom years of the nineties. Hundreds of thousands of guest workers were allowed into the United States in those years on special immigration quotas like the H-1B and the L visas.[2] In 2003, there were more than 865,000 foreign workers in the United States on one or another of these programs, some of them working for firms back home. For example, Infosys, a $1-billion-a-year Indian software company that specializes in outsourcing services, sent as many as 2,884 workers a year on this basis to the United States to work with customers.[3] Bringing in even larger numbers of foreign workers does not seem a viable solution for meeting shortages, however, because this tactic bumps up against political opposition. The resistance is even stronger in countries, like Germany, where legislators have defeated proposals for widening access for skilled outsiders. So when these companies can't find the workforce they need in their home societies, they are more likely to move offshore.

As any economist will tell you, facts about the availability of workers and space boil down to facts about the cost of workers and space. If wages for sewers and engineers went up in the United States, Italy, and Taiwan, more people would get education for those occupations. There would be more candidates for the sewing factories and for the electronics companies. If the Taiwan fabs were willing to pay higher rents, tracts of land that are currently being used for other purposes (perhaps agriculture or shopping malls or nature reserves) would soon enough become available for development.

True, there are some assets and capabilities that are in an absolute sense not available in one's home society and that can be accessed only by a move. If a pharmaceutical firm wants close and continuous access to the best biological and medical research in the world, it needs to locate near MIT and Harvard or Stanford. That's why—despite high rents, high salaries, and high taxes in those communities—virtually all the major pharma companies have labs around those universities. "Knowledge-seeking" investment abroad into countries with strong research communities—German pharmaceutical firms' movement into U.S. biotech clusters, for example—is becoming more common in a number of industries for which R & D is important.[4] It is especially important in the pharmaceutical industry. But most factors of production—land, labor, and capital in various forms—are available in advanced economies at a price. The question is whether firms are willing to pay the price it would take to buy additional units of such labor or land or capital. And if they do, will they still be competitive in global markets?

Cheap Labor

Overwhelmingly, the cost that firms have in mind when they locate production abroad, or contract out to foreign manufacturers, is labor. In the firms in which we interviewed, when managers explained relocation decisions many listed finding workers at lower wages as their main concern. Here the managers' explanations of their strategies mirror the public's worries about globalization and the conclusions of most mainstream economists. You do not need to be versed in standard trade theories and Heckscher-Ohlin, Ricardo-Viner, and Stolper-Samuelson models of factor price equalization to grasp the idea that when capital, goods, and services move freely around the world, eventually the wages of workers in rich countries are likely to fall as the wages of the poor rise elsewhere.

Most people believe that trade and foreign direct investment directly translate into a competition between the high-wage workers of the already developed countries and the low-wage workers of poor countries. They think wages of the well-paid workers of the West will sink when goods and services similar to the ones they produce—or the components of these products—can be made at lesser cost abroad, imported, and sold at lower price. They regard increases in foreign direct investment, too, as a catalyst of declining wages, when factories in the West are transferred to low-wage societies, leaving the original workforce to compete with other workers with the same skills in the home market. Even the threat of such relocations may lower wages if workers in the prosperous home countries hesitate to organize or to press for higher wages for fear of seeing their jobs disappear across a border. This "discouragement effect" is a major factor draining support for unions over the past decade. Union membership fell from 20 percent in 1983 to 13 percent in 2003.[5]

Managers usually do not regard calculating the savings on labor costs by moving activities from high-wage to low-wage countries as a difficult problem. They reason that whenever they can relocate an activity currently carried out in a high-wage country to a low-wage country, they reduce their costs. When our researchers asked managers why they were moving production offshore or outsourcing to foreign-based manufacturers, reducing labor costs was almost always high on the list of motivations; sometimes it was the only rationale for the move. Even in capital-intensive industries where labor costs are a tiny fraction of total costs, businessmen often describe the search for lower-wage labor as a survival issue.

In 2001 in Japan, we visited one of the world's largest synthetic-fiber producers, Toray. Its newest and biggest nylon-polyester filament plant is located in Ishikawa, in the Tatsunokuchi Hokuriku region, a historic center of Japanese silk production. In a bucolic rural setting surrounded by rice fields, the Ishikawa factory runs twenty-four hours a day, with only five workers per shift. When our team entered the factory, the manager had to turn on the lights. The factory floor had been totally dark, for robots were doing all the work of collecting, replacing, and packaging bobbins and spindles as they wound up the filament extruded from nozzles, unobserved by human eyes. Labor costs at the plant make up a mere 5 percent of total costs. Still, the plant managers told us wages were "too high," and they worried that one day production would be moved to

China and the Ishikawa plant would be closed. At 5 percent of total costs, we wondered, how could wage differences possibly matter? But in 2001, Toray was going through hard times. When people search for causes and remedies, labor invariably rises to the top of the list, even in capital-intensive industry. Even when the sums at stake are not large, labor costs appear variable and compressible while other costs seem fixed, as Marx observed long ago.

The first jobs relocated overseas in the 1970s were in industries requiring relatively low levels of skill: toys, clothing, shoes, printed circuit-board assembly. By the 1980s, the increasing level of skills that could be found in a number of low-wage Southeast Asian and East Asian countries, like Taiwan, Malaysia, and South Korea, made it possible to set up more complex manufacturing operations, like the hard-disk-drive industry in Singapore. Seagate Technology, the world's largest maker of hard-disk drives, first started making subassemblies in Singapore in 1982.[6] Only eight years later, Singapore had become the major world producer of hard-disk drives. Simple service jobs—medical transcription, processing credit card bills, back-office work—started moving in the 1990s. Today, companies can send a wide range of skilled technical and service jobs abroad and employ engineering staff in China, India, and Russia at less than half the cost of employing engineers at home.[7] Indian radiologists are reading X-rays for U.S. hospitals; IBM's R & D center in Beijing turns out some of its most promising new projects; and complex and heavily capital-intensive operations like semiconductor foundries are locating in China. IBM was reported in 2003 to be moving 4,700 programmer jobs to India and China, with salaries that in the U.S. would be $75,000 to $100,000 a year.[8]

True, there are constraints on relocating activities: Companies may not be able to hire all the skilled workers and technicians they need in a foreign low-wage society. Corporate managers recognize, too, that it may be impossible to close production facilities in their home country without bringing down on themselves too much political and social ill will. But when the foreign country apparently has enough workers and when home-country workers do not rise up in protest, then businessmen see decisions about gains and losses from substituting cheaper foreign workers as simple arithmetic.

Adding Up the Real Costs of Cheap Labor

A full calculation of costs, however, is much more complicated. First of all, there are countries, like North Korea or Liberia, where political risks are so high and the infrastructure so poor that even free labor and land would probably not be enough to entice foreign investors into setting up plants. Then there are countries on the edge: dangerous, but conceivable. Political risk is, of course, a category covering a wide variety of possible disasters. In countries like Indonesia and the Philippines, ethnic and religious conflicts, guerrilla movements, and political unrest make for a shaky investment environment. In countries like Burma, a business deal inevitably involves working with a highly repressive police and military. Strong feeling in Western countries about the abuses and violence of the Burmese regime means that companies thinking about investing there have to factor in the possibility of consumer boycotts back home. For example, in June 1996, the Massachusetts legislature—citing human rights abuses—passed a law forbidding state purchasing from any company doing business in Burma. A number of companies—like Motorola, Hewlett-Packard, and Apple—left. The U.S. Supreme Court struck the law down in June 2000 on grounds that it infringed the president's prerogatives in foreign policy. But even without a law, most companies are going to be wary about being associated with a country that evokes images of violence and repression.

Even in China, companies worry about lawlessness. There are many cases of holdups and kidnappings of Taiwanese and Hong Kong managers. Dealing with corrupt officials and local mafias is a constant preoccupation for foreign companies operating in China. Foreign investors worry, too, about the longevity of an authoritarian political regime that needs to keep the lid on the rising discontent of workers who have lost their jobs in the collapsing state-run sector of the economy. The restiveness of minority groups in the border regions of the country, like that of the Muslim Uighurs in Xinjiang in western China, also raises concerns about political stability. These concerns were often raised only obliquely in the interviews. For example, the CEO of a high-end French sportswear brand told us that the quality of the shirts they make in China was equal to that of the ones made in Italy. I asked, Why not make them all in China? He responded with mock derision, "Why, Professor Berger, and I thought you were a political scientist!"

A country like Haiti, which is close to the United States, with at least 70 percent unemployment and a minimum wage under $2 a day, might seem tempting for a labor-intensive industry. Levi Strauss must have thought so when it contracted the making of Levi 505s and Levi 555s to Grupo M, a Dominican manufacturer that set up sewing plants in 2003 in a free-trade zone (Ouanaminthe) straddling the border between the Dominican Republic and Haiti in order to recruit Haitian workers. Sweetening the deal was the International Finance Corporation of the World Bank's $20 million loan to Grupo M to build the plant. The IFC's condition was that workers' rights be respected. A union-organizing campaign was followed by claims of brutality, counterclaims from the management about political militants, the intervention of the Dominican military, a lockout, international protests, and picketing of Levi stores and headquarters in the United Kingdom. We cannot decide the rights and wrongs of this conflict on a site we did not visit, but the example demonstrates how setting up shop in a country with weak enforcement of rule of law, where order depends on repression, is likely to lead to disasters like this one. No level of wages could compensate for the losses of reputation for brand integrity, to say nothing of financial losses in such an episode.

Secondly, there are enormous differences among wage rates in countries around the world. But what matters in the bottom line is not wage rates but unit labor costs, the value of labor needed to produce a unit of a product or a service. Unit labor costs take productivity into account and illustrate that where well-educated, experienced workers use the latest equipment, even if wages are high, unit labor costs may be low. The value added by an average American manufacturing worker, for example, is twenty-eight times higher than that created by his Chinese counterpart.[9] The American workers are more productive because they are working with more and better capital equipment and because they make products that sell for higher prices. Better educated than the Chinese, Americans use equipment and run the factories more efficiently. Furthermore, there is less waste of valuable materials when well-trained workers catch and fix faulty runs quickly.

Even when factories in developing countries have the most up-to-date machinery, if it is not being used effectively, there will inevitably be breakdowns and defective products to correct, and as a result, unit labor costs will rise. This is, for example, a problem for Taiwanese electronics firms. Even though they have low-cost workers and engineers in Taiwan and now in China, their "overall equipment effectiveness" is only 84 percent, compared with world benchmarks of 95 percent.[10] This means machines are standing idle while problems are being fixed. In 2001, our team visited Brembo, an Italian maker of top-of-the-line disc brakes. In the lobby they proudly displayed photos of their iron-casting foundries around the world, along with output statistics. The Bergamo, Italy, foundry had 75 workers and produced 50,000 tons; the Pueblo, Mexico, plant had 674 workers and produced 90,000 tons. Why does it take so many more workers in Mexico? I asked. One manager, looking at the photos with me, replied that the Mexican plant happened to house many administrative personnel. Overhearing the conversation, a senior executive of the company interjected: "Nonsense. It's just that their productivity is low."

As our team visited shop floors, we asked the managers about the costs of making their products in their advanced-country plants as compared with making them in low-wage-country plants. The answers frequently showed a much narrower divergence in unit labor costs than in wage rates. An Italian cotton textile producer compared the costs of operations at their plant in northern Italy with costs in a brand-new plant they opened in northern India. They employ 676 workers (including staff and sales force) in Italy, and 450 in India. At the time of the interview (July 2002), a worker in the Italian plant earned $2,300 per month; a worker in India, $70 per month. Labor costs in Italy amounted to 25 percent of sales; in India, to 4.5 percent. But all the equipment used in India and most of the inputs, like dyes, have to be imported. Quality control costs twice as much. The efficiency of the Indian plant was 10 percent lower. The CEO estimated that the cost per meter of making the same fabric was more than twice as expensive in India as in Italy.

We heard a similar story from the manager of Emilia Maglia, an Italian company with a wholly owned subsidiary in Romania, as she walked us through the plant in Timisoara.[11] It illustrates in yet another way how difficult it is to calculate the costs of low-wage labor. Like the overwhelming majority of the firms we interviewed in new production sites, Emilia Maglia decided that it needed an Italian manager for its new Romanian operation. They recruited Signora Elena. Since she was to live and work full-time in Timisoara for years, her husband, a mechanic, had to be hired, too. Four years after the plant opening, Signora Elena and her husband are still running the plant. Similarly, in our interviews with Hong Kong companies with factories in China, we found that even in plants that were five to ten years old, Hong Kong managers (with salaries calculated according to Hong Kong living standards and not Chinese) still occupied the key positions.

HOW WE COMPETE

We Teach the Italian Mentality
SIGNORA ELENA FROM EMILIA MAGLIA, AN ITALIAN APPAREL MANUFACTURER

"We need to own and run the Romanian plant ourselves in order to get the quality we need. We want to teach them our Italian system and our Italian mentality. Sure, it would be easier to have agents and intermediaries or subcontractors and it would involve less investment. But we can't get the results that way. Over the course of a few years, we have really created an Italian working environment here, and we've passed along our mentality."

Elena was proud of how she had raised the productivity of the Romanian factory by teaching the Romanians the Italian ways of working. Then she pointed to a sleeve knitted of fine white yarn and a beaded sweater that were made both in Italy by subcontractors of Emilia Maglia and in Romania in their own plant. She ruefully explained that the sleeves were still 50 percent cheaper to make in Italy because productivity there is so much higher. Italian workers have years of experience with the machines and are able to set up rapidly for different products, to detect problems and fix them before work is wasted, and to maintain the equipment. For these reasons, many products are still cheaper to make in Italy, although Italian wages are about ten times higher than Romanian wages.

If the wage bill were computed in a way that included the cost of expatriate managers, with their elevated salaries, hardship compensation, transportation home, and housing, the simple numbers about the advantages to be reaped from relocation would be disproven. For some companies who have carefully figured out the real costs of offshoring, this has led to a decision to keep production at home.

HOW WE COMPETE

We Calculate the Real Costs of Cheap Labor
LUXOTTICA, ITALIAN EYEGLASS MANUFACTURER

"We are centralizing our process of production in Italy, and we're internationalizing our commercial structure. Our objective is to concentrate as much as possible in the Italian plants. We realized that the labor cost advantage, even in the Guangdong, China plants, was minimal if you took indirect labor costs into account. First of all, you need more supervisors in China than in Italy: 2 per 100 workers in Italy and 5 for 100 workers in China. And to bring workers from Italy to China costs three times as much as to employ them in Italy. The incidence of indirect labor costs in China is ten times the cost of labor in Italy. So sending our people to China ate up a lot of the advantage of cheap direct labor.

"To make two lenses cost $2.63 in Fuling, China; $2.49 in Waterford, Ireland; and $1.20 in Italy—with the same equipment. One of the issues is the waste of valuable materials. The savings from centralization in Italy are so great—the bottom line was that so many of those made in China are defective that labor savings were canceled out. The amount of downtime is very low in Italy compared with China. If machines break in China, it takes a month to get a technician in to fix it. For high-quality production, you need technical support—which comes from more advanced societies."

The Facts: Luxottica is an eyeglass frame and sunglasses manufacturer in Agordo, in the Belluno district of northeast Italy. It makes about 32 million frames a year, with $3.6 billion annual sales. The plant they opened in 1996 in China employs 1,200 workers. Currently, 75 percent of Luxottica's production comes from its Italian plants. More on Luxottica in Chapter 7.[12]

Other managers, convinced that they can raise the productivity on shop floors and eventually replace the "expat" managers with locals, continue to try to make the best of the operation in the low-wage country in the hopes of one day harvesting the fruits of low wages.

Of course, as productivity increases, wages rise. By 2004, a number of the biggest garment contractors in southern China pointed out that wages they are paying are now higher than those in many other countries, like Vietnam. They report that in the key production zones it is actually hard to find enough workers. With a population of 1.3 billion Chinese to draw on, it is difficult to imagine running out of workers. There are limits, though, on how many of these potential workers can be moved into the southern and coastal zones of China that now have the highways, power grids, telecommunications, experienced managers, and modern factories that make efficient operations possible. Pulling up and starting all over again in Vietnam or deeper into inland China is always possible, but it is enormously costly. At the end of the day, competing on low wages means perpetual flight into new territories, only to meet there the same hungry competitors that populated the last site.

Finally, as David Birnbaum, whose insightful and witty books on the global garment industry are the ultimate guide to thinking about low wages, argues: "There exists no direct correlation between labor rates and manufacturing costs."[13] Birnbaum provides many examples to back up his case, among them an analysis of five-pocket 501 jeans made in South Korea by a sewer paid $7.50 an hour and in Indonesia by a worker paid $0.20 an hour.[14] The F.O.B. [Free on Board—i.e., all costs up to shipping] price was only 15 percent higher for the South Korean-made jeans— although Korean wages were 3,750 percent higher. How was this possible? Denim fabric accounted for 70 percent of the cost; the remaining 30 percent included not only labor but trim, profit, overhead, and quota (now eliminated). Overheads in poor countries are often higher than those in more advanced countries, and in fact were lower in Korea than in Indonesia. A local entrepreneur looking to finance his current operations should pay attention to short-term interest rates, which vary from country to country and are highest in politically risky countries. The interest rate in 1998, Birnbaum reports, was 57 percent in Indonesia and 23 percent in South Korea.[15] Inflation rates, which vary from country to country, affect the cost of raw materials, transportation, and energy. These nonlabor costs average 80 percent or more of the F.O.B. price of a garment.[16]

Birnbaum figures that the total costs of direct labor in developing-world factories amount to only about 3 to 4 percent of the price of the product when it's loaded onto the ship, or about 0.75 percent of the retail price. If the impact of wages on total costs is so low even in the clothing sector, which is labor-intensive, one has to wonder how much it could matter in more capital-intensive activities, like electronics. Technology Forecasters, a consulting group, analyzed the outsourcing of electronics manufacturing and design services in many countries and found that lead firms often underestimate many of the costs, like supply-chain management, brokers' fees, and attrition in transportation, which are all associated with offshoring.[17] It concluded, based on sixty cases, that, on average, labor amounted to a mere 2 percent of a project's total cost.

But it's not just wages that seem lower abroad. Rents, energy prices, taxes, and environmental standards all look cheaper in developing countries than at home. These savings, however, do not translate directly to the bottom line. If land is less expensive (and sometimes is even given away by towns eager for new industries), the gas and electricity grid, highway and railroad networks, telephone service, police, and other public services are often poor and unreliable. It is standard practice in many places (like Timisoara, Romania) to require companies to build the roads and power lines that connect their plants to the main system. Often, they need their own generators because of power outages. In many places, they have to hire their own security guards. Even when bureaucratic regulators are less restrictive, they are often slow and arbitrary.

Corruption, too, adds unpredictability to dealing in these countries. Folk wisdom holds that Hong Kong and Taiwanese companies succeed in China because managers from the same ethnic backgrounds thrive in a climate of connections (*guanxi*) and side payments. On the contrary, our interviews showed how apprehensive even managers with common language and culture are about dealings when corruption is involved. Many of the Taiwan managers we interviewed argued that when the cost of the bribes they need to pay Chinese officials is factored into the equation, cost differentials between production in China and Taiwan are not so great.

Even worse than the price that corruption demands up front is the resulting worry about paybacks that might be demanded in the future. One Hong Kong equipment maker told us that every time he sends machinery to his China plant, a Chinese official offers to get the shipment in without taxes. What favors will be requested in return is left unspecified. The Hong Kong executive told us he would prefer to pay the tax once and for all, but he could not refuse this powerful person. As a result, every time he looks around his China shop floor at the machines, "each one looks like a bomb that could blow up in my face any day." Corrupt, or simply poorly trained, tax collectors and customs inspectors, weak courts, and freewheeling police make costs much less calculable in a developing country than in societies with rule of law.

The End of Trade Protection

The last remaining fortresses of trade protection are now under siege. Even agriculture, the most protected sphere of production in rich societies, is now facing more trade liberalization. In March 2005, a WTO tribunal determined that U.S. subsidies to cotton farmers increase their production and exports and thereby harm cotton farmers in other countries.[18] The United States is now obliged to lower its payments. This ruling against the United States in a complaint lodged by Brazil seems to presage the end of the untouchable status of national protection of agricultural commodities. Rich countries currently provide about $300 billion a year in various forms of aid to agriculture, and developing countries have long argued that these payments depress world prices and force unfair competition on farmers in poor countries. For manufactured goods, the big change was the January 2005 termination of the Multifibre Arrangement (MFA), which, under various names and guises in the postwar period, had sheltered the textile and garment industries of high-wage countries against imports from emerging economies. Fearing protectionist backlash in the United States and maybe hoping to hang on to some of the levers of control over domestic producers, Beijing in early 2005 announced export taxes, but they seem to have had little effect.

The impact of the end of quotas was immediate and dramatic: In the first few months of 2005, imports of Chinese clothing and textiles into the United States and Western Europe rose by more than 63 percent from a year earlier.[19] Despite the fact that the United States and the E.U. have put "safeguard" restrictions into place, the pressure of Chinese competition unfettered by quota restrictions is enormous—and not only for producers in high-cost countries in North America and Europe, who by now may well have already absorbed much of the impact of low-wage competition and adjusted one way or another. In fact, by 2003, 77 percent of the clothing Americans bought was already made abroad.[20] The blow of the end of the quota system will be heaviest for very poor countries. They had benefited from trade rules that gave them quota—a certain guaranteed access into rich-country markets—to develop their own industries. Now, with no quotas limiting what China and India can sell to the rest of the world, the fledgling apparel industries of Bangladesh, Cambodia, Honduras, and others are under great new pressure. In the first months of 2005, Bangladesh and Cambodia appeared to be holding out well, but Mexico and the Caribbean sank under the weight of the Chinese onslaught.

Clothing manufacturing has, in fact, been relocating outside of high-wage countries for the past forty years. As trade barriers and transportation costs started to fall in the seventies, most of the major American brands and retailers started to outsource production to firms in Asia. For some of them, like Liz Claiborne and Kellwood, it meant breaking off manufacturing from the business and outsourcing it to contractors abroad. Others were already outsourcing sewing in the United States and switched from U.S. contractors to overseas firms. Still others tried setting up their own plants abroad in joint or solo ventures. L. W. Packard, the woolen mill I described in Chapter 1, tried producing in Mexico in a joint venture with Mexicans. Like many others, Packard's president, John Glidden, had reasoned that free access to U.S. markets under the North American Free Trade Agreement (1994) would let him supply his old customers from Mexico, that Mexico was close enough to the United States to move goods rapidly, and that Mexican costs were low enough to compete with Asia. The 1994 devaluation of the peso cut costs almost in half (compared to U.S. costs) and made moving production to Mexico even more attractive.

Many people saw Mexico as a vast apparel factory for the U.S. market. Some U.S. textile manufacturers dreamed of a division of labor in which fabric would still be made in the United States, and garments sewn in Mexico. Firms like Burlington, Guilford Mills, and Delta Woodside planned to integrate textile production and garment making in-house using U.S. management and low-cost Mexican labor in Mexico. Many of the largest U.S. textile firms competing in the apparel segment invested in Mexico.[21] The idea was "one-stop shopping" for brands like Liz Claiborne, Ralph Lauren, and the Gap. Along with the Americans heading for Mexico were Asian firms selling to U.S. stores, and they, too, built factories in Mexico and Latin America. The Taiwanese, for example, were the third-largest investors in the Mexican textile and apparel sector. As big retailers like Federated Department Stores, Nordstrom's, and Wal-Mart stepped up the pressure on manufacturers to shorten lead times and to do rapid replenishment, Mexico's proximity to the U.S. market made it seem a natural production base.[22]

In their study on the mounting pressures that retailers in the 1990s were putting on manufacturers for rapid deliveries of an exploding number of products, Harvard Business School researchers predicted that an increasing amount of textiles and apparel would be made in Mexico and Caribbean Basin countries.[23] At the end of the nineties, this seemed an irresistible trend. At the beginning of the 1990s, Asians had sold four times as much clothing as had the Latin Americans to the United States, but a decade later, Mexico and the Caribbean Basin countries were outdoing Asian imports.[24] The Harvard study concluded "that the emergence of lean retailing is driving a regionalization of production in major U.S., European, and Asian consumer markets, because of the need to replenish retail stores rapidly."[25] And these shifts, they argued, would continue even after quotas disappeared in 2005.

Both L. W. Packard and the Harvard research team may have drawn too hasty a conclusion. By 2002, L. W. Packard decided Mexico had been a mistake. Because costs were rising rapidly and Mexican suppliers were unable to produce goods at a high enough level of quality, they closed the

Mexican operations. Other companies, like Burlington and Guilford, were coming to the same realization. As Mexican wages rose and disappointment grew over Mexico's inability to make high-quality products, over the relative inflexibility of Mexican plants, and over lead times that were still too long, many businesses started moving out and heading for Asia. Thousands of *maquiladora* plants folded. (*Maquiladora* factories are ones that produce only for export, and that benefit from special customs regulations allowing parts and equipment to come into Mexico tax-free and products to go out into the United States without duties and quotas.)

Most foreign direct investment in Mexico had gone into these *maquiladoras*, which fueled the rapid growth of the economy. When foreign investors started pulling up stakes and moving east, the effects were disastrous. In 2001 alone, about a quarter of a million Mexican manufacturing jobs disappeared. In part, this reflects the impact of the American recession, but there was also a deeper structural shift under way. The issue was not only rising Mexican costs but the weakness of the supply base in Mexico. In contrast, in China, businesses found suppliers able to produce the full range of inputs. Even fabric and finishing—the hardest parts of the process to do right—were beginning to become widely available in China. American brands started to realize that it might be about as cheap to fly clothing in from China as to make it in Mexico.

For companies who already had Chinese production bases, the shift was rapid. The story of the Taiwanese firm Hong Ho describes the experience of many. By the end of the 1990s, the company's prospects at home looked bleak. Like many Taiwan-based manufacturing companies, Hong Ho saw opportunity in Mexico's low labor costs, duty-free access to the U.S. market, and proximity to the U.S. border. In 1999, it launched an ambitious program to build textile and garment production facilities in the southeastern state of Yucatán, with plans to invest U.S. $60 million and hire 8,000 Mexican workers.[26] Early returns were promising, and demand from U.S. customers strong. Hong Ho announced a U.S. $10 million investment in a mainland Chinese textile factory, but the firm planned to continue expanding in Mexico.[27] By April 2004, Hong Ho's

Mexico strategy had stalled: Prices of NAFTA yarn were too expensive and local subcontractors too scarce and unreliable. Hong Ho halted hiring at 1,500 workers.[28]

Another Taiwanese firm we interviewed both in Taiwan and in Mexico realized too late that the only workers available for hire in their Mexican plant were those who lived near the factory. Once the local labor market had been used up, there were no more workers. Mexicans willing to travel long distances for jobs are likely to strike out for the United States; those who stay in Mexico are usually unwilling to relocate and live in dormitories around the factory. When our team visited the Taiwanese company's Mexican plant in May 2000, half the sewing machines stood idle. The Taiwanese managers requested permission to bring Chinese workers into Mexico, but the Mexican government refused. These companies are now pulling out of Mexico.[29]

Will All Production Move to China?

Even before the fatal date of January 2005, much of the world's textile and apparel industry was regrouping in China and preparing to move even more there very soon. With the results of the first few months of the post-quota world now in, the trend seems to be accelerating. Even companies with large and successful Mexican operations seem to be considering a move. Roger Williams, president of Warnaco Swimwear, a division of Warnaco, a $1.4 billion apparel business, said: "We will always go to the least expensive place. Once the issue of safeguards is settled, our comfort level will go up. There will be a shift to China over time."[30] Warnaco makes underwear and is the world's largest bathing suit manufacturer (under labels like Speedo, Catalina, Calvin Klein, and Anne Cole). Currently, Warnaco's plant outside Mexico City has 4,000 employees, runs 24 hours a day, and turns out about 20 million bathing suits a year.

Will *all* the industry move there? Industry lobbyists in Washington predict that 30 million of the 40 million jobs in apparel and textiles worldwide will change hands. Cass Johnson of the textile manufacturers association warned a 2003 meeting of industrialists: "If China is not stopped—textile and apparel industry in the United States is destroyed—630,000 workers will lose their jobs; 1,300 textile plants will close; everyone in this room will be out of a job."[31] A 2004 report from the U.S. Trade Representative's office concluded more diplomatically: "China is expected to become the 'supplier of choice' for most U.S. importers (the large apparel companies and retailers) because of its ability to make almost any type of textile and apparel product at any quality level at a competitive price."[32] The industry lobbyists also emphasized the foreign policy impact of ending quotas: "Not only will the United States lose more than 75 percent of its textile and apparel manufacturing sector, but millions of the expected 30 million job losses will occur in countries on the front line in the war on terrorism, such as Bangladesh, Sri Lanka, Malaysia, Thailand, Indonesia, Morocco, Tunisia, Turkey, Jordan, and Egypt."[33]

But it is unlikely that China will end up controlling the entire industry. Retailers and brand-name companies find it far too risky to put all their eggs in one basket, particularly when the basket is China, with great and unpredictable potential for internal political unrest and with the SARS episode fresh in everyone's memory. A World Bank study has predicted that China may end up after the end of the Multi-fibre Arrangement with as much as 50 percent of the world's clothing market, but of all the American, European, and Japanese textile and apparel firms we interviewed, only one was planning to have all its manufacturing done in China.[34] As costs rise in the easily accessible parts of China, even that 50 percent may come to seem high.

For a company that wants to put its eggs in a number of different baskets, though, the most likely options are other low-cost sites around the world. There will probably be fewer countries with significant textile and apparel industries than at present. Once quota is a thing of the past, there will no longer be an economic incentive to spread manufacturing across many countries. Production in many places will decline, with devastating effects on poor nations. Quota created not only the apparel industry of small Mauritius but also that of highly populated Bangladesh, where about half the country's manufacturing workforce is in this sector: 1.8 million jobs, mostly held by women. With declining orders from foreign buyers, many of these jobs will now disappear. The question is: Which countries are the most promising candidates for producing the clothing and fabric that is not made in China? A few low-cost countries, like India and Turkey, look like natural alternatives, since they have large-scale, up-to-date facilities and rather low wages. Vietnam is another likely survivor in this maelstrom, due to its low wages, relatively well-educated workers, and the strong presence of Taiwanese and Hong Kong investors.

Another reason why 100 percent Chinese production is unlikely is that for some textile products, Chinese capabilities are not particularly advanced. Almost 50 percent of the Central East European exports to Western Europe are rather expensive tailored suits and coats, and China is not strong on making these.[35] For the foreseeable future, our interviews and research lead us to conclude that such garments are likely still to be made in Eastern Europe, perhaps shifting eastward from Poland and Hungary toward Romania, Bulgaria, and Ukraine.

But there's yet another reason all garment manufacturing will not move to China: Fast deliveries and replenishment are services that still command a high price in well-to-do societies. People are willing to pay for having the latest best thing *now*, not a month from now. This factor privileges production in high-wage economies with large numbers of affluent consumers. Even in New York City, with high rents, high wages, and high taxes, there were still 33,200 apparel-manufacturing jobs in 2003 (down from 78,300 in 1994).[36] Clustered together with these manufacturing jobs are large numbers of better-paying jobs for designers, showroom employees, buyers, models, fashion journalists, retail specialists, and the like. Small New York City companies—with names unknown beyond the trade—do rapid knockoffs of hot fashion; they swiftly refill successful items that may originally have been ordered from distant foreign factories; and they do all this in under a month. In Los Angeles County, fashion is a $24 billion industry, and the city's biggest; there are still 68,000 apparel-manufacturing jobs. For many of the L.A. companies, too, fast turnaround is the key to doing well. (I'll turn to one of the most successful of these companies, American Apparel, in Chapter 9.)

If the only factor keeping textile and apparel production in high-wage economies were speedy replenishment, it's likely that very little would remain once trade barriers came down. In fact, even in the parts of the U.S. industry that specialize in rapid turnaround, like New York and Los Angeles, the numbers are falling—in New York by more than half over the past decade; in Los Angeles, from 103,900 in 1996 to 68,000 in 2003. Is the disappearance of most of this industry in high-wage countries now inevitable? Many people think so, or believe that the only measure that could prevent such an outcome would be reinstating quotas and trade protection. Whether or not it's a good thing to keep textile and apparel employment in our societies is another question, one I'll return to in Part Six. After all, these are slow-tech sectors with wages that are low for advanced societies; and there is tough competition from emerging economies.

Before thinking about how desirable it is to keep manufacturing in the United States, we need to step back for a reality check. Does Asian competition in an open international economy in fact leave *any* chance for a textile and garment industry in the West? Textile and garment making—with technologies that evolve very slowly, yet involve quickly acquired skills and easy-to-move operations—represents a critical case. Our team reasoned that if we could discover opportunities for these industries in high-wage economies, the lessons we learned would apply even more strongly across sectors requiring more skill, more capital, and higher rates of innovation. If *even* in textiles and garments we could find profitable businesses with well-paid workers, then it would be hard to argue that any industry in advanced economies is outright condemned by globalization. And that's exactly what we found. The Italian and the German examples show, although in very different ways, that survival and prosperity are real possibilities, even for textiles and garments. Even though the industry is declining rapidly in most of Europe, in countries like Italy employment levels are quite stable, with good jobs and profits.

No comparison could be more striking than the differences in the fortunes of garment and textile workers in the United States and Italy.
Between 2001 and 2003, 33 percent of the manufacturing jobs in the
apparel industry in the United States disappeared. In contrast, in Italy in
the same years, employment in textiles and apparel declined by only 6.5
percent.[37] There were 569,733 Italians employed in these industries
(2003) and 709,500 Americans (2004). (The U.S. population is roughly 5
times larger than the Italian: 293 million Americans in 2004 compared
with 58 million Italians.) In the stricken textile mill regions of the U.S.
South, there is despair about the chance of finding any job at all. You'll
find town after town like Kannapolis, North Carolina, where Cannon textile mills used to employ 20,000 people, the last 4,000 of whom lost their
jobs when the factories closed in July 2003.[38] In contrast, in the Italian
textile and clothing districts clustered in the northern and central regions
of the Veneto and Emilia-Romagna there is virtually no unemployment.[39]

If anything, the problem in northern Italy is finding enough workers
to expand production. Shortages have led some companies to invest
abroad, using neighboring Eastern European countries like Romania,
only a few hours away by plane. A wave of immigrants—legal and illegal,
Chinese, Albanian, Yugoslav—has poured into these Italian cities, filling the need for more sewing operators and generating a new group of
local entrepreneurs. In the province of Modena, in the heart of the Italian textile and apparel districts, 200 (out of 3,200) garment businesses
are owned by Chinese. About 6,000 Chinese are estimated to work in
them.[40] The promise of the industrial districts for newcomers is clearly
not yet exhausted, as demonstrated by the entry into the ranks of a new set
of immigrant enterprises. Newspaper exposés show that many of these
immigrant workers are laboring in bad conditions and for poor pay, as
their predecessors did in the sweatshops of the 1950s that lie at the origin
of today's model factories in the Italian districts. But given the great economic resources available in Italy—design, marketing, technical capabilities—and the political assets of a system where Leftist parties and
unions are still significant actors, there are real prospects of pushing these

firms up the ladder. The opportunities for companies to move into higher-value products and improve the working conditions and wages of their employees are undoubtedly present.

Same Drivers and Enablers, Different Outcomes

Over the past twenty-five years, the international economy has been enormously expanded by politics and by technological advance. The networks of international production and trade now encompass most of the world's population. There still remain a few nations, like North Korea, that try to systematically isolate their societies from the global economy. But for the most part, the countries that lie at the periphery or even outside international networks of production and exchange are destitute and politically-at-risk nations that do not attract even those foreign investors looking only for cheap labor.

Many poor countries suffer from dependence on commodities trade and from the unfair competition of the subsidized agricultural production of the rich West. The main problem, however, is not so much that these societies are exploited within the global economy as that they cannot get into world networks of trade, investment, and production. Much of the African continent, in this sense, is beyond the reach of globalization, and its poverty is reinforced by isolation and exclusion. Levels of political instability, violence, and corruption are so high in many African nations that they discourage both domestic and foreign investment. There may be very low wages, but the illiteracy, demoralization, and poor health of the potential workers do not attract new industry. When countries with large and desperately poor populations, like China and India, have become fully integrated into global production and trade, incomes and living standards have risen for many, although certainly not evenly or for all. As the international economy has stretched to cover vast new territories, the rules of the system have also changed greatly. As I have sketched out in this chapter, starting with the Bretton Woods agreement of 1944, there has been a slow and zigzagging advance toward the liberalization of trade. The liberalization of capital movements, on the other hand, started later than that of trade. It has reached a point today where huge sums of portfolio investing or foreign direct investment can be moved across borders rapidly with the stroke of a computer. The only factor of production that is still blocked at every pass by national border controls is the human being. A hostility to foreign workers that exists in many rich countries, together with security concerns born after 9/11, makes the cross-border movement of persons increasingly difficult. Globalization today is far more closed than the borderless world of the "first globalization" of the nineteenth century, when 55 million Europeans resettled themselves in the New World.

Earlier in the book, I argued that the technological advances that make it possible to reconstruct much of the productive system into modular networks are the *enablers* of globalization. The forces of competition, volatility, expansion, and destruction that have been set loose in this vast world of international production and exchange, on the other hand, are the *drivers* of globalization. In some objective sense, these *drivers* and *enablers* represent constraints and opportunities for all—but even managers in the same industries competing in the same markets do not perceive them in the same way or respond in the same way. Where Chapters 3 to 6 laid out a road map of the new Lego-land world of production, I move now to the field of practical implementation. The researchers at the Industrial Performance Center asked each of the managers in the 500 companies we studied what they make in-house (and what they outsource) and what they make in their own home country (and what they offshore). And why.

PART FOUR

Competing in a Modular World

There are different views [on outsourcing], and we're struggling with this in Fujitsu. Some say: "We should just be good at choosing the best components and package them with services." Other managers say: "If we use standardized parts, anyone can package them in the same way. Where's the competitive advantage for Fujitsu?" If there's no differentiating hardware, there is no way of succeeding in a "pure" service business. How would we make profits? From this point of view, we need to maintain advanced hardware capabilities. In my personal opinion, Japanese cannot be satisfied without making something. Japanese cannot feel safe just making businesses only out of ideas and concepts.

—Akira Takashima, Vice Chairman and
Member of the Board, Fujitsu Limited[1]

CHAPTER 7

Tracking Strategies
from the Grass Roots Up

F ujitsu's puzzle about what a business ought to create within its own four walls and what it should buy from others is a dilemma almost every company operating in today's global economy has to figure out. There are many opportunities to buy services and manufacturing from the tens of thousands of new businesses that now carry out one or another of the functions that used to take place inside integrated companies. Parts Two and Three laid out the drivers and enablers of this movement: the opening and expansion of the international economy and the fragmentation of production. What this chapter will ask is: Do all companies respond to these fundamental changes in the same way? Do they have to do so if they want to do well?

Our team set out to discover if companies in the same industries and markets came to the same decisions about which functions they should carry out in-house and which they should buy from others. To figure this out, we looked at the responses we had received in the interviews we conducted in 500 companies in East Asia, America, and Europe. In each interview, we asked CEOs, directors of R & D, and vice presidents for supply-chain management questions like: Which operations are you keeping in-house? Which are you outsourcing? Why? How do you weigh the trade-offs? Which competitors do you benchmark when you make your decisions? How is it working out? As I explained in Chapter 4, today there is much more choice about which activities remain within a company and which can be purchased. In the past, keeping production in-house and working with closely affiliated suppliers were basically the only ways to assure quality, speed, and skill. On each new project, teams of engineers and managers used lessons learned in previous rounds. These lessons often could not be written down or translated into rules, but had to be applied to the new situation by an engineer with previous experience.

Think about how a mask—the pattern that is used to trace out the design of integrated circuits on a semiconductor chip—used to be made and how it is made now. Today, the circuit is drawn on a computer so that digital instructions for the mask can be transmitted from one machine to another. The circuits on the chip are etched by an electron beam. In contrast, until the middle of the 1970s, the mask, much like a dressmaker's pattern, used to be cut out by hand with a razor by a skilled technician working together with the circuit designer and a draftsman. Cutting it in the right way was in good part a matter of experience and craft, and the designer and the cutter had to work closely together to get the right result. Exploiting this tacit knowledge was so important that companies built organizations around preserving and encapsulating it within their own walls. The organizations of the most successful vertically integrated enterprises, such as IBM and Hitachi, were centered around capturing the firm's formal knowledge (often protected by patents or in proprietary process technology) and combining it with the hands-on knowledge and the experience of employees.

Today, new software technologies allow brand-name companies to codify data that used to depend on personal judgments and extrapolations of past experience. These digital files are sent to suppliers on a diskette or over the Internet. Digitization allows the lead firms to provide such detailed instructions to suppliers that there can be seamless integration of the different steps—from defining a product to selling it—with a minimum of human coordination. (At least in theory. Reality often falls short of the ideal.) Still, modularity and the fragmentation of production can now produce the same or better results as vertical integration—and often at lower cost. As the competition from new rivals all around the world narrows profit margins, companies find themselves under tremendous pressure to figure out what they do best and to consider buying the rest from others who can provide the products or services at lower cost.

It's not only a matter of lowering costs. Modularity allows innovators to rapidly start new companies by specializing on the function they do best, while buying the rest. Now that a chip designer can send specifications over the Internet to a pure-play semiconductor foundry, "fabless" design companies—ones with no production capacity—can flourish. They do not have to focus on finding surplus capacity in some lead firm's fab or on shepherding their designs through the foundry process. When a sports shoe company like Nike can send a sketch of a new model with a CAD file to a Taiwanese supplier, it no longer needs to have its engineers in the plants in China working out the detailed production process. When Ulvac, a Japanese semiconductor vacuum equipment manufacturer, builds functions into its new machines that reduce the need for adjustments and fine-tuning by the foundry technicians, foundries can be located in new sites far from the mother companies, with their deep backbenches of highly skilled, experienced personnel.

HOW WE COMPETE

We Use the Expertise of Contract Manufacturers
YOUSEF ABBASSI, TECHNOLOGY GROUP COMMODITY MANAGER, CISCO SYSTEMS, AN AMERICAN TECHNOLOGY EQUIPMENT MANUFACTURER

"Contract manufacturers make a variety of products for lots of different customers, so they are the ones with the in-depth knowledge about the most efficient manufacturing processes. This expertise is a strong benefit for us. It reduces production costs, and at Cisco, outsourcing to CMs lets us focus on what we do best—research and product development.

"Cisco has been careful in its outsourcing strategy. A lot of manufacturing can be outsourced, but the question is how much control we should keep of key processes. Configuration and testing directly impact quality, and this is what the customer sees. So Cisco controls databases, quality control, and production monitoring, even when they are outsourced. For instance, data from contract manufacturers' quality-control systems can be pulled by Cisco at any time to find out everything about the product—who made it, where it was made, when, and more."

The Facts: Two Stanford University engineers founded Cisco in 1984. Twenty years later, the company had 34,371 employees and $22 billion annual revenues. In 2005, *BusinessWeek* ranked Cisco the fourth-best-performing company in technology hardware and equipment (after Qualcomm, Apple, and Dell).[1]

Who's Winning?

Understanding which functions the managers have chosen to keep in-house and which they have outsourced was reasonably straightforward. Figuring out which of these strategies are actually succeeding was much harder and ultimately a matter of the team's collective best judgment. Even with so large a pool of companies to draw on, we have not discovered one best solution—even for firms in the same industry making more or less the same products or services. First of all, finding winners and deriving lessons from them that others should follow is an exercise with a short shelf-life. Some of the brightest performers that were interviewed fifteen years ago in the *Made in America* project—like Digital Equipment (DEC), a computer company; L. W. Packard, a woolen mill ranked among the world's ten best; Mita, a Japanese office-machine maker; and GFT, an Italian clothing company making designer ready-wear—do not even exist as independent operating entities any longer. Even over five years of the Globalization Study, we saw astonishing reverses in the fortunes of the companies as we returned to check up on them in successive visits.

Take the case of Manufacturers' Services Limited, an electronics manufacturing services (EMS) company in Concord, Massachusetts. We first visited in October 2001, when the business was booming.[2] The firm had been founded in 1995, and set up its first plants in Ireland, where they received a hefty boost from the Irish government, eager to support industries likely to create jobs in a society plagued by unemployment. MSL specialized in build-to-order configuration of complex circuit boards, assembly, and testing. It excelled in "low-touch" assembly for a range of industries, like aeronautics and automotives, and it avoided focusing too heavily on telecommunications, as many other EMS firms had done—to their sorrow, once telecoms tanked after 2001. In 2001, MSL had $1.2 billion sales of contract manufacturing to companies like Palm, 3Com, IBM, Lexmark, Rockwell, Philips, and Honeywell. It seemed we had a success to analyze.

When we returned to MSL in March 2003, we met a new president, Robert C. Bradshaw, an industry veteran who had worked for IBM for many years, then for Solectron, and most recently had been president and COO for SCI before its purchase by Sanmina. From him we heard about the bright future of mid-sized contract manufacturers, like MSL, that concentrate attention on individual customers and diversify sales across a number of industries. We also learned about MSL's special strengths, which ranged from Six Sigma quality manufacturing to a hard-nosed human resources policy. (You don't need to put Cadillacs in benefits packages, we were told, to get good workers around the world.)

When we checked up again in December 2004 (on the Web this time), we discovered that MSL had disappeared, bought up for $275 million in October 2003 by Celestica, one of the big five global suppliers. In 2003, MSL's year-end sales had been $825.9 million (down one-third from 2001). It had shed 38 percent of its employees over the previous year. Industry analysts suggested (after the fact) that MSL's fatal flaw had been too many production facilities in high-cost locations like Ireland and not enough in China. Whatever the strengths and weaknesses of this company, the point is that the environment had changed radically over the course of three years. After 2001, all electronics contract manufacturers were struggling to deal with the sharp decline in the business of their IT customers. And all of them were rushing to build more capacity in China.

Very few, if any, companies do well forever, and our evaluations of them are always based on when we stop the clock. If we had written this book in 2001, MSL would have looked golden. It's a reminder that research has no silver bullets. It cannot identify long-term winners—just as the high-tech companies and dot-coms that starred in the business press five years ago are not the same as the most profitable companies today. (In 2004, with skyrocketing prices of energy and materials because of China demand, oil companies and metal producers rose to the top of the profits charts,[3] and there's no way to predict which firms will make the front covers of *Fortune* and *Forbes* five years from now.) While we cannot always be certain who the winners are even today, it's not for lack of data. But the mountains of information in company reports on profits, return on investment, price-equity ratios, cash flow, market share, and other, still more complex formulae do not tell us how to classify a business that looked strong at one point in our research and weaker at another. Is variance due to the business cycle? Or to short-term errors? Or are we seeing long-term consequences of strategic choices beginning to play themselves out?

The difficulty in identifying winners is not only a result of how rapidly the competitive landscape changes. It's the fact that even in the same environment there are multiple possibilities. We studied a large number of companies in the same industry—199 in electronics, 84 in autos and auto parts, 170 in textile and apparel. At each point along the value chain in the industries we analyzed, we mapped out the options available to companies. We looked at which functions each company decided to perform. Depending on their legacies and on the human and material resources available to them today, companies may have a wider or narrower range of opportunities. What we wanted to learn is why companies chose as they did, what the trade-offs are among the choices, and whether there is more than one right choice for companies operating in the same market.

Once we had collected the managers' responses, we examined whether all companies making the same products for the same markets came up with the same strategies. If they did, we reasoned, we would have confirmation of the "convergence hypothesis" I described in Chapter 2: the prediction that under common competitive pressures, businesses tend to gravitate toward the same set of best practices in organization and strategy. When instead we found different responses, we realized there could be at least two possibilities. We might be seeing lag, with companies who look different because they are failing to adapt to the new pressures of the global economy. And certainly we did find some laggards who will fail unless they change. But the diversity we witnessed went far beyond this: It revealed a *variety* of strategies that companies use to compete successfully in the same industries. As I will explain, our conclusions after analyzing the data were that this diversity is not disappearing and that there is no convergence on a single best business model. This is why a company can choose how it will use the capabilities made possible by its own legacy along with those it can leverage from suppliers and allies.

Whenever we did observe companies with different strategies that appeared to be doing equally well, one or another of the researchers would usually challenge the finding and suggest it was temporary. Are the Italian eyeglass frame makers that are profitable today while manufacturing at home on as sustainable a path as eyeglass frame manufacturers who have outsourced to low-wage countries? Even though their returns are high today, will they still be in five years? Or take the Japanese electronics firms with large manufacturing facilities in Japan. They have returned to profitability by exporting components to consumer electronics assemblers in China. They have also reduced their costs through alliances with other big electronics companies in order to share the cost of investment in expensive new semiconductor and LCD fabs. Can they succeed long-term without outsourcing their manufacturing, as most of their American competitors have?

If Samsung, one of the few remaining vertically integrated giants, is riding a triumphal wave of success in components and consumer electronic products, and does most of it in-house, is it an exception to the rule? Or an alternative model? We often could tell losing strategies when we saw them, such as L. W. Packard's desperate gambit of shipping all its machinery to Inner Mongolia for a joint venture despite no prior China experience and no L. W. Packard personnel on the ground to monitor operations. But conclusions about companies that are doing more or less equally well will always be based on our judgment calls.

Which industries, which products, which operations can survive and prosper in advanced countries? Which are condemned? These are the questions we started with. As we met with corporate executives in hundreds of companies in fast-tech and slow-tech industries, we began to see that the core strengths of innovative and successful companies are not located in the products themselves, but rather in the capabilities a firm possesses and develops for carrying out particular functions.

A Look at Functions, Not Products

Beyond Commodities

On December 7, 2004, IBM announced the sale of its personal computer division to Lenovo, a Chinese computer manufacturer. The sale was the symbol of the arrival of China in the American IT industry and the end of an era for an American company that had pioneered personal computing. The revolutionary innovation that IBM introduced into American life twenty-three years earlier with its 5150 Personal Computer had finally reached commodity status. Personal computers can now be made all over the world and margins have become vanishingly thin. In any personal computer, much of the value of the product comes not from the brand-name firms but rather from components purchased from no-name suppliers. A graphic that appeared in the *New York Times* on December 4, 2004, showed a breakdown of the components in an IBM ThinkPad X31 selling for $2,349. This particular machine was assembled by Sanmina-SCI in Mexico, but other ThinkPads were being assembled in IBM plants in Shenzhen, China.[4]

Around the world in one laptop

IBM

Personal computers that have the I.B.M. name on them are built from an international array of components. Here is a look inside an I.B.M. ThinkPad X31 selling for $2,349.

ASSEMBLY
Mexico.

MEMORY
10 manufacturers world-wide, the largest in Korea. COST: 512 megabytes for about $60.

CASE AND KEYBOARD
Made in Thailand. COST: $50.

DISPLAY SCREEN
Two of the major screen makers are Samsung and LG Philips in South Korea. COST: A 15-inch screen is about $200; 17-inch about $300. Costs are estimates of what manufacturers pay for components.

GRAPHICS CONTROLLER CHIP
ATI. Made in Canada. TSMC. Made in Taiwan. COST: $30 to $100.

MICROPROCESSOR
Intel. Made in the U.S. COST: Intel's Centrino chip includes wireless capabilties, $275 to $500.

WIRELESS CARD
Intel. Made in Malaysia. COST: If not packaged with the microprocessor, $15 to $20.

BATTERY
Made in Asia to I.B.M. specifications. COST: $40 to $50 for a typical laptop battery.

HARD DRIVE
Made in Thailand. COST: Laptop hard drives range from $1.50 to $2 a gigabyte. A typical drive is about 40 gigabytes.

Source: New York Times Graphics

The sale wasn't entirely unexpected. From 2001 on, IBM had been losing money in its personal computing division.[5] Even before selling the unit, IBM had moved all manufacturing of the desktop PCs to Sanmina-SCI — a global supplier providing contract manufacturing services to a number of brand-name firms. The laptops were being assembled in Mexico and Scotland and in a vast factory in Shenzhen, China, whose 4,000 workers represented 40 percent of the total IBM PC workforce. But none of these moves had been enough to make PCs into a business with a good future, IBM decided. Samuel J. Palmisano, the CEO, explained the sale to IBM employees by arguing that information technology companies have two options: "invest heavily in R & D and be the high-value innovation provider for enterprises, or differentiate by leveraging vast economies of scale, high volumes and price." IBM was choosing the first route.[6]

Like many other companies the MIT globalization research team has studied over the past five years, IBM decided to withdraw from making a product it defined as a commodity and refocus on the more profitable businesses of services and high-end hardware: software for systems solutions, servers, and specialized components, like those that will be the engines of Sony's new game consoles. Philips, the largest European consumer electronics company, followed IBM and announced they were selling their computer monitors and low-end flat-screen TV business to TPV Vision Inc., a Taiwanese original equipment manufacturer (OEM) and supplier of displays and tablet PCs with operations in mainland China. TPV's parent company is Pou Chen, a business that has made a fortune as the world's largest contract manufacturer of sneakers for brands like Nike, New Balance, Reebok, and Adidas. In 2002, Pou Chen's Hong Kong-based subsidiary, Yue Yuen, made 130 million pairs of shoes. For Philips, TPV will be making computer display screens.

In 2001, when Pou Chen was just starting in the electronics business, we asked managers at their vast industrial park at Huang Jiang, Dongguan, China, where electronics plants sit side by side with the shoe factories, how a shoe company could get into the electronics industry. They told us, No problem! Only the commodity is different: The business and procurement practices for shoe contract manufacturing and for electronics contract manufacturing are the same.[7] There are many good Taiwanese and mainland engineers who can be hired to do either job. And Pou Chen has also set up joint ventures with established Taiwanese electronics firms, like Chi Mei Optoelectronics Corp., in order to get expertise in its new line of production.

While IBM and Philips are getting out of commodities, Pou Chen (or TPV) is expanding its commodity business. This raises the following question: What *is* a commodity today? Have all personal computers and displays become products that can be made by so many different manufacturers in the world that competition over price will inevitably drive their margins to the floor?

That depends. If personal computers and displays (or sneakers, for that matter) are looked at only as stripped-down manufactured objects, they are commodities. But many products today are sold bundled together with services. They bring together manufacturing with design and delivery and brand in combinations that create valuable products that are difficult to emulate.

HOW WE COMPETE

We Create Fashion
LUCKY JEANS, AMERICAN CLOTHING COMPANY

A pair of Faded Glory blue jeans made in Mexico can be bought for $10.77 at the Farmington, Maine, Wal-Mart. Because these pants can be made by almost any apparel company anywhere in the world, they are true commodities. A pair of Lucky blue jeans, on the other hand, sells for around a hundred dollars. Lucky, a branch of the American clothing designer Liz Claiborne, incorporates design services that identify and create fashion; high-quality components—denim, zipper, trim; stonewash and sanding finishing treatments that give each pair a distinctive look; and advertising and branding that make Lucky jeans seem unique and desirable. About a third of them are sold in hip Lucky retail shops. Lucky does not carry out all these functions within its own walls. The components are purchased from suppliers; the sewing and finishing are done by Latino workers in Los Angeles factories owned by Koreans (and closely watched by Lucky managers). But the product definition, design, marketing, and branding are Lucky's. It's the ability to conceive the product and combine these functions that makes Lucky a producer of a valuable product and not merely a commodity.

Even though Lucky's parent company, Liz Claiborne, is outsourcing and offshoring its mainlines, it will likely keep Lucky in Los Angeles, since its design and the finishing treatments change so quickly in response to consumer trends. Juicy Couture, another cool clothing company Liz Claiborne acquired, also remains in L.A.—for the same reasons.

For further proof about why we should think about functions, not products, consider two of IBM's direct rivals in PCs: Dell and Sony. Neither of them is exiting the personal computer market. Are they making a mistake? How can it be a good business for them if it is not for IBM? From one point of view, they are all making personal computers—and we might expect them to face the same pressures and come to the same conclusions. But each company has bundled personal computers together with different services and products, making them in the end different businesses. Sony has a wide range of businesses, from electronic components to consumer electronics, music, movies, games, and a finance company. Dell, on the other hand, basically specializes in distribution and logistics, and starting from PCs has extended its formidable capabilities to other IT hardware. Dell's business is providing highly valued services to customers by making it possible for them to customize options easily and cheaply. Customers can, in effect, "design" their own computer, buy it online, and Dell will deliver it to them in a matter of days. Dell focuses on its core strengths: marketing and distribution. In fact, the company is now extending the scope of its business by providing the same services to customers purchasing printers and television sets, and over time will widen to even more products.

Who makes Dell computers and where? A long article on Dell in the *New York Times* (December 19, 2004)[8] quoted the CEO, Kevin D. Rollins, as saying that Dell makes them in the United States: "None is outsourced; none is made in other countries and shipped in." The *New York Times* journalist noted in passing that this was not quite accurate, since Dell laptops are assembled abroad. Nonetheless, the reporter concluded: "Computer equipment accounts for the bulk of Dell's revenues, and it is still produced by Dell workers inside Dell factories." This statement shows how much confusion there is about production in a modular world. In fact, as I noted earlier in the book, the only operations that take place in Dell factories in the United States are those involved with final assembly—in other words, screwing in the parts and burning in the software options selected by a customer.

Suppose a customer chooses a 2-gigahertz processor, an 80-gigabyte hard drive, 2 gigabytes of RAM preinstalled, a video card, an Ethernet card, 802.11G wireless, a DVD RW drive, 4 USB slots, a firewire connection, and a 17" LCD monitor with 1400 × 1050 resolution. All of these components, as well as the computer body, are made by suppliers whose trucks line up outside the U.S. Dell plants to ensure a seamless flow of parts. The microprocessor is likely made in the United States (Intel or AMD), as is the software (Microsoft). The rest (monitor, motherboard, hard drive, mouse, casing) was probably made with chips designed in a fabless house in the United States or Taiwan, with memory chips that could come from the United States, or Korea, or Japan, or Taiwan, and then assembled in Taiwan or China. Dick L. Hunter, the vice president for manufacturing operations, estimated, "Our top 30 suppliers represent about 75 percent of our total costs. Throw in the next 20 and that comes to about 95 percent. We deal with all of those top 50 daily, many of them many times a day."[9]

At the final assembly part of operations, Mr. Hunter explained what happens in Dell's U.S. plants: "We receive the parts; we screw them on; we bolt them on and—increasingly, we snap them together. We download the software the customer has selected. There's not a lot of touch involved in the process. It's a remarkably orchestrated process, and one person can do this in about four and a half minutes."[10] While these are the only operations that take place in the final assembly plant, Dell considers itself to be "producing computer equipment" in the United States. In the same sense, a leading-brand sneaker company that attaches soles and uppers—both manufactured in China—to each other in Los Angeles can advertise "Made in the U.S.A."

As we learned in interviews with Taiwanese original design manufacturers (ODMs), they find themselves doing a growing amount of design services for Dell, in addition to manufacturing the parts. But Dell still controls the vital part of design: knowledge of the customer and ability to respond rapidly to new demands.

HOW WE COMPETE

We Know the Customer

DICK HUNTER, VICE PRESIDENT FOR MANUFACTURING OPERATIONS, DELL, AN AMERICAN COMPUTER COMPANY

Dick Hunter told us: "We know what the customer wants because we get feedback from thousands of them every day. We disseminate some part of that—whatever is necessary—to our suppliers. We also have our own design teams working on integration of the components and on industrial design. We're not in the business of improving the processor—that's up to Intel—but when we hear from customers that the machine is eating up the battery supply, we give this feedback to Intel and they work on processors that can give better battery life. The result was the Centrino. So we do play a vital role in design."[11]

As for R & D functions, while IBM chief Sam Palmisano explains his company's basic choice is to "invest heavily in R & D and be the high-value innovation provider for enterprises," Michael Dell questions whether there's anything great about spending a lot on R & D. In fact, Dell spends less than 1 percent of sales on R & D.[12] Michael Dell explained his philosophy in a 2004 interview: "A lot of companies say they're better than us because they spend more on R & D. What are they better at? A lot of the R & D spending is actually spent to protect things that are proprietary, of no benefit to the customer. We only do the kind [of R & D] that benefits the customer. We don't try to reinvent things that other companies have [invented]. We don't develop things nobody knows what to do with. We develop things people want to buy—and buy in volume. Innovation can occur in supply chain and logistics, manufacturing and distribution, and sales and service."[13] The strategy has been very successful: In 2005, *Fortune* named Dell "America's most admired company." Dell's shareholders' 2004 return was 24 percent—compared with Hewlett-Packard's 7.3 percent.[14] Scott McNealy, chairman and CEO of Sun Microsystems, points out that while Dell and Amazon spend practically nothing on R & D, Intel spends 14 percent, Microsoft, 21.1 percent, and Sun, 17.2 percent. "Which type is right? Both are. Amazon is right to focus on its supply-chain expertise, from the earliest concept all the way through to delivery, because that is its core strength. Sun is right to focus on R&D because that is our core strength."[15]

Creating a Big Bang

When MIT researchers visited Sony at its Tokyo headquarters in 2001, 2002, and 2004, we learned about a business based on choices that are very different from IBM's and Dell's about what to keep in-house in order to make best use of resources and capabilities. In 2003, Sony was the world's largest consumer electronics company, but its sales and profits had been falling since the end of the nineties. Suddenly, in 2003, Sony shares fell by 25 percent after large quarterly losses. Sony announced it would cut jobs and lower costs by reducing the number of components used in making its products.

By 2005, the company still seemed to be in trouble. Profits in the electronics and game division were falling, and the company had lost out in areas in which it should have had a strong lead. The company that had pioneered portable music players with the Walkman in 1978 was left in the dust by Apple's iPod. Sony engineers' insistence on using only proprietary technology meant that Sony machines could not play MP3 files, which most people who download music want. For other consumer electronics products, like TVs, Sony makes both components and products, but it has not been able to drive costs down on the components as its competitors Matsushita, Sharp, and Samsung have done. In a dramatic move to reverse the company's fortunes, in March 2005 the board named a foreigner, Sir Howard Stringer, as chairman and CEO. Prior to that, Stringer had headed Sony's American movies and music businesses, and with tight cost controls and successes like *Spider-Man 2*, had made them into highly profitable parts of the company.

Stringer was brought in to transform the company, and his first statements as chairman laid out a mission not very different from the vision of his predecessors in the office: to build on the synergies of a company that pioneers across a broad range of activities, from component making to consumer electronics products like DVDs, cameras, and cell phones, to game machines like the PlayStation Portable, to content businesses like games, movies, and music. Stringer said: "We would accelerate cross-company collaboration, thereby revitalizing the company and promoting creativity. Growth cannot be achieved just through cost reduction. We need new projects, new ideas, new strategies, new alliances and a shared vision."[16] What's gone wrong, Sony's board and senior managers seem to believe, is not the fundamental structure or reach of the company. They see a problem in the *execution* of objectives as divisions continue to battle over turf, and the synergies imagined on paper between extraordinary engineering talent and great content divisions have failed to materialize. Stringer's job is to bang heads together (or remove them) and succeed with the old vision.

The Sony vision has always been that of a company that grows by inventing blockbusters. The company boasts an impressive track record of products that have transformed the way we live and play: the tape recorder in 1950, the transistor radio in 1955, the Trinitron color TV in 1969, the Walkman in 1979, the CD player in 1982, the camcorder in 1983, the digital camera in 1988, and the PlayStation video game console in 1994. Each of these products not only enjoyed tremendous success; they created entirely new markets. When Ken Kutaragi, the legendary creator of the PlayStation and former executive deputy president, told investors the bad news about the company's performance in 2003, he said: "It may appear as though Sony is being sucked into a black hole. . . . But we hope to create a 'Big Bang' that will lead to new business."[17]

Sony's Big Bang hopes are focused on a new processor it is developing with Toshiba and IBM. The Cell chip is a multicore semiconductor composed of several processors handling many tasks at the same time and able to move large amounts of data over broadband networks.[18] It is much more powerful than today's chips; its processing capabilities place it in the ranks of the world's top supercomputers.[19] Sony plans to use it initially as the motor of the PlayStation 3, a video game console due on the market in 2006. But the company hopes it will be the process driver for digital phones, cameras, high-definition TVs, and workstations. If incorporated into personal computers, it could create a product with capabilities a technological quantum leap beyond today's Windows- and Intel-based machines. With so many hopes pinned on far-out innovation, it's not surprising that Sony spends heavily on R & D (6.4 percent of sales in 2003).

We asked Dr. Teruaki Aoki, Sony's executive vice president: Why not cut costs by using outsourcing? Why make Sony Vaios in house? Why not have these personal computers and laptops made by contract manufacturers, as Dell does? He told us Dell and Sony have completely different business models. He sees Dell's business as dominated by corporate sales—a high-volume, low-margin business. From his perspective, Dell is a single-focus company with a blockbuster product, as Sony would be if it were mainly a business to make PlayStations, he said. (Between PlayStation's introduction in 1994 and 2004, Sony sold 170 million PlayStation game consoles. They were responsible for 68 percent of Sony's 2004 profits.)

But Sony is not just PlayStations; it has an astounding number of product categories—about 100,000—in electronics, movies, music, games, financial services, and software. Within each branch, the array of products, components, and services is extremely wide. Sony electronics products range from the most advanced new semiconductors to cell phones, personal computers, and batteries. From year to year, the profitability of each segment varies greatly. This diversity makes Sony less vulnerable to business cycles. Our question was whether the spread of Sony's resources across so many functions meant that the company was keeping in-house activities that could be done more cheaply and as well by others. So we asked Aoki to explain Sony's strategies on the Vaio, a personal computer, and the PlayStation.

Why does Sony not outsource as much as Dell? Or, in its electronics businesses, why not use the Taiwanese foundries the way a company like Cisco does, instead of making so many of its own chips? There are real limitations in outsourcing, Aoki argued. It adds another layer between customers and the manufacturer, and information flows are filtered and slowed. This leads to the buildup of inventory, and to the kind of situation brand-name firms faced when the dot-com bubble burst and contract manufacturers ended up holding a large inventory of unsellable goods. The independent contract manufacturers just cannot do model changes at a fast enough rate for most Sony products, which have three- to six-month life cycles (in contrast to the PlayStation's five-year life cycle).

Besides, Sony can negotiate better prices on parts from suppliers than those contract manufacturers get in purchasing parts. Moreover, contract manufacturers do not have a strong incentive to push back on the cost of parts, because they would have to pass on some of the gains to their customers. While Sony does use original equipment manufacturers and original design manufacturers for making some of the PlayStations and the cheaper Vaios, it is building its own plants in China to take back the low- to mid-range Vaios within its own walls. The Sony trend, Aoki explained, is to build 100 percent Sony-owned factories in China rather than outsourcing. Our team found this strategy in other Japanese companies as well. Of the Japanese managers we interviewed in electronics who are offshoring production, 86 percent told us they were using their overseas plants; only 7 percent reported using subcontractors. Of the American electronics managers who were offshoring, 46 percent used factories they owned and 31 percent used contract manufacturers. (Others did not—or would not—say.)

Fifty percent of the Vaios, by value, are top-end expensive computers, with design and technical features that change every few months. Sony makes them in its Nagano, Japan, plant and plans to keep doing it that way. Aoki showed us the latest Vaio: a beautiful, superslim laptop with a gleaming black, lacquerlike finish. The two MIT researchers in the room immediately reached out to touch the machine and to heft its light weight. To make a small form-factor product like this thin Vaio takes special components and very difficult manufacturing techniques that cannot be perfectly controlled or standardized. Only in Japan are there metal polishing suppliers capable of producing such a finish. If Sony wanted to use a Taiwanese OEM to make such Vaios, they would have to teach them how to make the parts. That would take too much Sony engineering time, Aoki calculated.

Then he came to the heart of the matter. Though the Taiwanese ODM companies will eventually catch up, Sony does not want to teach them how to do this too quickly. Because outsourcing can lead to leaks in intellectual property, Sony tries to prevent this, or at least slow it down during the window of opportunity of new-product introduction, when the highest margins are made.

HOW WE COMPETE

We Don't Set Up Our Own Competitor
DR. TERUAKI AOKI, EXECUTIVE VICE PRESIDENT, SONY,
A JAPANESE ELECTRONICS COMPANY

"We constantly have to think: Are we creating a competitor? We can delay this if we give each vendor only one part of the process to do, whereas if we used them as ODM, they could do everything. We need to 'black-box' the technology in our products so others can't get it quickly. Basically, the best use of ODMs is to fill in low-end product lines. . . . Besides, if we went to modular production, there'd be no profit for us. Sony's profits come from components, not from assembly. We made $2 billion in revenue from [internal] chip sales this year. We need to drive down costs, but not to move production out of the company. We should only ask contract manufacturers to work on parts that do not add that much value."

Our team felt that Sony may be missing a big chance—not only to lower its costs, but to use open standards and common components that others can build on in order to benefit the entire industry, as IBM is doing in giving away software patents. Sony's announcement in mid-2005 that it was deepening its technology cooperation with Samsung suggests a step in IBM's direction. The balance between black-boxing—protecting intellectual property—and creating products that others can plug into is one of the toughest calls today.

American-led firms also worry about their intellectual property disappearing when they deal with Taiwanese ODM companies. A manager at a telecom equipment company explained that though the Taiwanese ODMs were very efficient, they bring a lot of intellectual property risk—"they scare the hell out of us"—and so the decision was to use Flextronics (a U.S.-based contract manufacturer) instead.

The discussion with Aoki turned from personal computers to the PlayStation. While the high-end Vaios change so rapidly that Sony wants to keep a competitive edge by protecting the new technologies in-house, the PlayStation has been a rather stable product and one made in very long runs. Why not outsource all of the PlayStation, components and assembly? While some key components are made by suppliers—Sanyo, Texas Instruments, Cirrus Logic, On Semiconductor—and assembly takes place in a Taiwanese contract manufacturer (Foxconn) plant in China, it's Sony's components (some made in a joint venture with Toshiba) that remain at the heart of the PlayStation.[20] Sony components amount to more than 50 percent of the material cost of the PlayStation, and Aoki claimed that if Sony outsourced them, it would miss out on much of the value in the business. With the Cell chip coming on as a driver that will make PlayStations light-years faster and more powerful than the competition, why give up making components?

As for fabbing Sony chips in a Taiwanese foundry like TSMC or UMC, Aoki told us that even if Sony trusted the pure-play fabs with its intellectual property, there would still be too much risk, because Sony needs so many chips a month (2 million). "If we cannot get the required amounts at the right time, we lose the whole business. It would be far too risky to ask someone to make these components." (One of the engineers on our team wondered why Sony would find this so risky, since fabs typically make about 15 million chips a month.) Still, when strategizing about the future of the PlayStation and the personal computer, Sony is not focused on getting rid of these products, as IBM has, or on driving down their costs and providing other services to the customers, as Dell does. Its main drive is to transform its products by radical innovation with the Cell chip.

When we asked a Toshiba senior manager why they were keeping notebook computers in-house, he, like the Sony executive, pointed to the competitive advantages they get from having first access to new components that are made in Toshiba—such as the wireless communication feature that in 2002 put Toshiba notebooks back on top of notebook sales.[21] The Toshiba and the Sony managers both recognized that Dell's costs are lower because Dell holds less inventory and does more outsourcing; in fact, they costed out the differences for us in the interviews in great detail. But they believe the competitive advantages they gain from keeping components and products together in the same company are worth it. As the Toshiba manager explained: "We remain together as an integrated group because we see a strong potentiality to create new products out of the pieces of our existing and upcoming capabilities, and a Dell cannot do this."

Ten years from now, we may look back and conclude that either IBM, Dell, Sony, or Toshiba had the best strategy for dealing with outsourcing, but today the question is open. Meanwhile, IBM has withdrawn from personal computers altogether. But at present, the Dell, Sony, and Toshiba models work. Yet even these models use different kinds of corporate resources when embedding qualities and services in their personal computers. A Dell customer is buying easy customization, logistics, marketing services, and a brand along with his machine; the Vaio or Toshiba customer is buying innovative technology, extraordinary design, and a brand along with hers. Since a commodity is a product or a service that many companies can deliver, it's clear that none of these companies is making mere commodities.

Making a Medical Device into a Fashion Statement

As we looked at other industries in our study, we found many cases, like personal computers, in which the "same" good could be made either as a plain-vanilla commodity that producers all over the world could turn out or else bundled with valuable features. Are eyeglass frames commodities? After all, they can and are being made all around the world in plants with low-wage and low-skill labor. We visited eyeglass companies in Hong Kong, China, Italy, Japan, and Germany to determine how the industry was faring. Some of these firms are world leaders in the optical industry, like the Carl Zeiss Group, headquartered in Oberkochen, Germany. In 2003–2004, the group had 13,700 employees and $2.7 billion in sales. Zeiss focused on high-tech optical technologies for microscopy, optoelectronics, and medical applications. When the team interviewed Dr. Franz-Ferdinand von Falkenhausen, the president, he told us that German companies like BMW, Daimler, and his own had learned that it was a mistake to give up on making products for mass markets. While it might not be competitive at the lowest end, Zeiss could build good consumer products in the middle range. In 2004, Zeiss decided to acquire Sola, a company making ophthalmic lenses, and merge it with its own consumer lens division in a new company: Carl Zeiss Vision. With the approval of the merger in March 2005 by antitrust authorities, the new company starts out as a global player with 9,000 employees and $1.03 billion a year in revenues.

Luxottica and Sàfilo, with headquarters and factories we visited in 1999 in a high mountainous district of northern Italy, are world leaders in the optical industry and specialize in prescription frames and in sunglasses. Luxottica had $3.61 billion sales in 2003; Sàfilo, $1.16 billion sales the same year.[22] Luxottica is the leading optical retailer in the United States and Canada, with 2,500 Lenscrafter and Sunglass Hut stores. It has its own house brands, like RayBan, Vogue, and Persol, and it licenses brands like Prada, Versace, Chanel, Brooks Brothers, and Anne Klein. Sàfilo licenses such labels as Burberry, Diesel, Giorgio Armani, Gucci, Nine West, and Yves Saint Laurent. Given their diversity and size, these are not exactly niche businesses. Luxottica employs 38,000 people worldwide. Even Sàfilo, the smaller of the two, sold 26 million frames in 2003. They are also very profitable businesses. A high proportion of their sales are in the American market. Of course, as the U.S. dollar sank in value relative to the euro since 2003, both companies suffered. But still, Sàfilo's operating margin in 2003 was 11.2 percent (down from 16 percent the year before), and Luxottica's was 15.9 percent (down from 18.9 percent in 2002).[23] It's a different industry, of course, but it's worth noting that Dell, one of the world's most efficient and profitable information technology companies, had 2004 operating margins of 8.8 percent.[24]

Both Luxottica and Sàfilo carry out within their own four walls all the stages from product definition (with some input from the brands they license) through production. Luxottica also controls a significant part of its retailing through its own LensCrafter and Sunglass Hut stores. Luxottica describes its strategy as "full vertical integration [with] direct control over all significant components of the eyewear production and distribution process, including design, production, and worldwide distribution both to wholesale customers and to a large number of end-consumers through its retail division."[25] Seven of Luxottica's production facilities are in Italy, one in China. The Chinese plant (Dongguan, Guangdong) has 1,200 workers; its output goes to the low end of the U.S. market and to Chinese domestic stores.

When Luxottica bought Bausch & Lomb in 1999, it came into possession of RayBan and its factories in Nuevo Laredo, Mexico, and San Antonio, Texas. Luxottica closed the factories, packed up the production equipment, and shipped it off to Italy to install in plants there. Even though Italian wages were higher than those in the plants on the United States-Mexican border, the quality and productivity of the North Americans were just too low compared to the Italians. It was far better, the managers told us, to consolidate production within plants where Luxottica's skilled Italian workers could control the processes closely. For the same reasons, Luxottica has been gradually absorbing into its own plants work that used to be done by its subcontractors in the small towns around Luxottica's home district.

Making eyeglass frames is hardly rocket science, and manufacturers have sprung up in low-wage countries like China, Slovenia, and Hungary. There are prescription frames that sell today for as little as $18 in the Danvers, Massachusetts, Wal-Mart, and sunglasses are even cheaper. Yet 25 percent of the world's frames are still made in Italy by high-wage workers in companies like Luxottica and Italian factories in industrial districts in the Venice region. Some of the difference between Italian frames that sell for several hundred dollars and the Chinese frames has to do with using more expensive materials, like titanium. But the most important difference, and one that explains most of the price differential, is that the $18 frame is a "lens holder," as one of the Italian executives described it, and the $300 frame is a fashion accessory. The Italian companies have succeeded in transforming medical devices that were objects of necessity into fashion that is an object of desire.

By licensing brands like Chanel and Dior, the glamour of haute couture has been incorporated into glasses. For licensing to work, though, the value of the brand has to be visible and protected. Sàfilo and Luxottica need staff capable of working with the brands and translating the trends of the year into frame designs. If Prada tells Luxottica that this year's fashion is retro chic, Luxottica designers need to be able to convert this idea into a shape for glasses. Most important, Luxottica and Sàfilo designers have to divine the idea even before the Prada or Armani designers appear in their offices. For this they need to breathe inspiration in the same air where fashion is created—that means Milan, not San Antonio or Beijing.

Are the only options in eyeglasses, then, the high-value vertical integration in which branding, design, production, and retail remain in-house—or else the production of commodity frames that can be sold at Wal-Mart? No: Consider Zoff, the start-up we visited in June 2003 in Tokyo.[26] Zoff opened in 2001 with six people in the shop and five in the back office. When they started the business, the average price for eyeglasses in Tokyo was around $280. Ten retail stores controlled around half of the market, and profit margins were around 80 percent. Retailers bought frames from wholesalers, who paid for licensing brand names. Manufacturing of both lenses and frames had already mostly left Japan for China. Zoff realized that they could reduce prices if they could bypass the wholesalers and source directly from Chinese manufacturers. They figured out how to sell glasses for well under $100 per pair. But the idea was not just price cutting. It was to change the image of glasses into fashion items so that customers would buy twice as many, with different pairs to match different outfits and for formal and informal occasions.

Today, Zoff designers send computer-aided design (CAD) files over the Net to Chinese factories and buy lenses in Korea. Zoff salesclerks hand customers their glasses forty minutes after they walk into the shop and order. Eye exams can also be done in the store. With these new services, Zoff has created a whole new business out of eyeglasses. By the end of 2002, they had $19 million in sales and ninety employees in Japan. Two years later, they had $28.7 million in sales and 145 full-time employees and 100 part-timers.

The lesson our team drew from personal computers and from eyeglasses is that highly valued products and services can be created at virtually every point along the chain of functions. The critical difference between companies lies not so much in their industries as in the functions they choose. Commodity status is not inherent in things in themselves; in fact, almost anything that has value for people can escape commodity status if a company can embed in it properties that potential rivals find difficult to replicate. In making these valuable services and material objects, companies choose different functions in the sequence of operations that links product definition to sales. To capture the dynamics of these strategic decisions about combining capabilities and products, we need to zoom in on functions and map out companies—not by their end products (Is Dell selling computers or services? Are Luxottica and Sàfilo selling fashion or eyeglasses?) but by the activities in which companies specialize.

CHAPTER 8

Brand-Name Firms, No-Name Manufacturers, and Everything in Between

The team started analyzing the data we collected in interviews by mapping out two sectors—electronics and textile/apparel—as a chain of functions arrayed in sequence.[1] In both industries, there were vertically integrated brand-name companies like Samsung or Zara that made components (e.g., chips, fabric) *and* products (e.g., cell phones, blouses). Others made components only (like Intel's chips or L. W. Packard's woolen fabric). Some did design only (like the integrated-circuit design companies) or design and retail (like Liz Claiborne and Kellwood). A company like Samsung does it all—from definition to design to manufacturing to sales (some such firms even do after-market services). Still others do little or no manufacturing in their own plants and outsource it all (like Liz Claiborne and Cisco); others do only manufacturing (like the Taiwanese original equipment manufacturers or Flextronics, the American contract manufacturer). The team grouped companies according to the functions they carried out in-house and those they outsourced (as well as those they kept in their own home country and those they moved abroad)—decisions I'll discuss in Part Five.

Making Products and Components?
Or Product or Components?

Vertically integrated firms are ones that do it all: from design to sale both for their components and the final product. The classic model in the American electronics industry was IBM in the seventies. IBM designed, manufactured, and sold components, and designed, manufactured, and sold typewriters, computers, and a wide variety of other products to businesses and consumers. Companies like Texas Instruments, Motorola, Siemens, Hewlett-Packard, Philips, Hitachi, Fujitsu, Toshiba, NEC, and Matsushita were organized along the same lines in those years. Today, no major American electronics corporation operates this way. IBM's major business has become business services. While IBM still makes some of the semiconductors it uses in its hardware, it has turned much of the manufacturing of the components it uses and of the products sold under its brand over to contract manufacturers. Texas Instruments shed product manufacturing and now focuses on making components. Motorola spun off its integrated-circuit design and semiconductor manufacturing as an independent company, Freescale, with an IPO in 2004 (as Siemens had spun off its semiconductor division as Infineon, in April 1999).

The Japanese vertically integrated electronics companies have given up many fewer of their in-house functions than the Americans. In the companies we visited (twenty-five Japanese electronics firms in fifty-seven different interviews over the years 1999 to 2004), we heard echoes of their internal debates over how wide the scope of the activities carried out in-house should be. Sony, Toshiba, Matsushita (Panasonic), NEC, Sharp, and Hitachi all make both components and final products. Like Dr. Aoki at Sony, many of the managers in these firms argue that keeping component making in-house is vital to competitive advantage. Sharp, for example, sees its strength in liquid crystal displays (LCD) production as a way of introducing very rapid changes in products like TVs, cell phones, and solar panels, and at the time of writing, enjoyed the highest profit margins in Japanese consumer electronics.[2]

Since 2000, Sharp has opened five new plants for component manufacturing in Japan. The Kameyama plant inaugurated in January 2004 is a vertically integrated facility that manufactures LCD components and also assembles LCD television sets. In January 2005, Sharp announced that this factory would start making the most advanced LCDs—eighth-generation substrates for forty-five- to fifty-inch LCD TV panels—thus moving out in front of the Samsung-Sony seventh-generation plant in South Korea.[3] (Substrates are thin sheets of glass with chemicals pressed between them. Each generation has larger sheets, so more, or wider, panels can be cut out of each piece. The eighth-generation sheets, which are as big as a king-size bed, are dauntingly complex to make and manipulate.) Because Sharp is still doing much of its manufacturing in its own plants in Japan, there have been no major layoffs in the company, although workers have been shifted from making household appliances like microwave ovens to other activities. The number of Sharp employees in Japan has been stable over the past decade (1994–2004): 30,000. However, Sharp's "spiral strategy" of selling both components and products means that it can find itself competing with its own customers—for example, when it sells LCD panels to European mobile-phone makers that compete with Sharp's own brand-name mobile phones. But even here, Sharp sees an opportunity to entrench its standards for LCD more broadly across consumer electronics firms and to fend off plasma displays, the competing technology.

For many Japanese, American, and European firms, like Philips and Siemens, the high cost of building new wafer fabs makes it just too expensive to keep all or even most chip making in-house. The American companies have outsourced most of their semiconductor manufacturing to the pure-play foundries in Taiwan. Again, pure-play "fabs" are semiconductor-manufacturing plants that make chips to customers' designs and specifications but do not develop their own products or brands. Even Jerry Sanders, CEO of Advanced Micro Devices, famous for once dismissing outsourcing by proclaiming that "real men have fabs," finally came around to it and tried to bring about an alliance with the second-largest Taiwanese fab, United Microelectronics Corporation. Though that project eventually fell through, at the time he explained his change of heart as "an innovative response to the tectonic shift that has changed the fundamental economics of the worldwide semiconductor industry."[4]

Aside from outsourcing to the fabs, there are other ways companies can deal with the costs of high capital investment and still keep their hands on the steering wheel. There are a growing number of alliances among multinationals and foundries for building new plants. Over the last five years of restructuring Japanese industry, even traditional rivals have built alliances in order to survive by sharing the cost of investment in new fabs. Hitachi and NEC merged their memory-chip businesses in a new company called Elpida. Toray and Matsushita are jointly investing in plasma-display panels factories. (The one they are building now involves an $862 million joint investment.) Hitachi, Matsushita, and Toshiba are investing together in a $1 billion plant to make LCDs for the flat-screen TVs that each of them makes. These giants previously had go-it-alone strategies, but today, even if they are still unwilling to transfer production to the pure-play foundries, they need to find partners.

Looking at the Japanese companies, our group debated whether the Japanese are becoming more like American companies that are focusing on core capabilities and outsourcing the rest. Are the Japanese moving, however slowly, toward dividing into companies that make either components or products? Does the success of a company like Sharp show that there is still vitality in the vertically integrated model? Or do its thin operating margins demonstrate, rather, the fragility of the model?

There is one example of a vertically integrated company whose extraordinary success we could not question: Samsung. The South Korean company rose from near-bankruptcy in the 1997 Asian financial crisis to become the world's third-largest information technology company (after IBM and Hewlett-Packard). In 2004, Samsung reported $10 billion of net profits—an amount twice that of Japan's top ten electronics companies combined.[5] Samsung's market capitalization—only about a quarter of Sony's in 2000—today is almost twice as large. Samsung makes both components and consumer electronic products. It is the world leader in dynamic random-access chips (DRAM) and near the top in flash memory, LCD, and other basic components. It makes flat-screen TVs, mobile phones, digital music players—and all in its own factories. Its scale, efficiency, and heavy investment in manufacturing components make Samsung a low-cost producer of consumer electronic products. Its CEO, Yun Jong Yong, said, "If we get out of manufacturing, we will lose."[6] But Samsung has not only continued to excel in successive generations of semiconductor chips; it has also turned around its image as a maker of rather clunky consumer products to winning international design competitions with some of the world's coolest electronic gadgets.[7]

If there's a Samsung model in the textile and clothing industry, it is Zara, a family-controlled Spanish clothing company that has experienced extraordinary growth over the past five years, with $5.6 billion sales in 2004 and net profits that rose almost threefold over the period 1999 to 2004, years when most of the European apparel manufacturers were in serious trouble.[8] Zara is a vertically integrated company that concentrates multiple functions in-house: from weaving and dying about 40 percent of the material it uses, to designing the garments, cutting them, organizing all the logistics of distribution, and owning and operating some 600 shops—mainly in Europe, though there are a number of Zara shops in cities like New York. It subcontracts out all the sewing—mainly to about 500 sewing factories operating near Zara's headquarters, plants, and distribution centers. About half of Zara's products are made in this tight circle of mother firm and dedicated suppliers in the region around La Coruña. In contrast, Zara's principal competitors, H & M and the Gap, have no in-house (and very little in-country) production. Benetton in 2002 still procured 70 percent of its products in Italy, but only 30 percent of them were made within the company.[9]

Zara stands out from all its closest counterparts because of how fast it moves garments from the design stages onto the racks in its stores. Zara stores renew their offerings every two weeks, with new items coming in all the time. Customers come in often to see what's "in" that week. Because Zara gears its production to demand and produces in smaller batches than its competitors, it ends up with fewer pieces of clothing to sell at less than full price. Its net margin on sales is therefore higher than its rivals'. In 2001, Zara's net margin was 10.5 percent, Benetton's 7 percent, H & M's 9.5 percent, and the Gap's, in a bad year, near zero.[10]

HOW WE COMPETE

Speed Takes Control

ZARA, A SPANISH CLOTHING COMPANY (FROM AN INTERVIEW WITH A SENIOR EXECUTIVE OF A LARGE AMERICAN CLOTHING BRAND— WHICH HAS NO IN-HOUSE MANUFACTURING)

"The King of Speed is Zara. Everybody wants the short-cycle, speed-to-market Zara model, but unless you control your mills the way Zara does, quick-turn is nearly impossible. Without this kind of local control, you won't switch product development from six to seven months to two months. Zara has it all in one box: from design to fabric to assembly to transportation. Other wholesalers have production everywhere—Sri Lanka, Jordan, South Africa—and 80 to 90 cents per garment to ship by air will kill your profit. Moreover, unless you control your mills, as Zara does, you cannot convince mill owners to leave their lines open and machines available for last-minute runs."

Since the major American brands have long ago sold off their manufacturing and outsourced production mostly to Asia, the Zara model is inconceivable for them. This demonstrates how legacy shapes the range of current options. In clothing as in electronics, there are many fewer vertically integrated companies making components and products today than in the 1970s, but the beast is certainly not extinct. In companies like Samsung and Zara, true vertical integration still has vitality and good times ahead.

From Vertical Integration to Brand Plus

The story of Hewlett-Packard over the past twenty years illustrates the dilemmas that companies that were once vertically integrated giants now face as they try to raise profitability by outsourcing functions that were once carried out in-house. HP, as I explained, has moved most of its manufacturing out of its four walls. The only major part of the business remaining under the company roof is printing and imaging. HP was a pioneer in thermal inkjet technology and produced the first inkjet printers in the 1980s. The sale of ink cartridges in the United States was a $34 billion business in 2004—and worth more than twice the amount of printer sales.[11] For HP, ink cartridges are among its highest-margin products. At the end of 2004, the printing division earned $3.8 billion in operating profits for HP—about three-quarters of HP's operating profits.[12]

When in 2003 and 2004 investors grew impatient with the management of Carleton S. (Carly) Fiorina and her failure to make the HP-Compaq merger she had pushed so hard pay off in higher profits and market share, they started demanding that HP spin the printing division off as an independent company. In the competition over PCs, HP was still losing ground to Dell; in corporate computing (storage and servers), HP was not able to match IBM's margins and profits; and the company failed to meet Wall Street forecasts in seven out of twenty quarters. Analysts figured that the value of the printing business if it were split off would be equal to almost the entire value of HP's market capitalization—although HP's other businesses earn $56 billion in revenues.[13] Fiorina fought against any breakup of the company's activities until February 7, 2005, when she was fired. Whatever the outcome of the battle over HP's structure will be, the breakdown in Fiorina's relations with the board was clearly what caused her ouster. As her successor, Mark Hurd, moved into office, he insisted he would resist moves to break the company up.[14]

While controversy swirled around the fate of Carly Fiorina and the future of the printing division, our team was interviewing HP managers in the trenches.

Deciding Whether to Outsource or In-house
MIKE FAWKES, SENIOR VICE PRESIDENT, OPERATIONS, IMAGING AND PRINTING GROUP, HEWLETT-PACKARD, AN AMERICAN TECHNOLOGY COMPANY[15]

"Several variables enter into the in-house vs. outsource decision—like trade-offs (labor costs, capital costs, etc.), competitive advantage questions (intellectual property, proprietary processes, etc.), and product life-cycle. The manufacturing strategy for HP's printing business has evolved to the point where we outsource 100 percent of printer hardware production but keep in-house virtually 100 percent of inkjet cartridge production. We make about 40 million inkjet hardware units per year, but in excess of 400 million inkjet cartridge units per year.

"Our hardware business has relatively short product life-cycles, whereas our inkjet cartridge life-cyles are ten years or more. Our hardware business uses industry-standard assembly processes compared to our inkjet cartridge business, which uses proprietary, highly automated processes. As a result, the labor content of our hardware business is relatively high, but with a very low capital cost. Ten or fifteen years ago, we were convinced that our in-house manufacturing strategy for printer hardware provided an advantage. Over time, the emergence of highly efficient contract manufacturers displaced that advantage, and HP became a leader in using these contract manufacturer partners.

"On the other hand, our inkjet cartridge business has relatively low labor content but a high capital cost. The economic value of outsourcing cartridge production would be limited, because the design is proprietary, so HP would be the only customer. We would not be sharing external capacity with other lead firms if we went to a contract manufacturer. And we consider the intellectual property in our inkjet cartridges and their manufacturing processes to be a source of real competitive advantage for HP."

Fawkes summed up his company's strategy by explaining that HP has very different kinds of businesses. Ink cartridges involve a lot of HP intellectual property in both their design and in the manufacturing process; the inkjet printers themselves require HP proprietary design, but the manufacturing processes for making printers are generic; and computers need only generic design and generic manufacturing skills.

He said it's possible to make money in all these businesses, but in different ways: "For example, in the PC industry, the component manufacturers like Intel and Microsoft and the companies with superior business models using a direct-selling model [e.g., Dell] can make money. Our printer hardware business enjoys the advantages that come from a product-design differentiation combined with the economic benefits of outsourcing. For our inkjet cartridge business, we combine the advantages of a superior product design with a highly efficient, capital-intensive manufacturing process."

The story of how Hewlett-Packard's Barcelona, Spain, inkjet printer subsidiary grappled over twenty years with choices over in-house production or outsourcing and over location shows in microcosm the enormous changes in the organization of industry over the past twenty years.[16] HP opened a manufacturing plant in Barcelona in 1984 and started making printers there in 1993, a time when companies worried about whether the European Community would end up as "Fortress Europe," with trade barriers that would make it prohibitive to bring in goods from outside. They began with 50,000 printers a month, and the volume rose rapidly. HP decided not to risk expanding their own plants, because in a downturn they would stand idle. So the choice was between automation and outsourcing. One of HP's U.S. facilities had tried the automation solution and found it to be complex, rigid, and expensive. Their Singapore plant had tried outsourcing, and the Barcelona plant followed that model. First, they used local manufacturers, and older, less complex products were handed off. But the locals were too small, and there was the risk that HP would become responsible for their survival if they gave them too much business.

HP started looking to Eastern Europe and turned to the large global contract manufacturer Flextronics, which was already operating in Hungary. By 2000, Flextronics and SCI were making a million printers a month for HP in Hungary. Some of the high-end printers were still being made in-house in Barcelona. Then came the downturn and the painful decisions about what to cut and where. The managers in Barcelona realized that "HP would never be world-class at product assembly. We are paid to create, not to improve on the same process for the rest of our lives." They closed down the assembly operations in Spain and moved it all to Hungary and to Asia. In 2004, HP moved the Hungarian manufacturing to Ukraine because the high euro-dollar exchange rate made Hungary too expensive. But it would not remain in Ukraine very long. In 2005, HP decided to shut down in Ukraine and move the operations to China. While wages were low in Ukraine, all the other costs of working there were just too high. At the same time, it turned out, under pressure of the crisis, that HP engineers were good at designing low-cost printers—a "fundamental breakthrough"—so much of the design work has stayed in-house in the United States. (Some design is also being done for HP by ODM firms in Asia.)

Components Only

Equally rare is the electronics component company that still carries out in-house all five functions of component making—definition, design, detailed design, manufacturing, and marketing. Most of the companies that make chips today, like Analog Devices, Infineon, ST Microelectronics (a French-Italian semiconductor maker), and Texas Instruments, make some components in-house but also outsource some to the pure-play fabs, as customers or as joint-venture partners. When our research team met with senior executives from ST Microelectronics, they explained that they do outsource about 20 percent of their chips to the fabs but that their basic strategy is to keep all the vital functions in-house in order to be able to deal with very diverse customers — some of whom, like Nokia, do most of the design, while others want ST to do more of the design and customization.[17] Keeping a wide range of functions in-house allows ST to deal with customers in different markets with different needs. ST also has its own fabs so that it can ramp up rapidly during the profitable window of opportunity of new-product introduction, when ST might have trouble getting enough attention and capacity from the pure-play fabs, who, after all, work for lots of customers. Finally, ST believes it needs to retain key competencies in all functions as a kind of hedge on the future: Who knows where in the chain of functions the highest value will be created tomorrow? If ST gives up developing its capabilities in some part of the process, they may lose out on breakthrough opportunities. Like ST, Infineon, Texas Instruments, and Analog Devices all have mixed strategies, outsourcing some of their semiconductors and making others in-house. Where ST's outsourcing seems to be a kind of production buffer for excess capacity, some of the other companies distinguish by component type what will be made in-house and what gets "fabbed." Analog Devices, for example, sends its digital signal processors out to be fabbed but keeps in-house the sophisticated data converters that require nonstandard silicon technology.

Intel is the leading example of an electronics component company that does it all in-house. Intel has the largest share of the world semiconductor market, and it sells 83 percent of the microprocessors used in PCs and servers, a $27 billion market. Intel does not make consumer products, though it did in the past and the idea keeps resurfacing.[18] Intel is unique as an electronics component company for having a brand that many consumers recognize. The "Intel Inside" logo tells the consumer that invisible though the Intel microprocessor may be from the outside, it's in there, giving the product a value even greater than that which the brand on the box conveys.

"Intel Inside" is what components producers aspire to, but rarely achieve, in virtually all industries, electronics or not. In automotives, Bosch and Brembo are component names that consumers recognize. Even Solstiss, weavers of traditional lace in Caudry, France, who sell to haute couture apparel companies, told us that their long-term hope was an "Intel Inside" reputation that would force high-fashion labels to identify "Solstiss" as a component in expensive gowns and underwear with lace trim.[19] Currently, the lace makers of Caudry have a virtual monopoly on the production of the world's finest lace, because they have bought up most of the remaining stock of Leavers looms. These looms are the only ones that can weave lace of the highest quality, and Leavers, the British company that made them, went out of business years ago. The Caudry weavers know that the Japanese are working to improve machines that produce similar lace and are setting them up in China. So it may only be a question of when the differentiation created by the Caudry quasi-monopoly on the looms disappears. From then on, Caudry lace has to be able to survive on creativity and brand recognition. Despite the success of Solstiss, most component companies in fashion (as in electronics and autos) remain unknown to their ultimate users.

Shigenobu Nagamori is the founder and president of Nidec, a company in Kyoto, Japan, that makes small precision motors that are built into many of the world's cutting-edge consumer electronic products and into industrial equipment. Nidec has captured 70 percent of the world market for hard-disk-drive motors and digital camera shutters. Like Solstiss, Nagamori recounted his dream of a future in which consumers demand "Nidec inside."[20] Although that day has not yet dawned, Nagamori does see a tremendous shift in the balance of power between component producers and large companies in recent times. Big companies like Toyota used to be able to dictate terms to suppliers, typically small companies with less-skilled and lower-paid workers than those at Toyota. But this is no longer the case. Over the years, he said, components became increasingly complex and vital to the performance of the final products, like Nidec's disk-drive motors, or Kyocera's high-quality materials for semiconductors, or Murata's chip capacitors. Today, he claimed, these component manufacturers have become more profitable than the large assemblers. Moreover, these strong component capabilities may well give the suppliers a leg up in new generations of final products. A company like Nidec, he imagined, could be making electric cars in the future.

Building a Design-Only Business

Intel does it all, but most companies in the electronics components business have a scope that extends over fewer functions. Companies like Nvidia, Broadcom, Qualcomm, SanDisk, and Xilinx that concentrate on design of integrated circuits (ICs) and definition of new IC products offer services to a variety of different markets—multimedia, wireless, and PC chip sets among them. Some firms are even more specialized and, like ARM, one of the most successful of a cluster of innovative IC fabless design houses in Cambridge, U.K., offer blocks of code that are used in others' designs as well as in their own full-fledged chip designs. Innovative design companies do well by developing chips that can be used in a variety of different electronic products and selling the same chip to several original design manufacturers (ODMs) or original equipment manufacturers (OEMs). The leaders in fabless design have been American companies, and still today, much of the frontier work is being done by these firms.[21] The companies locate in regions like Silicon Valley not only to recruit from the wealth of human talent in these places but also to draw on the research in universities and other local institutions that has been funded by government contracts.

Outside of the United States and Europe, there are relatively few fab-less IC design firms with real innovative capabilities. The highly trained and creative talent they need to recruit is a scarce resource in most countries. Taiwan stands out as an exception, having grown the second-largest group of IC design firms in the world. These firms benefit from very close relationships with strong pure-play foundries; in fact, a number of them have broken off from semiconductor companies. Mediatek, for example, was founded by engineers who left United Microelectronics Corporation (UMC) in 1997, when UMC became a pure-play foundry. Mediatek has 700 employees in Taiwan, 80 percent of whom work in R & D on optical storage drives, like CD-ROM, DVD-ROM, CD-R/RW, DVD rewritable drives, and DVD player chipsets. It was ranked by *BusinessWeek* as the most profitable information technology company in the world in 2004, with a return on equity (ROE) of 55.2 percent.[22] VIA and Realtek are other Taiwanese leaders in IC design. VIA makes chipset designs that are manufactured in Taiwan foundries and in National Semiconductor facilities in Oregon for most major American PC makers. Realtek is the leading supplier of Ethernet chips—even besting Intel on this.

Most of the Taiwanese firms prosper either by custom-designing chips for local OEM and ODM customers, or else by making standard chip designs that are sold in the market. Today, few of the designs of these Taiwanese firms are leading-edge technology that they develop themselves—but these businesses do deliver quite sophisticated, reliable, and reasonably priced products to a wide range of industries. A number of them, like VIA and ALi, are sending engineers to China to set up design houses to work on chip design for the Chinese market and for the new fabs (SMIC, Grace) being established on the mainland with Taiwanese management and investment. The China-based firms specialize in detailed design and use blocks of code that other companies have developed to customize products for mainland users. The days of innovative IC-design houses like the ones in Silicon Valley have not yet arrived in China, although as our team discovered (see Chapter 11), there are a few foreign-invested firms there that are advancing rapidly.

Brand or No Brand?
Contract Manufacturers and Beyond

The last twenty years have seen an enormous expansion of contract man-ufacturing in all its forms and in virtually all industries. By definition, contract manufacturers do not have brands and make their profits from assembly, along with various design and logistics services that support manufacturing. In the global electronics industry in 2003, about 17 per-cent of the cost of all goods sold were made by contract manufacturers.[23] The big five North American electronics manufacturing service busi-nesses — Flextronics, Jabil, Sanmina-SCI, Celestica, and Solectron — are global giants with plants around the world that make myriad products for lead firms.[24] The rapid-fire growth of contract manufacturing in the 1990s mainly took place within these companies.[25]

IPC researchers waiting in the San José Flextronics lobby noted on display a list of what Flextronics was making that month (October 2001) and where: Philips car radio front panels (Hungary), Microsoft mouse (China), Sony Internet terminal board (Guadalajara, Mexico), Cisco fast Ethernet switchboard (San José), Ericsson switch and rack (Hungary), HP copier document feeder (Guadalajara), Palm Pilot (Guadalajara; Malaysia; San José), Unipath fertility testers (Australia), Iomega Zipdrive enclosures (Colorado), and much more. These global suppliers, like the pure-play fabs, all emphasized in their interviews with us, as they do on every occasion, that they do not compete with their customers and will not develop brands. Their business is manufacturing.

A newcomer to the ranks of the giants is a little-known Taiwanese con-tract manufacturer, Hon Hai Precision Industry.[26] Under the name Fox-conn, it makes products for companies like Hewlett-Packard, Sony, and Motorola, and it also manufactures and sells a wide variety of components, mainly for personal computers. Hon Hai has become Taiwan's largest manufacturer (in terms of sales), and it is the largest exporter in China. In

2003, it employed 38,000 workers. Even as other electronics contract manufacturers have struggled through hard times after the boom ended in 2000—laying off workers and closing down plants, many of them only recently acquired—Hon Hai continued to grow explosively, to sales in 2003 of around $10 billion. Its profits have been rising rapidly, too. Hon Hai's edge is to have been among the first Taiwanese firms to set up operations in China, in Shenzhen in 1988. It has focused on fully exploiting the possibilities for low-margin manufacturing in China, and it is thought to have the lowest costs in electronics contract manufacturing.

Most contract manufacturers, however, find themselves in a very different league. They are typically much smaller than the lead firms they deal with and in constant search for some way of loosening dependence on their customers and warding off the cutthroat competition in manufacturing. It is fascinating to look at how this search is playing out in Taiwan. There, contract manufacturers have been the main motors of an extraordinary growth trajectory that brought the society from miserable poverty and underdevelopment in the fifties to high-technology industry. Today, those who stick with OEM manufacturing alone are under more and more pressure from brutal price competition as the demand for personal computers and telecom products falls and as product begins to pour in from cheap mainland Chinese factories. The dilemma of Taiwanese OEMs and ODMs today is a microcosm of the possibilities and constraints for contract manufacturers who are trying to break out from being producers with skills that almost any other factory in the world with lower costs can easily replace.

In the case of the electronics contractors, a few customers dominate their lives; in 2002, 63 percent of their sales were to only five companies: HP/Compaq, Dell, Sony, Apple, and IBM.[27] The contractors are generally medium-sized companies who do almost all of their manufacturing in Taiwan or mainland China. Under pressure from both their customers and from mainland Chinese competitors whom they can observe catching up, the Taiwanese need to differentiate their products and services from pure commodities. To escape bottom-feeder competition over price, one strategy has been to develop design capabilities; the other way up is branding.

Building an international brand is difficult and expensive, particularly for companies from societies with small domestic markets—like Taiwan, with a population of only 23 million. Yet there are great success stories. One of the most impressive is that of Giant bicycles, a contract manufacturer that has reinvented itself as a world-class company.[28] King Liu founded the company in 1972 and, until the early eighties, mainly made bicycles for Schwinn. In 1981, Giant started to market small lots under its own label. Schwinn's response was to form a joint venture with a mainland Chinese bicycle manufacturer and to cut off orders to Giant. But the move paid off. Giant has become one of the world's largest producers of bicycles, and it sells 70 percent of its production under its own brand. Creating the brand involved heavy investment in design centers in Europe and the United States as well as in Taiwan, and sponsoring sports events and bicycle races around the world. As Giant grew, it expanded vertically, setting up a Chinese plant in Kunshan, Jiangsu Province, to manufacture aluminum tubes and another to make carbon fiber. Many of the components of Giant bikes are purchased from suppliers—Michelin and Continental tires, Lee Chi derailleurs, and Shimano brakes. Giant then designs the product, fabricates the frame, and does the assembly. Giant makes about 600,000 high-end bikes in Taiwan that are mainly sold in U.S., European, and Japanese markets, and about 2.5 million low- to mid-range models in China for export to stores like Toys "R" Us and for sale on the Chinese domestic market, where the Giant brand reigns as number one.

Thunder Tiger, another Taiwan brand triumph on a smaller scale, is a toy company that in 1980 started developing its own brand of remote-controlled model airplanes and cars and marketing them in the United States and Japan.[29] It grew by spending 7 to 8 percent of its sales on advertising in the United States and sponsoring competitions. As we walked around the plant in Taichung, Taiwan, the founder, Aling Lai, showed us $4,000 toy helicopters being made side by side with real aerospace and medical equipment components—Thunder Tiger's diversification beyond toys. Suspended from the factory ceiling floated a drone aircraft that showed that Thunder Tiger was aiming at military clients these days, not just civilian hobbyists. This case, upgrading from toys to military procurement, is perhaps unique, but it does show how contract manufacturers can break out of the mold. At the time of our visit in 2000, there were 280 employees in Taiwan; Lai predicted numbers would go down to 168 when they transferred production to their new China facilities. But five years later, in 2005, there were still 220 employees in Taiwan and 498 in China. The skilled workers and technicians that allow Thunder Tiger to make its astounding range of products are more available in Taiwan than they would be to a small company in mainland China.

But despite success stories like Giant and Thunder Tiger, the overall chances for electronics contractors to become brand manufacturers are not good. The reason is that the lead companies do not want to make competitors out of their contract manufacturers. This problem is not specific to electronics. We heard about it from Giant and in many of the textile and apparel interviews, too. For example, when Fang Brothers, the giant Hong Kong clothing contractor, started its own brand and opened retail stores, Liz Claiborne stopped using them as a manufacturer. Lead firms fear the loss of intellectual property and design and suspect that even the ODM contractors who do not have brands are just waiting to leap into the market under their own colors at the first possible opportunity.

When Acer, the largest Taiwanese electronics products company (and the fifth-biggest global producer of personal computers), tried to develop its own brand of personal computers, it lost much of its OEM business, since it looked to customers as if the company was eating their dinner. Acer had been earning about half its contracting-manufacturing revenues from IBM. When Acer started selling personal computers under their own brand name, IBM stopped buying from them. OEM clients also were concerned that Acer would give priority in production to its own branded products rather than theirs. As one of the Acer managers said wryly, "When there's a first wife, the second wife worries."

On a second try, Acer split off a part of the company in 2001 to become a brand producer.[30] The spin-off, BenQ, makes digital cameras,

PC peripherals, notebooks, and liquid-crystal-display televisions and in 2004 had sales of U.S. $5.1 billion. By 2003, BenQ had become the seventh-most-recognized brand name in China, but about 60 percent of its business was still as an ODM firm for other brands. BenQ made a dramatic leap forward as a brand-name company in 2005, when it acquired Siemens' mobile handset line. For the next five years, products will be co-branded with a BenQ Siemens logo. Headquarters will remain in Munich, Germany (where there are 6,000 employees), and BenQ will gain the prestige of the 158-year-old German firm, along with its European customers and valuable technology. Making the deal even sweeter, Siemens is basically paying BenQ (with cash, services, and purchase of a minority share in the Taiwanese firm) for taking over its loss-making unit.

We asked Dick Hunter, the vice president of manufacturing at Dell, whether Dell had a problem doing business with contractors that were developing their own brands.[31] He recognized that the models that Wistron (another Acer spin-off) and BenQ are selling under their own labels have family resemblances with the computers these companies make for Dell. But he said Dell's ability to identify the needs of its huge customer base and to evolve its products rapidly leads to differentiation that makes Dell machines stand out even from those marketed by its contractors. Dell's response was far more tolerant and confident than many others we heard. It's unlikely that contractors can develop a brand without doing mortal damage to relationships with its old lead customers. The possibility of losing multinational clients—like Schwinn and IBM—who take their business elsewhere still makes this a very risky, as well as an expensive, option.

Power in the Supply Chain

"Only fools own factories," Patric Hollington told us in the office of the Paris shop on the Left Bank that sells the elegant, unconstructed menswear he designs and has manufactured to order in natural fiber fabrics. On the rainy day in May 2002 we met him, Hollington was just finishing up a meeting with a Portuguese manufacturer whom he was trying out as a possible replacement for French factories. The Italian suppliers from whom Hollington buys most of his denim, linen, corduroy, and wool fabrics are flourishing, and he has been able to coax some French textile firms into making new products for him. But all of his sewing has been "Made in France," and the big question is whether his French subcontractors will survive. Every one of the five he deals with has gone bust at one time or another. When Hollington's largest subcontractor went bankrupt a few years ago, Hollington thought for a while about buying the factory and running it himself, but his main investor told him it would be madness. Finally, a Bordeaux company bought it and production started again; but soon thereafter another French supplier was bought by Germans. From 2002 to 2005, Hollington's sales grew by a third, and thanks to customers he met at the "Pitti Uomo" trade show in Florence, he received big new Japanese orders. But Hollington continues to worry about whether it's safe to count on other companies making his clothes for him.

Hollington owns a very small business, but even for the largest companies our team interviewed, this dilemma is a real one. When major functions like manufacturing are not in-house, the fortunes of even big companies become dependent on other players in the supply chain. In a world of great instability of demand and of fragmented producers, no economic actor can control its own fate and fortunes completely. Firms cannot easily replace one set of providers with another. The issue of maintaining the right set of functions for doing well in the future arises most often over design services, where questions about which parts of technical design need to remain within the lead firm and which to transfer to subcontractors hang in a kind of gray zone. Concerns about protecting intellectual property weigh heavily, as do worries about getting enough factory space when they need it. Semiconductor firms with strong design capabilities, for example, worry about shifting all of their fabrication to the East Asian foundries for fear that they will not be able to get enough capacity rapidly enough when they want to ramp up production of a new product.

Companies try to mitigate the perils of dependence by spreading the work among multiple contractors. They often establish some kind of ceiling on the maximum amount of business they do with any single supplier. Dick Hunter at Dell told us: "We have no hard-and-fast rules, but we are concerned if there's too much from one of them—and they, too, are concerned. Our top thirty suppliers are doing 75 percent of our business, so that means they are doing a lot of their business with us. But otherwise, there would be problems with consistency."[32] Other brand-name companies told us they had a 20-80 rule: 20 percent of the suppliers should do no more than 80 percent of the business.

There are other ways, too, of trying to lower the risks. Some companies, like ST Microelectronics and Analog Devices, keep a lot of manufacturing in-house, even while sending some to the fabs. Others run pilot plants so that they have ways of continuing to learn about the manufacturing processes of the products and services they are contracting out. Keeping a close eye by sending teams of engineers from the lead firm to "live" in the contractor's plant and monitor operations is another. For the contractors, of course, there is the mirror-image problem of relying on a limited number of customers, any one of whom might fall onto hard times.

In the American apparel business, the big players are now companies that own brands or retail stores—but they have no more manufacturing. The big names include Ralph Lauren, Jones NY, Liz Claiborne, the Gap, and The Limited. A company like Kellwood (with $2.6 billion net sales in 2004) holds several hundred brands, including Sag Harbor, Briggs, Calvin Klein Women's Better Sportswear Collection, and Phat Farm. Although these giants do not own any manufacturing facilities, their size brings leverage, and they can control production by filling a supplier's facilities with their products.

We Control a Factory Without Really Owning It

A SENIOR EXECUTIVE IN A BIG APPAREL COMPANY FRANKLY LAID OUT FOR US THE PROBLEMS OF TRYING TO CONTROL PRODUCTION IN FACTORIES IT DOES NOT ITSELF OWN, VIRTUALLY ALL OF WHICH ARE NOW OUTSIDE OF THE UNITED STATES.

"A Jones, a Liz, a Kellwood, a Ralph—if they find an excellent factory, they want to control it. They can only do that by placing a large enough order to consume the factory's production. How does this work? The CEO of Liz Claiborne or of Jones NY or one of the others will say to Kenneth Fang, president of Fang Brothers, Hong Kong, one of the world's largest manufacturers of apparel—we'll give you an order for 30,000 units per month; which factory will you give us? If you're a Liz Claiborne or a Jones NY or a Kellwood, and you find a good factory, you want to control it, hence to do the lion's share of the manufacturing in that plant. Say it's Liz [Claiborne]. They'll say: We have to control our own destiny. The physical plant Liz is in, Liz controls. Fang may own it, but to all intents and purposes it is your plant. The wholesaler doesn't own it, but he's in it. Fang then uses the revenue from the contract to build another factory that will be dedicated to a different wholesaler, thus diversifying his risk.

"The most critical question for a wholesaler to a manufacturer is Which plant will I be in? And the order needs to be large enough so you are the only client in the plant. If you work with the Fang Brothers, you expect quality. But unless you demand to see the plant, Fang may subcontract your order to a less-competent garment assembler. You have to say, 'I want to see the plant.' If not, you'll be outsourced to some little subcontractor Fang finds down the street. You control manufacturing [even if you do not own it] by having it in your own plant. Fang, after all, is only going to expand to the predictable level, the valley of his demand, not his peak, and the rest he'll subcontract. Checking out the plants is what your agent is doing in Hong Kong and what you do on your trips to Asia. This is a gray area contractually. Highly specified contracts don't work very well in the garment business. With the big boys, let's say Ralph Lauren and

Kenneth Fang—both are kind of hooked—put in a win/win or lose/lose situation. The bets are too big for both sides to default on an agreement. Small wholesalers, without a lot of bargaining power, get screwed. They don't have the power and can't make the fixed-cost investment in managing a plant. The letter of the law is kind of immaterial in these cases."

The lesson here is that size brings leverage, and large firms can control production by dominating a factory without owning it.

On the other side of the table, we know from our interviews that companies like Fang Brothers are warily observing the ups and downs of their customers and adjusting their responses to these demands for control over factories accordingly. When we asked a manager in one of the large footwear contract manufacturers what kind of ceilings a brand like Reebok or Nike or New Balance places on how much production to take from a firm like his, he said, No, you've got it wrong: We have to decide how much business *we're* willing to do with them.

In addition to figuring out how to keep control of production when it takes place in plants that contractors own, American brands face an even greater challenge in confronting the retailers that control the distribution function in the industry. Some of them, like Warnaco or Ralph Lauren or Liz Claiborne, sell some of their clothing in their own stores. But the majority of those we interviewed sell most in department stores or to large discount retailers like Wal-Mart and Target. Over the past twenty years, there has been an enormous concentration in American retailing.[33] Just a few big companies dominate the market. One of the senior executives in a big-brand company described for us the transformation of relations between the brands and the department stores: First, department stores pulled the hot brands in to set up stand-alone brand shops in the stores. Then, when retailers got stronger, they began requiring the brands to reach certain fixed gross margins. If they did not meet those margins, they were forced to pay back the stores.

As one apparel senior executive told us: "Power relationships totally shifted, even for the hot lines." Retailers added more and more requirements, like having the contract manufacturers attach the price tags and put the clothes on hangers. He continued: "If you slipped up on a single item, you'd be penalized. It was impossible to be perfect to that degree. There were so many rules that sooner or later you're going to get nailed. Charge-backs became a revenue stream for the retailers—though they'd never admit it." As a result of retailer power, the smaller brands could not keep up, and many were squeezed out.

The same manager argued that today the brand wholesalers are becoming powerful enough to push back. "It's a situation of the megas versus the megas. You've got a $4 billion Liz [Claiborne], a $3 billion Kellwood, and a $4 billion Ralph [Lauren] pushing back against, say, the Federated Department Stores." What's at stake is who holds inventory, who bears the risks, and how the profits get divided up. The struggle plays out, in fact, among three sets of players in the supply chain: the contract manufacturers (like Fang Brothers or Luen Tai), the branded wholesalers (like Liz Claiborne, Ralph Lauren, or Kellwood), and the retailers. At each of the points on the chain of functions that links clothing to the final customers, giant firms now control much of the terrain in the United States.

If "megas versus the megas versus the megas" characterizes part of the U.S. apparel scene, an increasingly large part would be better described as the struggle of all against Leviathan.[34] The greatest retail success of the past twenty years is Wal-Mart, a chain of discount mass-market stores founded by Sam Walton in Bentonville, Arkansas, in 1962. By 2004, Wal-Mart had $245 billion net sales, 1.5 million workers, and revenues equal to about 2 percent of U.S. GDP.[35] Wal-Mart imports from China are around $18 billion a year. The Wal-Mart phenomenon is also playing a major role in driving change through the whole economy. A McKinsey Global Institute study of the extraordinary productivity gains in the U.S. economy from 1995 to 1999 found that the increases were concentrated in just six sectors of the economy.[36] Retailing alone explains about a quarter of the productivity increases, and about a sixth of these retail gains took place in general merchandise. Wal-Mart was responsible for much of this, the research concluded.

Wal-Mart's low prices reflect a mix of factors: not only low-cost imports, but low wages and benefits for workers in its stores, tightening pressures on its suppliers, and pioneering innovation in using information technology to manage the supply chain.

HOW WE COMPETE

Working with Wal-Mart
THE PRESIDENT OF A MAJOR SPORTS APPAREL COMPANY (OVER $1 BILLION SALES) WE INTERVIEWED EXPLAINED HOW WAL-MART GETS BRANDS AND MANUFACTURERS TO LOWER PRICES.

"We do 50 percent of Wal-Mart's [he named a piece of clothing almost every American wears at some point in the year]. We sell them branded products and also some private label. If you understand Wal-Mart and you wait for them to push you on price, you're not a very good vendor. You don't understand them. Wal-Mart has a philosophy of 'one plus.' It's not always the least expensive [that they're looking for], but it's a very good value at a very low price.

"If I sell them something for $10 this year, then try to sell it to them for $10 next year, they're not going to be happy. Everything you do has to be 'one plus' better than the year before. We worked hard at finding fabrics that are less expensive. We've actually gone in and offered to lower our price. They have a tremendous number of vendors that understand that concept."

Not every brand or supplier is willing to submit to this kind of pressure. (The president of one of the juniorwear firms we interviewed called them "the devil, the evil empire," and said he did not want their business. He sells to Target, JCPenney, and a number of department stores instead. Others did not go so far in talking with us about Wal-Mart, though we heard a lot of anger about being vulnerable to so gigantic a customer that no real negotiation is possible.) But it is hard to avoid dealing with a retail chain so vast and omnipresent. Moreover, Wal-Mart shapes the selling of a wider and wider range of products. In 2002, it became the second-biggest electronics retailer in the United States. Having captured much of the market for the lowest-price consumer electronics, it is now pushing up the ladder into expensive items like flat-screen TVs. Wal-Mart's practices with suppliers and brands have spread beyond its walls and are now widely followed by chains like Circuit City and Best Buy.

Do Networks Create Equality Among the Players?

As the world of production has fragmented, mutual dependence has replaced the old hierarchies that put lead firms on the top and suppliers on the bottom of the pyramid. The company calling the shots often seems to vary with phases in the business cycle or with changes in the product mix. When there's a high demand for chips, the pure-play foundries are king and the customers clamber for space in the production schedule. When the gods of fashion decree lace, the Caudry lace makers rule. But things change, and the other players have their day, too. From this evening up of the relations of power has emerged a vision of a world in which networks replace hierarchies. A new model appears of equality and partnership between players who are at different points in the supply chain.

But are these partners really so equal? In fact, we found it is usually the case that one firm in the network exercises more power than the others. That firm, though it has no ownership rights in any of the others, gets to decide how the production chain will be divided up and recombined and what role in the division of labor will be assigned to each of the players in the network. Decisions about how to restructure the production process and who gets to make what and when are made by some players, but not by all. The key player acts as the systems designer, or, as Masahiro Aoki, a Stanford professor who writes about the networked economy, put it: a "helmsman" firm.[37]

In most of our interviews, it rapidly became clear whether a firm was a helmsman or an ordinary oarsman. There were some cases with roughly equal collaboration among contracting firms, but we heard about far more in which partners were clearly unequal. In these cases, orders are passed from the lead firm to the others. The lead firm's employees make frequent visits to the contractors' plants to monitor operations. Although they may negotiate over price, essentially the lead firms are price-setters and the outsourcers are price-takers, and the wishes and whims of the lead firm ordinarily win out over the preferences of the other parties.

HOW WE COMPETE

Who Calls the Shots?

AN EXECUTIVE FROM TIMISOARAWEAR, A ROMANIAN APPAREL COMPANY, DESCRIBED ITS RELATIONS WITH BRAND-NAME COMPANIES FOR WHICH IT DOES MANUFACTURING TO SPECIFICATIONS.[38]

"Our German clients work on a cut-and-make basis, because they always think they know best. They continually watch over our shoulders and tell us how to do everything. The Germans have their own technicians who are in the plant every day. One of the biggest German customers gives us the patterns and we do the grading. But mostly they're unwilling to send us patterns by e-mail or Web, because they're afraid we'll be able to get their secrets and know-how! I could reconstruct their system and grading anyway from the data they have to send us. Our oldest German client we do grading for—but they are not even willing to have us buy trim, though we could cut their costs if we did.

"Even with long-standing German customers, we have endless negotiations about every conceivable problem that could possibly come up. One of these German brand-name firms had 60 percent of our capacity. Two years ago, they wanted to place a big order and insisted on a lower price. We hesitated, and they cut us off with a single fax—even though we'd been doing business with them for years. We had a rough time recovering from that loss.

"A lot of these companies simply have no respect for us. Take Armani. They came and looked us over and said, Well, maybe you'd be OK for one of our labels, but not for the others, but we've got to think about it. After all, making Armani in Romania is a hard decision. I finally just told them: We've got to think it over, too! It's a hard decision for us, too."

One prominent Taiwanese laptop computer maker told us half jokingly, half bitterly, that no matter how much travel his engineers did, he dared not let them use business-class seats, for fear they would be seen on the plane by a customer who would conclude there was still "fat" that could be shaved off his prices. Clearly, the lead companies and not the outsourcers are calling the shots in these situations.

What's the Best Location in the Network?

If firms carrying out different functions along the process of production are so unequal, which functions should a firm choose as its core capabilities—if it has a choice? It might choose those functions on which it earns the highest returns (measured as profit, or return on equity, or return on investment). Take the case of Barbie, a Mattel brand doll. In 2003, Mattel's sales were about $3.3 billion, and Barbie purchases were responsible for more than half. In 1996, Barbie sold for $9.99 in a California Toys "R" Us. A *Los Angeles Times* reporter tracked down all the countries that manufactured some part of Barbie and figured out how much of the $9.99 was produced in different places.[39] Her body was made of vinyl plastic pellets from Taiwan (and the ethylene to make the pellets was made from Saudi oil); her nylon hair came from Japan; her cardboard and paints came from the United States. Only her clothing came from China, where the doll was finally molded, assembled, painted, dressed, boxed, and shipped out from Hong Kong. When Barbie left Hong Kong for the United States, she was worth $2, including about 35 cents' worth of Chinese labor.

From this reckoning, though, we cannot tell which company at which point in the chain is making the highest profits. Brand-name firms do not always earn the lion's share of the profits. A 1999 report on the profits and return on shares earned by a number of Hong Kong and Taiwan contract manufacturers compared with the lead firms to which they sold goods showed that the suppliers often were more profitable than the brands.[40] Economists who have modeled relations between lead firms and contract manufacturers report that profits go up only when the lead firms are strongly dominant.[41] Otherwise, the lead firms do better by keeping their own production facilities or by sharing plants with other lead firms—just as the Japanese are currently doing in deals like the merger of the DRAM (memory chips) divisions of Hitachi and NEC in Elpida and the merger of Hitachi and Mitsubishi semiconductor divisions in Renesas.

The uncertainty about whether it is more profitable to be a brand firm or a supplier is not only a dilemma for electronics. Recently, in the automobile industry, the proportion of pretax profits going to the assemblers is 24 percent, while the suppliers capture 28 percent, the after-sales activities 43 percent, and the dealers 5 percent.[42] In the case of Barbie, the brand and the retailers are collecting 80 percent of the price of the doll. But they may have very high costs as well. Perhaps the Japanese company that makes the nylon hair is getting a higher rate of return on its capital than is the American retailer. If so, there might be little incentive for the hair manufacturer to push itself farther along the value chain and to try to develop a brand name itself or to innovate by designing new kinds of dolls.

Short-term profits may not be the only consideration. The hair manufacturer may find itself in a very competitive part of the market, with lots of rival firms equally able to make hair—which, after all, is not too complicated—and willing to drive down prices by squeezing their costs. In this situation, the functions a firm should aim to capture are those difficult for others to replicate easily. Parts of the manufacturing process that are distinct or complex, parts that are covered by patents or require tacit knowledge that takes long to accumulate—these make good choices because they help protect the firm against cutthroat competition. Equally important, the firm will be in a stronger bargaining position with others in the chain because its contribution is unique—or, at any rate, hard to replace.

Another factor that firms take into account in choosing functions is risk. If a firm makes only the hair for Barbies, no matter how profitable the function is today, the company stands at risk if Mattel, the brand-name firm, does badly or if Barbie dolls go out of fashion next year. Even in the lowest-end producers, competing only on price, we usually found them making some efforts at an R & D function to come up with new products that would help them diversify and thereby lower the company's risk.

Finally, the desire to wield power in the chain and maintain control over the firm's own destiny looms large as firms decide which functions to concentrate on. Firms carrying out different functions along the value chain are interdependent, but not equal, and the power disparities allow some firms to dictate terms to others. Many managers we interviewed saw the value chain as a kind of bullwhip, with some firms wielding the handle, and others, at the far end, being swung from side to side in large, uncontrollable arcs. Holding a valuable brand name gives a company a strong grip on the handle; so does offering services no one else provides. The relative size of firms and their share of the market in their own sector are also key variables. For example, the larger a subcontractor making laptop computers is, the greater its share of the market, the more resources it has, relative to competitors, for providing unique or difficult-to-replace design services, and the more power it will have when dealing with the brand-name firms.

In electronics, some subcontractors have achieved almost as much power as the lead brand firms have. The big five global suppliers I mentioned earlier (Jabil, Solectron, Flextronics, Sanmina-SCI, Celestica) had become so valuable to their customers that during the nosedive of the telecoms and electronics industry in 2001, lead firms like Cisco Systems, one of the fastest-growing firms of the nineties, agreed to shoulder much of the cost of the excess inventory that had ended up on the shelves of the contract manufacturers.

HOW WE COMPETE

Recognize the Dangers of Overoptimism

TIMOTHY STURGEON, A MEMBER OF OUR TEAM, HAS RECOUNTED CISCO'S EXPERIENCE DURING THE COLLAPSE OF THE DOT-COM BUBBLE.

"The end of the boom period of 1992 to 1999 exposed some spectacular instances of poor inventory planning. Cisco alone wrote down nearly $2 billion in excess inventory. As late as the first half of 1999, the problem for companies supplying the hardware to power the 'dot-com revolution' was in keeping up with demand. Cisco purchasers ordered twice, and in some cases *three times*, the volume of components and finished products that they needed to fill current orders from customers. The company knew the lesson, learned the hard way by other Silicon Valley firms such as Apple Computer, that the worst blunder they could make in selling to highly dynamic markets was to be unable to meet sudden spikes in demand for their most advanced products. In new markets, where buying patterns and customer loyalty is yet to be established, being unable to ship finished products to customers means losing the chance to dominate new market niches. During the boom, this strategy worked well for Cisco. They were able to keep up with the radical growth in demand for Internet switching gear and accumulated an 80 percent market share, which in turn drove the company's share price into the stratosphere. When the market collapsed suddenly in the fall of 1999, Cisco—and its suppliers—found themselves with huge volumes of excess inventory."[43]

Why did Cisco pick up the costs of inventory still held by its suppliers? Chris Lewis, chief financial officer of Jabil, an electronics-manufacturing services company, which does 20 percent of its business for Cisco, explained that Jabil's profits (5 to 6 percent) are too thin to bear this kind of risk. Why, Lewis asked, would Cisco "yank us out of business, so they can save a dollar and make $31 instead of $30?"[44]

The issues of relative power, irreplaceability, and resilience are all at stake when firms decide to maintain within their own walls functions that give them control over their own destinies. Managers in the small and medium firms we interviewed clearly felt that to gain more control over their situation, they needed to reduce their dependence on the whims and fortunes of their main customers. One solution is obviously to find more customers for the same services, but the other approach has been to broaden the range of functions the firm provides so as to have more diverse customers. Timisoarawear, the Romanian clothing subcontractor I described earlier, started business in the early nineties working for German firms on a pure "cut-and-make" basis; in other words, the Romanians cut and sewed the garments, and the foreign customers provided the fabric, the patterns, the detailed technical instructions, and the trim (buttons, zippers, linings), and arranged for pickup and delivery of the final goods.

In order to liberate themselves from these clients who pushed them on price and whose agents hovered over their shoulders at every step of operations in the factories, Timisoarawear managers started a full-package supply business, mainly with English customers who had given up manufacturing in their own businesses. For these customers, Timisoarawear buys and finances the purchase of fabric and trim and provides a lot of the technical design services for manufacturing. Full-package now represents about 35 percent of Timisoarawear's business. These customers send their designers to the Romanian plant from time to time to discuss collections, but they have no full-time people monitoring production in the plant. Timisoarawear recently created a brand to sell in Romania and opened a number of retail outlets for it. On this line, the company has full control over all functions from design to sale to the customer. Timisoarawear does not know yet if its own brand or full-package supply can replace the "single-function" cut-and-make business, or even be as profitable, but it feels it has captured a greater zone of autonomy and initiative in controlling its own situation.

The stakes in the world of fragmented production are much the same as they have always been: profit, power, opportunity, and security. What has changed is that now it is possible to realize these by building a business on virtually any point in the value chain. Twenty years ago, the integrated companies still ruled. Today, a component manufacturer, a fabless design company, a brand with no manufacturing, a manufacturer with no brand, and many more combinations are all discovering new ways to compete.

PART FIVE

Make It at Home?
Or Offshore?

CHAPTER 9

Made in America?

The first thing a visitor to American Apparel's Los Angeles T-shirt factory will see are large banners strung across the front of the bright pink building: "American Apparel Is An Industrial Revolution!" and "Legalize L.A.!"[1] We wondered about the banners, and we wondered how anyone *can* make T-shirts in the United States and compete with T-shirt makers from low-wage countries around the world. *Why* would anyone even try to do it in the United States now—when the barriers and the transportation costs of importing from Asia are falling rapidly? Marty Bailey, the vice president for operations, explained to us that what makes this booming business work are sexy, close-fitting styles in high-quality ring-spun cotton; a great talent for promoting the company's image; and the ability to send out 75 percent of their orders the same day they are received. The majority of their products are "imprintable" T-shirts that they sell to wholesalers, distributors who customize the T-shirts with designs or printed messages. American Apparel has about 60,000 wholesale customers, with the biggest doing only about 4 to 5 percent of the sales. Recently, American Apparel has been opening its own retail stores—the newest one is on Newbury Street, Boston's upscale shopping neighborhood, and a passerby sees in the window the T-shirts hanging next to a big sign: "Made in Downtown L.A." The clothing is aimed at customers who are thirteen to thirty-five, fit, and thin. About a quarter of the products are sold online on American Apparel's very cool Web site, www.americanapparel.net.

The T-shirts could undoubtedly be made for less in Asia. But buyers don't want them in a month; they want them today, Bailey said. "The main issue is delivery times. We're extremely reactive. We have 5 million pieces on hand, and 75 percent of our business is from calls we take and send out that day. If I did this work abroad I'd save 15 percent, but I couldn't be as fast. My inventory in pieces turns four to five times a year, and my bread-and-butter items in inventory turn fifteen to seventeen times a year." The average wholesale order is only 270 pieces. No order is too small, though AA charges more for them. If the business was off-shored, there would be no way of moving this number of orders so rapidly to so many different customers.

All the cutting, sewing, and assembly of the garments takes place within AA's four walls. Four other Los Angeles companies do the dyeing and bleaching. Sewing factories are high-pressure, unpleasant workplaces under the best of circumstances, but American Apparel's is one of the few we have seen where many workers looked up from their machines and smiled at the boss and his visitors; Bailey greeted quite a few of them by name. In East Asian plants, workers typically look down more closely at their machines and move more rapidly as bosses and guests walk by. In one plant in Dongguan, China, the manager wanted to demonstrate to us the discipline he had instilled in the plant by shouting out a command for everyone to freeze in place. We politely refused the offer and assured him that we were already convinced of his point.

If workers seem happier in the American Apparel plant (unfathomable cultural differences aside), it could be because American Apparel's 3,200 workers are earning on average about $12.50 an hour and benefits—high for the industry in the region. As we walked around the factory floor, we did not hear much English. Like other L.A. sewing plants, the labor force is mainly Mexican immigrants. (The banner out front suggests that immigration regulations are a concern for them.) The company offers workers subsidized bus passes, lunches, legal assistance, English lessons—and medical benefits.

As for the banners out front, it's clear from our interview, the Web site, and the coverage of American Apparel in the media that Dov Charney, the founder, has a broader agenda than just making money in the rag trade. Charney wants to show that it's possible to make even T-shirts in the U.S.A. and pay workers a good wage and benefits. American Apparel advertises that its clothes are "sweatshop free"—made by people with decent earnings under good working conditions. The integrated production strategy is a way of achieving both competitiveness and fairness. The mission statement on the Web site reads: "Ultimately, it is vertical integration, an efficient system that cuts out the middlemen, that enables the company to be sweatshop free. Because we do not outsource to local or developing-nation sweatshops, the entire process is time-efficient and the company can respond at breakneck speed to demand. This enables us to be competitive within the global market."

No one really knows how much more customers are willing to pay for "sweatshop-free" goods, but when consumers see television programs filming children in factories or terrible working conditions in plants making brands they buy, the backlash against the brand is usually very costly, as Nike and Kathy Lee Gifford discovered. If American Apparel is trying to incorporate "sweatshop-free" production in its cool company image, for most other businesses we interviewed the objective is more defensive: avoiding disaster. One publisher, for example, explaining why she does not send children's books to be produced in Asia, said: "Do you know why environmental and code-of-conduct issues are important? Your brand depends on them. Can you imagine if our books, created primarily for American children, were manufactured by mistreated children in India making a penny a day! It can really damage your reputation and your brand. I would rather pay 5 or even 10 percent more for peace of mind with respect to these issues and to intellectual property. Think about cases like Nike or Kathy Lee Gifford!"

For some goods, the label with a particular country of origin matters. Many of the Italian textile and clothing managers we interviewed told us that "Made in Italy" labels communicate a level of quality and distinctiveness that command higher prices than apparel made elsewhere. Some products seem inextricably rooted in a particular locale. When Fang Brothers, the giant Hong Kong contract manufacturer, decided in 2000 to develop its own cashmere label, they purchased Pringle of Scotland.[2] Pringle had a 185-year-long history, a prestigious brand, troubled finances, and a very antiquated factory; Fang Brothers has very modern, large production facilities in China. Should Fang close the Scottish factory and use Chinese plants to make Pringle sweaters? Or update the Scottish plant and keep the old workers? After lots of discussion, the Fangs decided that "Pringle of Scotland has to be in Scotland." They hired Kim Winser, a top-notch British manager who had been an executive at Marks & Spencer, to run Pringle. They opened a shop on Bond Street, then a flagship store on Sloane Street in the heart of an upscale London shopping neighborhood, and relaunched the brand.

Few of the American companies we visited, however, explicitly mentioned that keeping production at home was valuable in and of itself. Jim Davis, the CEO of New Balance, a top-ranking sneaker company with headquarters in Massachusetts, is one who believes it is important to maintain a U.S. manufacturing base, although as Herb Spivak, the New Balance executive vice president for operations, told us, "If accountants were in charge, we'd never make a shoe in the U.S." New Balance has been doing well, and had about $1.5 billion sales in 2004.[3] It has five wholly owned plants in Maine and Massachusetts and works with a Taiwanese contractor's plant in California. New Balance employs 2,300 workers in the United States (out of 2,600 worldwide), and it has added 500 blue-collar jobs in the United States over the past ten years. Production floor workers make about $13 an hour plus benefits. Mr. Spivak noted that Chinese wages are $0.40 an hour, and that this advantage is only partly counterbalanced by tariffs levied on imported shoes when they enter the United States. Other major sneaker brands, like Nike and

Reebok, are manufactured wholly outside the United States—mainly in China and Vietnam. New Balance is the only athletic shoe brand making some of its footwear in its own plants in the United States.

Of the 36 million sneakers New Balance sold in the United States in 2004, 8 million were made—in part or in whole—in the United States; the others were imported from China, where they were made by contract manufacturers like Pou Chen. Understanding what making them in America means, however, takes—as in the case of Dell computers—a closer look. Two million of the 8 million pairs are made in a plant that Pou Chen, a Taiwanese company that is one of New Balance's major overseas contractors, runs in Ontario, California. In that plant, soles and uppers come in from China and are glued together. The other 6 million pairs are assembled in New Balance-owned plants. Of these, 400,000 (1 percent of the total) are composed of wholly U.S.-made components— soles and uppers; for another 2 million, New Balance stitches the complete upper part of the shoe. All the others are assembled by attaching soles made in China to uppers composed of a mix of Chinese and U.S. materials. Depending on how much domestic content is in the upper, the label on the sneakers will read "Made in USA" (when there's more than 70 percent value added in the United States) or "Made in USA of Imported Materials."

Fast Fashion Works at Home

If making things in the United States matters to the managers of American Apparel and New Balance, it does not necessarily matter very much to most consumers. Getting the latest fashion while it's fresh does. For New Balance, like American Apparel, what makes it possible to do well in the U.S. market with fierce competition from foreign-made products is a business model focused on fast response to retailers: filling orders quickly, holding just the right amount of inventory, and being able to replenish orders right away—in contrast to the four- to six-month lead times needed for placing and receiving orders from the contractors in China. In many of the companies that we studied, the ability to get goods to final customers rapidly turned out to be one of the most important offsets to the lower labor costs of overseas production.

Take the story of Joel and Judy Knapp, who are "manufacturers"—which in Los Angeles parlance means they develop brands (JKLA, Judy Knapp, and others), design, make samples and markers, market, but do no cutting or sewing ("cut, make, trim"). They make blouses and pants for plus-size women and sell them mainly through large stores like JCPenney, Sears, and Lane Bryant. The Knapps do about $82 million in sales a year and have forty employees. Their clothing is produced by ten to fifteen L.A. sewing and printing contractors, all Koreans.

As imports flooded into the U.S. market, the Knapps' business survived by meeting a demand for stylish clothes for older, heavier women and by rapidly designing and delivering new pieces. Judy Knapp, the creative inspiration behind the business, told us that customers used to choose from collections the designers presented five times a year. But demand increased for special items and modifications, and by 1988, they were up to eight or nine collections a year. Today, customers request particular garments and adaptations of the samples on a nonstop basis. The designers meet every other day or two to exchange reactions to the looks they are seeing in the shops and on TV. They focus on "what can we sell to a zillion people" and talk about colors, style, buckles or flowers this season, the feel of the clothes. Meanwhile, stores are calling in all the time and saying what they want. Collections have dissolved into a continuous stream of new products.

Knapp makes samples right in L.A. Buyers want to see the styles in "cute junior size 8," though the clothes will eventually be made for much larger women. If the buyers like the model, they want preproduction samples for fit. At this point, the cap sleeve that barely covered the top of the size 8 arm is redesigned to drape more forgivingly around the size 18 arm. That takes another three or four days. The buyers then have more requests about fit. The pattern maker, who's been with the Knapps for twenty-five years, keeps making adjustments. Then they make the "markers," the patterns for cutting different sizes.

Deliveries are scheduled three and a half to four weeks after the fabric arrives at the contractors. Getting the fabric takes a day if the suppliers have it in stock—or a month if it has to come from Korea. The Knapps think it's important to provide rapid replenishment, and they showed us two blouse reorders they had received that day for 12,000 each. They would go out that week. Through the back-and-forth between designers and buyers and fabric suppliers and sewing contractors, people are in constant discussion and negotiation. The result is speed and responsiveness at levels that are not often available from overseas production.

Fashion and rapid reaction are valued not only in the clothing industry but in many of the companies we visited—even those making books and balloons.

HOW WE COMPETE

We Get It There by Christmas
DRAKE MCFEELY, PRESIDENT AND CHAIRMAN OF W.W. NORTON, LIKE OTHER AMERICAN PUBLISHERS, TOLD US THAT HE SENDS VERY LITTLE PRINTING OFFSHORE.[4]

"The huge disadvantage of printing overseas is that it takes time. It's expensive to ship books if you do it by air, and if you do it by boat, it's slow. Most of what we do in publishing requires fast turnaround. If it's a book printed in the U.S., we can get a reprint in two to six weeks. But if it's overseas, it could take up to three or four months. You print a book in July so that you can ship it to bookstores in September-October so that it can make a wonderful Christmas gift. If it turns out to be an even more wonderful gift than you had anticipated and you need more books, you're sunk if the book was printed in Asia or in Italy, because you can't get a reprint until after the season."

Our team heard the same response from all of the U.S. publishers we interviewed—editing, designing, and printing the book (in black-and-white) stay in the United States because it's so valuable to be close to customers and to respond rapidly to demand. And books are too heavy and too inexpensive to send by air.

Even a toy like a balloon can be time-sensitive enough to warrant making in the United States. Anagram Corporation makes helium-inflatable metallic balloons in plants in Minnesota, China, and in a *maquiladora* factory in Mexico.[5] Sales are about $100 million a year. Although decorative trim is made in China and attached to the balloon in Mexico, the main body of the balloon is manufactured in Eden Prairie, Minnesota. A turkey balloon sold at Thanksgiving time has "feathers" that come from China to the United States, is put together in Mexico, then returns for sale—typically in a big, discount party-goods store. The Anagram factory in Minnesota has 417 workers (up from 200 ten years ago). Almost all of them have high school diplomas; 10 percent have degrees from technical schools and junior colleges in town; 10 percent are college graduates. Workers in the Minneapolis plant make about $15 per hour, plus health benefits and contributions to 401(k) accounts. Workers in the Mexican *maquiladora* plant that attaches the decorations to the balloons make about $2 per hour; the Chinese workers in Shenzhen make about $1.89 per day.

Why not move all of the balloon making to China or to Mexico? Paul Ansolabehere, the chief operating officer (COO) of Anagram, explained that because of machinery they've invented, the Minnesota factory is the fastest one in the world. "It just doesn't make sense to move it; we couldn't find the kind of educated workforce we have in Minnesota to run it." He told us about patents the company holds that shop-floor workers helped develop.

HOW WE COMPETE

Automation Plus: Smart Workers Equal Speed

ANAGRAM CORPORATION, AN AMERICAN BALLOON MANUFACTURER

"This is a fashion business. If a Brother Bear balloon is hot today, it'll be dead in six months. Fast as they come, they die. That means we need to get it out fast, and we can manufacture and ship in a week. We couldn't do everything in China, because it just takes too long to get stuff. My goal is to use automation to bring down the costs. Costs are rising in China now, and there's overcrowding on the roads and [with] shipping. Airfreight is a possibility, but I don't think the seasonal nature of our business would let us do that at a good price. Also, we sell to a large U.S. market, and so by remaining in the U.S., we reduce our shipping costs."

Fashion and speed matter in electronics, too. In 2004, when our IPC team researchers visited Kenwood, a Japanese consumer electronics company, we learned about the role these factors played in Kenwood's remarkable comeback from near-death to profitability.[6] I will return to this story later in this chapter and describe why Kenwood brought some manufacturing back to Japan as part of a turnaround strategy. When Kenwood moved production of portable mini-disk players from a factory in Malaysia to their Yamagata, Japan, plant in 2003, they discovered they could exploit short-lived consumer trends. It used to take thirty-two days to get portable minidisk players from Malaysia to stores in Japan. Now when the players are made in the Yamagata plant, they can order them at 3 P.M. one day and ship them out the next day. The managers calculated that bringing production back to Japan lowered total costs (including raw materials and transportation) by 10 percent.

And there were unexpected benefits, too. For each holiday and special event, it turns out that customers like different colors. One-month lead time was just too slow to pick up on these trends. But by producing in Japan they could do it fast and cut down on "dead" stock. Kenwood sold 25 percent more players in 2003 than the year before.

Cutting Out the Slack

Speed is not hardwired in geography. It is a function of organization and of transportation costs. Information technology can accelerate supply-chain operations in distant locations, as many managers told us. For example, a company I will call Alpha, a clothing "manufacturer" in Britain, makes 120,000 tailored jackets, slacks, and skirts a week and sells them to big retail chains.[7] Like Liz Claiborne, the Knapps, and Kell-wood, this London "manufacturer" has no factories. Alpha's chairman and managing director said he got his inspiration for how to organize the business from reading an article about Airbus—"for me it was a life-changing idea." The article he read argued that as long as Britain kept the technology for making the wings of the plane, and let the seats and all the rest be made in the cheapest places, Britain would always have good profits and jobs from the wings.

Ten years ago, Alpha closed its factories in the United Kingdom and moved production to subcontractors in Romania that work exclusively for this British business. About eighty people work in the London offices of the company, dealing with customers, doing design, and developing the software systems used to coordinate the supply chain. The Romanian subcontractors have huge plants and employ about 10,000 workers. Alpha buys fabrics (synthetics), buttons, hangers, plastic bags, and all the rest in the Far East and supplies them to the Romanian factories. Transportation takes about four weeks on a ship from Asia to Romania. Production takes another four to five weeks (down from twelve weeks five years ago). Then the goods are shipped directly to customers in Britain—taking another seven days of transportation. It takes almost three months from order to the customer. In order to get good enough quality to be able to ship clothes directly to customers from Romania—without having to add more time while company inspectors look them over in London—Alpha stations fifteen of its own employees in the Romanian subcontractors' factories on a permanent basis to work on reducing defects.

The biggest issue, though, is how to build an organization that cuts out every minute of slack, starting before the customer ever places an order—a decision Alpha has learned to anticipate and to help shape—through final deliveries to the stores.

HOW WE COMPETE

We Figured Out the Coordination Puzzle
ALPHA, A CLOTHING MANUFACTURER IN GREAT BRITAIN

Alpha's chairman: "We decided that if we are only going to employ as few people as possible in the West End of Central London, we really needed to solve the basic problem of coordination. One garment equals twenty bits. It needs a hanger, a bag, a lining, a button, zipper, so it comes to about twenty pieces. The multiplications are all very easy, so if we have 4 million garments, we've got 4 million times twenty bits to coordinate from the supply chain. We have to get the supply chain, which is worldwide, to actually supply 4 million times twenty bits from wherever it is in the world to wherever it's going in the world within certain time frames and within certain specifications."

As we looked at the data from Alpha, our team concluded that the company specializes in the same functions as Dell. However different the products, both of these businesses have learned to excel in coordination and distribution, while leaving the manufacturing to someone else—under Alpha's or Dell's close monitoring.

To pull all the pieces together rapidly, Alpha combines standard software like Microsoft Excel with proprietary software and uses them both over the Internet (with firewalls providing more or less access to data to different players in the system) and also over a virtual private network that's open to the factories. These software technologies allow Alpha to work with the factories and their customers as if they were all sitting in the same room.

Take pattern cutting. Alpha has ten big customers and knows which jackets have sold best for each of them over time. When a customer asks for another jacket, Alpha goes to its electronic library, picks out the last bestseller, and uses that block of computerized instructions to create next season's jacket. Alpha's chairman told us, "It's like the good old days when you cut a pattern by hand and you put the cardboard pattern on the back of a lorry and sent it to the factory. Only now it's totally integrated, and they just pick it up from the library on our network. In a lot of the factories, we don't use patterns at all anymore. The pattern for the sleeve, say, is picked up electronically from the library by a cutting machine, and it goes back and cuts out the sleeve without a pattern."

Since the fabric is coming from East Asia, why not make the clothes there, too? we asked. Aren't labor costs lower there? Alpha's senior executive had firm convictions on this point. He explained that the Far East does not have much experience making tailored garments, while Romania does. He pointed to one researcher wearing an unlined casual jacket and said that one could be made in Hong Kong, but—gesturing to mine, which had shoulder pads, lining, and a close fit—that one had to be done in Europe. Moreover, having all your factories in one region means you ship full truckloads and save on transportation. You put time into developing skills, and the contractors learn how to do "quality." "You develop factories you now love." And then: "To be fair, in Romania they are earning about three bowls of rice and a cup of tea every day. For how much less are you going to find anyone to make stuff for you?"

Labor costs are just not that important, he said: "In reality, the amount of money that a physical machinist gets for sewing up the garment is so minute, it is so low, that it is actually a stunning irrelevance. Everyone keeps focusing on the wages you pay in each country, but it has more to do with the efficiency of the factory as to what price you pay for making. So if the efficiency of the factory is running at 50 to 60 percent, then why not get it to 80 percent, and you're there." Here again we heard the lesson that even in a labor-intensive activity like apparel, wages are a very small part of the total cost picture. It's productivity and unit labor costs that matter.

Bob Zane, senior vice president for production at Liz Claiborne, a U.S. women's clothing brand that did over $4 billion sales in 2004, also emphasized that the real gains come from making the supply chain work more rapidly and seamlessly.[8] He described how ten years ago (1995) the company was sourcing from 512 contractors in 45 different countries. The strategy then was "country-of-the-month sourcing," with orders shifting around all the time to plants that could do it a few pennies cheaper. But this failed to take into account the overhead of managing so many sourcing partners. Whatever was saved by getting the suppliers to compete with each other did not compensate for the infrastructure needed to manage so many of them. Today, Liz sources from half as many vendors (250) in ten fewer (35) countries. In fact, 75 percent of all Liz merchandise now comes from only thirty different factories. There have been enormous savings from the new system. Zane expects to continue to bring down the number of suppliers and to expand the range of functions carried out at the suppliers—transferring functions now still performed in Liz offices in the United States.

The End of Distance?

As the organizational possibilities of coordinating extended supply chains have been changing, so too have transportation costs. As Chapter 6 described, in the mid-nineties, around the time that NAFTA was established, consumer electronics and textile/apparel makers thought that locating production in Mexico would give them a chance to simultaneously lower the costs of production and reap the advantages of rapid deliveries to

U.S. customers. Mexico disappointed on both counts. Costs rose rapidly, and Mexican infrastructure and Mexican factories were unable to get a flexible mix of goods into U.S. markets quickly. The cost of airfreight from Asia also began to fall. When we started our interviews in 1999, managers told us that only very light and expensive items, like notebook computers or cashmere sweaters, could be flown to the United States from China. Otherwise, the goods had to come on ships, and final customization would have to take place in the United States or close by. By the time we concluded our interviews in 2004, virtually every company we were seeing had a much longer list of what they could bring in by air from Asia.

American brands started to realize that it might be about as cheap to fly clothing in from China as to make it in Mexico. Bob Zane, the Liz Claiborne vice president, said he's pulling out of Mexico and many other Caribbean sites and locating 50 percent of his sourcing in China. Were it not for "country risk," he might do it all there. What about time to market? we asked. He told us that if he does it right, he can get airfreight from China down to the same price as transport from Mexico. An executive at a big electronics manufacturing contractor explained what "doing it right" means, using the example of a Microsoft mouse, which his company was making. At the time of the interview in 2001, making the mouse in China saved 30 cents over other locations, and it cost 20 cents to ship from China. "If you are global, you can optimize this. Location is a balance of volume, labor costs, engineering, inbound and outbound transactions costs, and time to market."

In Los Angeles, we met with the president of a company I will call Adamwear, a women's fashion business with fifty retail stores and a private-label business for department stores.[9] Adamwear does about $110 million of annual sales. The owner of this privately held company is also its chief designer. In the United States, he employs about fifty people as designers and sample and marker makers; another 450 work in his retail stores. In 2004, 30 percent of Adamwear clothing was made in the United States, though this is on the way down to 5 to 10 percent. The president is also shifting much of his Latin American and Mexican production to

Asia. He explained: "More than half our products are flown from Asia. It's costly, but would you rather own unsold, outdated inventory or pay a little more?" In China he works with agents — independent middlemen between brands like his and the sewing contractors.

Adamwear's president told us he is now sending some sample-making to Asia via the Hong Kong agent. Not all of it — the prototype sampling will always remain in Los Angeles, close to the designers. The president used an analogy to explain Adamwear's outsourcing strategies: "If I were a chef at a five-star restaurant, I wouldn't be the guy getting up at 5 A.M. to kill the chicken or staying around to 1 A.M. to clean up."

One big L.A. textile "convertor" told us how he had resolved to make a big, one-time switch — from 98 percent domestic suppliers in 2001 to 70 percent imports in 2003, mostly from Asia and China. A convertor takes orders for fabric from brands and retailers and then finds suppliers to make up the fabrics. The company president we interviewed had made his decision to outsource after watching most of his competitors and eight out of his twelve major U.S. suppliers go out of business. "Since the end of 2003, geography literally doesn't matter anymore for us. The question of where we source depends purely on delivery times. For example, we're doing a 290,000-yard program for Wal-Mart. We sent an order to our supplier in China on Friday, and today [Wednesday] they've already sent us a sample. Two weeks from the order, the supplier will start shipping to us, and twelve days later the goods will be here. The cost of finishing and dyeing in China are only a fraction of what they are in the U.S. We can't understand how they do it."

He told us that as far he could figure, China was going to own the textile industry, and the only mystery was why they did not take it all over but left some for others. He described the quality of his Chinese suppliers as "very very good." They inspect 100 percent of the fabric and flag all the defects. His Chinese suppliers have now started doing a lot of product development, and all his team has to do is "fine-tune it." Wasn't he worried that eventually the Chinese would deal with the retailers and brands directly and cut him out? He sounded confident that he still held a winning hand: "Mentality-wise, the Chinese don't know how to deal directly with U.S. companies."

Clustering

The Los Angeles fabric supplier I have just described has a special expertise: how to manage relationships with U.S. brands and retailers. He believes this skill is difficult to learn and irreplaceable, and hence that his business will remain anchored in the United States. Again and again in the interviews, managers described deciding about outsourcing and offshoring on the basis of assessments of where they find people with essential skills for doing the job. In a first pass at sorting out what makes production and jobs stick in advanced countries, we find knowledge or skills associated with activities that can only be performed in the location in which they are consumed. Immobile assets include such things as coal mines, which are stuck in the ground and create mining jobs that by and large people do not want any more (if they have a choice), but also expert communities with intense face-to-face daily exchanges of knowledge, like university research laboratories or Silicon Valley. To get into the flow, you need to be there in person. Such cluster communities attract high-technology industries and high-paid, desirable jobs. Jobs associated with these immobile resources—whether mines or high-tech clusters—cannot be offshored, or are less likely to be offshored, because their value is best realized in a particular locale.

Firms also cluster in certain locales to be close to other firms whose capabilities they need to combine with their own. We visited the Itema Group in Bergamo, Italy, one of the most prosperous of the Italian districts. Itema's three loom brands—Somet, Vamatex, and Sulzer—make them the largest weaving machinery company in the world.[10] They have built and sold about a quarter of a million of the world's installed looms, and their 2003 sales were $962 million. Many of the components that go into a loom are purchased from suppliers—about 80 percent of the value of the loom. These components come from 380 suppliers, most of whom are Italian—and mostly (70 percent) located near Itema's factories in Bergamo. In order to expand its sales of looms in China—the most rapidly growing market for textile machinery—Itema needs to be able to make at least some of their models near the Chinese customers. But they cannot find in China, or anywhere else in the world, the cluster of specialized and highly skilled suppliers they have around them in Bergamo. So any expansion of production abroad, let alone any transfer of production, is likely to be very difficult and slow.

A cluster of interconnected firms concentrated around a core industry is usually associated with higher wages. Michael L. Porter, a professor at Harvard Business School and the author of books on competitive strategy, is studying how synergies of location in regions in the United States with clusters of firms making goods and services for sale outside the region produce flows of information and coordination that raise incomes.[11] Porter has found that a person employed in one of the traded goods or services clusters in the United States earned on average $44,956 in 2000, in contrast to the average U.S. earnings that year of $34,669. While clusters usually call to mind high-tech concentrations of industries, like information technology companies in Silicon Valley or the Route 128 area outside Boston, in fact activities as different as winegrowing, photonics, medical devices, moviemaking, NASCAR stock car racing, and financial services are also found in clusters.[12]

As we looked across the firms we visited, we saw a range—from the most mobile activities that are easy to offshore (like portfolio investments) to the least mobile activities (like gardening). There are a number of potentially sticky points where companies face real dilemmas and choices about location. At some of these junctures, there are high rewards in profitability and jobs associated with strategies that draw on knowledge and skills that companies are most likely to be able to find and develop in their own home society. One Italian men's trouser maker told us he had to start offshoring some of his production because of labor costs—an Italian sewer earns twice as much as a Portuguese sewer, he explained, and four times as much as a Romanian. The productivity of the Romanians is only 70 percent of the Italians', but the Portuguese produce at the Italian level. So we asked, Why not move everything to Portugal? He was taken aback: "But, but . . . our success comes from innovation, and the environment here is a lot more stimulating! All the accessories are available here—the belts, the finishing facilities, the finishing techniques. Here's where we dream up products. The R & D certainly needs to stay here, and some of the rest." Like the Sulzer, Somet, and Vamatex looms, such businesses may be less sticky than coal mines or housekeeping jobs or university research laboratories—but they emerge from our research as strong magnets for attracting durable and valuable work. Which opportunities a company seizes at these points depends in large measure, as we will see, not so much on the product or the industry but on the kinds of resources that have been built up in the firm through previous experiences—that is, those that draw on its legacy.

The Limits of Modularity: When Outsourcing Doesn't Work

Despite all the advances of modularity over the past twenty years, there remain many activities in which processes and connections among them cannot be captured and expressed in digital code. These are areas on the cutting edge of technology where knowledge has not (or has not yet) been standardized, or areas involving continuous back-and-forth between engineers and workers involved in different functions—like design and manufacturing. When coordinating the different phases of production from design to market still depends mainly on knowledge, judgment, and craft of experienced employees, it helps to have human beings meeting face-to-face and working out problems, rather than communicating over the Internet. There's likely to be a high premium on recruiting and retaining people with high levels of technical training. Today, such education is best provided in the universities and research centers of advanced countries. But this advantage over others in the world is rapidly shrinking. Over the past fifteen years, developing countries like India and China have taken giant steps forward in building universities capable of turning out men and women with formal skills equivalent to those they might have acquired in Western universities. Universities like Tsinghua, Peking, Zhejiang, Fudan, and Shanghai Jiaotung in China and the Indian Institutes of Technology are graduating scientists and engineers at levels close or equivalent to those of the finest institutions abroad.

Above and beyond the education and skills provided by formal school learning, however, there is knowledge shared and transmitted in long-established research communities like Silicon Valley or Hsinchu Science Park in Taiwan, or around Cambridge University in England, or within the four walls of one company over time. These understandings translate into knowing how to move bright ideas into practice, designs into manufacturing processes, test runs into full-scale production, and innovations into products people buy. The accumulation of such experience over time in centers of high productivity and innovation leads to the crystallization of tacit, informal knowledge in particular localities. These are the places where cutting-edge work tends to be carried out, for, by definition, this is work that has not yet been wholly mastered, routinized, and codified.

Even in electronics, where the advances of modularity have been so rapid, there are many areas in which the interface between functions cannot—or cannot yet—be modeled and standardized. Firms that are pioneering in these areas look quite different from segments of the industry that are modular. In firms developing new products, engineers from different divisions of the company may need to be pulled in on an ad hoc basis to solve problems.[13] It may not be at all clear how to specify and stabilize production processes. The same engineers may have to move back and forth between different phases of product definition, design, test runs, and full-scale implementation, without any a priori or stable division of tasks emerging for a long time, if ever. In electronics, the difficulties of fragmenting production may be especially evident in phases of radical innovation. In other industries, like autos and auto parts, as Chapter 4 explained, getting the vital parts of the system to work together may still require "integral" and centralized, rather than modular, architectures.

Ulvac Technologies is a Japanese company specializing in vacuum technologies used in production equipment for semiconductors, flat-panel silicon and polysilicon display screens, disk and magnetic media, and many other industrial processes. Dr. Chikara Hayashi, Ulvac's eighty-three-year-old former chairman, is a physicist with strong scientific contributions in particle physics as well as a keen interest in the connections between R & D and industrial performance. He spoke with MIT researchers on four visits to Ulvac laboratories and factories between 1994 and 2004. Despite the general debacle in the electronics industry after the collapse of the telecom and dot-com booms at the end of the nineties, Ulvac expanded greatly, particularly because of its capabilities in making production equipment for flat-panel displays. Its net sales climbed from $847 million in June 1999 to $1.5 billion in June 2004; its net revenues increased by a factor of twelve over the same five years. Ulvac had 3,712 employees in 2004 (up from 2,600 ten years before). The company listed on the Tokyo Stock Exchange in April 2004.

Dr. Hayashi explained that for the kind of products that Ulvac develops, there is no clean hand-off possible between R & D and commercialization. The information needed to move from a prototype to producing on a larger scale cannot be standardized and translated into digital code. Bringing the functions together "still requires all our effort," and that's why outsourcing is not possible. As for offshoring, many of the skills that are needed can be found only in Japan—indeed, some only in the Aomori region in Japan. The issue is not just the skills of Ulvac engineers but the skills of its specialized suppliers in areas like electroplating and polishing, and the meshing of Ulvac skills with the suppliers' skills.

Other considerations also make it essential to keep these activities together in Japan. Ulvac wants to protect its intellectual property and sees the dangers of joint ventures and outsourcing as demonstrated by how the Koreans once used Japanese technologies to develop their own high-tech industry only to become fierce competition. Ulvac is building companies in China, but they are basically new businesses for the company and not parts that are being hived off of Ulvac Japan and sent to a low-wage production site. (Here Ulvac's strategy resembles that of the Italian industrial district firms, which I will discuss again later.)

After twenty years of investment in China, Ulvac has accumulated experience in several major cities. In Ningpo, China, for example, Ulvac has developed a vacuum pump business to supply parts for refrigerators and for older-model displays. With three Japanese engineers on site, the plant now does a lively business and "makes a product you can almost sell in Japan." Ulvac has plants and service centers in the U.S. and a number of Asian countries; as the semiconductor and display industries have developed in Korea and Taiwan, Ulvac has followed them. But the core activities across the entire sequence of production are still located in Japan—in key plants at Chigasaki for display technologies and at Fuji Susono for semiconductors.

If functions cannot be broken apart, they cannot readily be geographically separated. When the production sequence is nonmodular, much tighter and more intimate forms of collaboration are needed to tap the tacit knowledge of the participants. They are likely to need face-to-face relationships to make it work. So nonmodular activities are more likely to stay home. When and if they become more modular—either because new technologies allow the rich information that used to flow between people to be captured in software, or because, as Liz Claiborne explained about clothing design, it becomes profitable to make products that are just less complex—then these operations become more vulnerable to relocation outside the home society. Once the production process can be fragmented, people with specific talents and expertise can be located in one part of the organization, and other activities can be dispersed.

Even in industries where some of the functions can be broken apart and relocated at a distance, other functions may still clump together. When companies cannot provide complete enough instructions on what they need—because their standards are so demanding, or because they do not know how to specify the details in advance—they are likely to keep the functions together and at home. Brand-name companies like Liz Claiborne, Ralph Lauren, and the Gap basically specialize in branding, retail sales, and product definition, which means imagining clothing to match up with lifestyles. Virtually all of their manufacturing is outsourced, and much of it to Asia. But thus far they still feel the need to keep most design in-house, along with product definition, merchandising, and retailing. The reason is that they cannot yet describe how to create their collections well enough to pass it over to designers at their distant contractors.

This may be changing. In our interviews we discovered that many of these big brand-name companies are contemplating partnerships with a limited number of mega contract manufacturers. The contractors would do the design function—in the language of electronics, become ODMs. A senior executive at one of the apparel brands told us he has hundreds of designers in his offices in the United States and too many of them "think they are Yves Saint Laurent," he said. In other words, they want to select their own piece goods from their favorite small mills in Italy and not the big mills in China. They want to work directly with the sample makers. The senior executive sees this system as expensive and not worth it for, say, a blouse that will be sold for $25. A designer ought to be able to go to a supplier and ask: What can you do for $5? The brand, in his opinion, does not need to choose a fabric mill or a thread count. The kind of designers he wants to have working for the company might well be people working for the contractors. Most design activities should shift to the contractors, he thought, who should be banging down the door proposing designs, yarns, fabrics—not passively waiting for orders from the brand, he said.

When Offshoring Leads to More Integration

Interestingly, when activities are broken off and moved to developing countries where skills and experience are in short supply, we often found more integration and less modularity in the operations abroad than in the originating society. The explanation of more integration abroad is that bringing work within a company's own four walls gives it more control over quality and delivery times. When contractors are new, workers are inexperienced, and supplies have to be transported over crowded, potholed highways, companies are apt to push for bringing more functions in-house. So, for example, we found that U.S. companies like Warnaco were more integrated in their Mexican operations than back home, and Hong Kong companies like Fang Brothers more integrated in their mainland China plants (or in their Pringle subsidiary in Scotland) than in Hong Kong proper. Sometimes, instead of carrying out more functions in-house, a company can twist the arms of its longtime suppliers in its home country to join it in the move offshore. I discussed this trend in Chapter 4 as it related to the auto industry. Major U.S., Japanese, and European assemblers required their parts suppliers to set up plants near them in Mexico and China. Taiwanese companies have usually favored this approach. Often when we visited a Taiwanese firm in mainland China, we found it in a zone surrounded by the same Taiwanese companies it worked with back home. It seemed as if a fragment of home territory had been broken off and implanted in a new setting, but that all the old relationships continued more or less unchanged.

Looked at from another perspective, modularity and the shedding of functions on one side may induce bunching up of functions at other points along the value chain. In the past, when American multinational corporations (MNCs) set up operations abroad (often, as we've seen, in order to be able to sell in foreign markets), they usually tried to clone their organizations back home. Companies like GM, Ford, and IBM ended up reproducing integrated structures in the foreign society. Today, in an increasing number of locations, the multinationals can find foreign suppliers who offer a broad range of capabilities across the functions of the production process. A multinational can therefore outsource, rather than re-create its whole organization abroad. In order to pare down the business to only its most profitable areas, the multinational company is likely to push its foreign suppliers to take on even more functions.

This leads to a kind of competition among contract manufacturers for the business of the lead firms that stimulates the contractors to extend their offerings along the value chain. Suppliers often increase design and other services they provide in hopes of wooing new customers and making it harder for lead firms to switch their business away from them. On the other side, though, lead firms are reluctant to enter into deals that make it very costly to switch from one contract manufacturer to another. If, for example, Hewlett-Packard has an order from Circuit City and wants Flextronics to deliver to Circuit City, who should own the information technology that makes this direct response possible? If Flextronics were to own it, would HP be locked into the relationship with Flextronics and no longer free to switch contractors? Or free to switch only by risking massive delivery disruptions in getting HP products into Circuit City stores? The worries about how much integration to buy from the suppliers and how great the risks are of lock-in were ever-present in the interviews. Our questions about these issues were also among the most difficult for managers to answer, for here we had ventured onto the terrain of proprietary information and competitive benchmarking—and so details were hard to come by.

How to Use China—and Still Keep Jobs at Home

Our interviews in Japan identified another kind of home-based skill that makes companies more likely to keep production at home, rather than moving it out to low-wage countries. We learned that a key factor in the remarkable resurgence of Japanese electronics companies has been domestic manufacturing. Much of the manufacturing that remains in Japan has been transformed by a shift away from assembly-line production toward production in "cells" or "pods." In cell production, small groups of workers assemble whole products. Our question, though, was why the Japanese are keeping manufacturing—in cells or not: Why not move it to China? As I will discuss later in this chapter, the answer was that the skills of the Japanese workers keep the cells at home.

In the United States, manufacturing has mainly changed by subtraction: Productivity increases have made it possible to do more with fewer workers. Of the manufacturing that remains, some has been transferred to large contract manufacturers, and they are moving much of it abroad. The Japanese, too, have sold off some factories to contract manufacturers, but far fewer than the United States has. Even when they have done so, as several of the managers at large global suppliers emphasized to us, the Japanese did not really want to buy outsourcing services. They used the sales to get rid of old factories. As one manager told us, "The Japanese sold culls."

In Japan, the sale of plants to global suppliers was also a way of reducing the workforce without having to lay off the employees. Because Japanese are so opposed to layoffs, firms cast about for alternatives, and transferring the plants has been one of them. They found other ways, too, of lowering labor costs. As Steven K. Vogel, professor at the University of California, Berkeley, describes, the Japanese first tried to trim financial and overhead costs, then reduced overtime, bonuses, and new hires, and offered voluntary early retirement. Only as a last expedient did they fire people.[14] A 2002 government survey found widespread recourse to these other options and stated that only 7 percent of all companies actually fired workers.[15]

The Japanese have massively invested in China over the past ten years, but they seem to have done so in ways that use the potential of China quite differently from the ways that American firms have.[16] First of all, the Japanese have kept more of their production in China in their own affiliates, rather than outsourcing this production to contract manufacturers. Of the Japanese managers in electronics we interviewed, 86 percent of those who were offshoring told us they were locating production abroad mainly in their own plants—in contrast to 46 percent of the U.S. managers. The American managers we interviewed in electronics companies were more likely to use subcontractors abroad (31 percent of them mentioned this as their main choice), in comparison with only 7 percent of the Japanese electronics managers. Even where we found Japanese using contract manufacturers in China, as at Sony, managers said that in the future they wanted to expand production by building more of their own factories in China. Our conclusions about differences between U.S. and Japanese companies in China can only be tentative, since they draw on our interviews rather than on large-scale survey data (which, to our knowledge, does not exist).

Second, some Japanese firms, like Matsushita, the Panasonic brand, have made huge investments in developing fully integrated companies in China. These companies operate with a cost structure that allows them to sell at "China prices" that can compete not only with other multinational companies in export markets but also with domestic Chinese producers within the China market. Here, too, we find a major difference from American uses of China—designed either to lower the cost of production of goods that will be exported (like U.S.-brand clothing outsourced to Chinese companies) or to make goods to be sold in the upper end of the domestic Chinese market (like Motorola cell phones). The Japanese strategy, in contrast, is what Chunli Lee, professor of economics at Aichi University, Japan, calls "full-set integrated localization." By this he means that a company does everything from design to component purchasing, production, and sales in China.[17] This strategy involves head-to-head competition against domestic Chinese businesses in low-end, high-volume products.

The example Professor Lee provides is of Matsushita's production of a microwave oven in Shanghai that sells at a price quite close to a Galanz (a domestic Chinese company) model. Compared to Matsushita's previous model, this "Made in China" microwave (MX20) was 37 percent cheaper. It used 30 percent fewer parts, almost all of which were made in China (the transistor and steel came from Japan). In order to achieve these savings, Matsushita has partnered with some Chinese domestic companies, such as TCL. Other Japanese companies following this "full-set-localization" model have entered into similar alliances—for example, Sanyo and Haier. By following the same "integrated localization" pattern when making its DVD players and TVs, Matsushita has come up with a low-end China strategy that's quite different from that of the Koreans, or Sony, or U.S. and European mobile phone companies—such as Nokia, Motorola, or Ericsson—that have aimed at selling higher-end products in China and exporting higher-value goods.[18] Matsushita's expansion in China has been part of a broad cost-cutting strategy that cut its domestic workforce by 19 percent and restored its profitability.[19] At the same time, the company increased R & D spending and turned out a succession of blockbuster new products in digital cameras, plasma TVs, and DVD recorders. In 2002, Matsushita had a $3.6 billion loss; in 2005, its profits are expected to rise to $2.9 billion.

Finally, even as the Japanese have moved some of their manufacturing to China, they also see major advantages to be gained in keeping certain kinds of production and a significant share of manufacturing in Japan. Keidanren, the Japanese business association, describes a vision of Japan's role in 2025, where "Made in Japan" will evolve into "Made by Japan,"[20] and where Japanese businesses will be "positioned in a broader global context, providing Japan's knowledge and technology to drive economic development around the world, not just on Japanese soil." But this widely shared perspective still includes a major role for production in Japan. In a large-scale survey of Japanese manufacturing companies in 2002, managers were asked to predict what impact they thought the next three years of overseas investment would have on their domestic operations.[21] About 42 percent responded that they thought there would be no effect, since their overseas investment was aimed at exports.[22] Another 40 percent said that while some domestic production would be offshored, the domestic production would shift to high-value goods that could fill in the gap. Only 22 percent said they thought that domestic production would decline. A 2002–2003 White Paper report by Japan's Ministry of Economy, Trade, and Industry (METI) found that, all other factors being equal, the more profit a company generates, the more likely it is to produce in Japan.[23] The differences between these findings and the U.S. picture are striking. The restructuring of the electronics giant Hitachi, for example, offers a remarkable contrast to U.S. companies like IBM, since Hitachi's new strategies still emphasize the importance of manufacturing—and of manufacturing in Japan.[24]

CHAPTER 10

Building on a Legacy at Home

Over the past three years, the Japanese economy has experienced a recovery from its long slide into stagnation and recession in the 1990s. At the end of 2004, the profitability of Japanese big companies was climbing, and corporate debt was at its lowest level (as percent of GDP) since the mid-eighties. Much of the new dynamism builds on a Japanese lead in the new components and products of digital consumer electronics. The Japanese companies that have done best over the past three years are component electronics makers, like Nidec, and businesses, like Canon, Matsushita, and Sharp, that have been leaders in creating new consumer electronics products, such as digital cameras, cell phones, flat-screen TVs, and DVD recorders.[1] These products contributed 12.6 percent of the growth in Japan's domestic industrial production in 2003.[2]

Equally important, the recovery of the Japanese electronics industry is contributing to a massive transformation of Japan's situation in the international economy, as China has replaced the United States as Japan's top trading partner. This reversal generated a $14 billion trade surplus in Japan's balance of trade with China in 2004—in contrast to the

U.S. $162 billion trade deficit with China in the same year—the largest deficit the U.S. has ever had with a single country.[3] Japanese firms have been able to ride the rising tide of Chinese capabilities by massively exporting to China the vital electronic components for new generations of consumer electronics products being assembled in China and exported to the world. Flash memory, hard-disk drives, charge-coupled devices (for digital cameras), large-substrate LCDs, and plasma displays are among the most important of these components. Neither the Chinese nor the Taiwanese have yet mastered the technologies for making them, though as Chapter 11 points out, they are narrowing the gap. Because of the complexity and rapidity of innovation in these components, the Japanese have a long lead. The Apple iPod is a typical example. It was dreamed up by Apple in California, but its most valuable working parts come from Japan, from companies like Toshiba and Nidec, and are assembled in the factories of Taiwanese contract manufacturers in mainland China.

Why the Japanese fare so well in digital consumer electronics has to do, among other things, with their skill in squeezing complex circuitry into small form factors; with the boost their domestic market provides because of Japanese consumers' enthusiasm for such novelties; and with control of innovation in both the component and the product value chain. In contrast to American electronics companies, which today usually focus either on making components (like Intel and AMD) or on making products (like Dell and Apple), many more of the Japanese enterprises have kept both components and products within the same company. And compared to the Americans, they have kept more of the functions involved in making components and products within their own walls—although the Japanese, too, now use somewhat more contract manufacturing than in the past. The Japanese dominance in digital consumer electronics has built upon the legacy of strength in electronics that Japanese companies established in the seventies. Theirs is a victory won by bringing old strengths to bear in the development of altogether new products.

Among the jewels in this legacy are the human resources of a manu-facturing workforce well-educated in primary, secondary, and technical schools and abundantly endowed with skills that are maintained and upgraded on the job. Japanese companies invest heavily in on-the-job training. The characteristic features of Japanese-style management—just-in-time production and continuous improvement processes—depend on the superb skills of shop-floor workers and on their willingness to go the extra mile for the company. Even in the worst years of the economic downturn, Japanese companies were reluctant to lay off workers. There is a strong social stigma attached to letting workers go in Japan. Mr. Takashima, the Fujitsu vice president we interviewed, told us that one of the main factors leading Fujitsu to keep manufacturing under its own roof was that "if we got rid of all manufacturing, we'd have to get rid of 50 percent of the workforce. We couldn't survive if we did that, because other stakeholders, like governments who procure our services, couldn't accept our doing such a thing." In many of our Japanese interviews, man-agers said that if they fired people, it would become impossible to keep their best employees or to recruit good new ones. Managers told us they felt that losing workers who had developed such a deep understanding of how things worked in the company would destroy valuable and irre-placeable resources.

For all these reasons, Japanese managers were interested in any pos-sibilities for keeping manufacturing in-house. While the idea of using "cells" or "pods" instead of assembly-line production has been around for a long time, it really started to take off in Japan around five years ago. In 1999, Canon was one of the first large companies to break up its assem-bly lines into cells, and others—like Sanyo and Sony—began to use this system around the same time.[4] Once they implement cell production, factories are able to produce small batches in quick response to shifts in consumer demand, and therefore can cut down on inventories. Cells also require less dedicated special-purpose machinery, since the workstations are set up to facilitate assembling a very diverse mix of products by hand.

We Do It Faster, Better, and Cheaper In-House

WHEN OUR TEAM INTERVIEWED MATSUSHITA MANAGERS, THEY TOLD US WHY THEY NEED TO KEEP PLANTS IN JAPAN, EVEN AS THEY ARE EXPANDING IN CHINA. ONE EXPLAINED:

"Take LSI [large-scale integration: putting lots of circuits on a single chip]. Many U.S. companies specialize in a core competence, a piece of the value chain. Panasonic does it all: system LSI, design, manufacturing, production equipment, and marketing. LSI and assembly are the core areas that should be in-house. We place small integrated circuits with hundreds of pins [leads] on both surfaces of the board with only a micron of tolerance between layers. This cannot be done in China, so we use our Yamagata, Japan, plants. Circuit density is key. This determines our competitiveness. We do this faster, better, and cheaper in-house. With highly sophisticated products, you have to be first. Manufacturing in Japan means we can be speedy. This is the road to victory in the market.

"We can put knowledge about system design from all over the company into the LSI design. If an outsourcer made the component, it might not work as well or fit as well within our final product. In the past, we could buy key components from the outside, but now, system LSI determines everything, so we do them inside the company. There are, of course, some components we still purchase from the outside.

"Products that don't require the state of the art we do outsource, but only as an exception—when demand exceeds capacity. As long as our factories can do it, we use them.

"Cellular production has really been important. New ideas for improvement may come from this area. If someone else is doing your assembly, you don't learn these things, you can never get feedback, you can't get specific information like 'You can't solder this way if you design like that!'"[5]

The Facts: Matsushita is the world's largest consumer electronics company. In 2004, its sales (consolidated for the group) were $72 billion. The company's resurgence after a number of bad years was marked by a 54 percent increase in operating profits from 2003 to 2004.

Fujitsu, too, told us that even under tremendous pressure to reduce costs, they still think they need to keep a lot of domestic manufacturing. The company has been struggling to reduce its debt and to restore profitability. In February 2005, Fujitsu sold its LCD and flat-panel-display businesses (to Sharp and to Hitachi)—although these were areas in which Fujitsu had been a leading innovator.[6] Fujitsu also sold off major blocks of shares it held in two big Japanese technology companies, Fanuc, the world's largest producer of industrial robots, and Advantest, a maker of computer-chip testing equipment. Akira Takashima, vice chairman and member of the board at Fujitsu Limited, explained that even with these changes, they realize they need to keep some manufacturing in-house. When they tried outsourcing a component to an American contractor, the end result was poor quality, so Fujitsu decided to bring it back into the company. Takashima said: "Domestic production allows production to be close to design. We can't change production in response to design changes so easily if our factories are in Taiwan or in China. It's just hard to communicate small changes, and when things go wrong in the quality of the product, we need to get this information back rapidly to the designers." He told us that in Fujitsu's cell-production system there is so much automation that labor costs are minimal. He added that automation has the added value of greatly reducing waste.

Cell production has been critical to the revival of Japanese electronics, since it makes it possible to change models quickly. Every few months, top-of-the-line cell phone manufacturers will add new functions, like cameras, video, music, and ringer tones. And while it's possible to produce long runs of stable products like PlayStations successfully in China, because of the lack of experience of the managers and the workforce, it's not possible to execute rapid shifts from one product generation to another.

Almost every Japanese executive we interviewed complained about "job-hopping" by the managers and technicians they hire in China. Although the prestige of working for a big U.S. brand trumps working for a Japanese multinational, high turnover of skilled personnel is a problem for American companies, too, who are constantly having their employees poached. Companies like Motorola pay higher wages and also tie housing loans to the job in order to keep experienced employees. Because of high turnover, foreign companies often lack people in their China plants with previous experience of carrying out product transitions. The workforce, too, lacks the broad skills that would make new-product introduction smooth. Chinese workers typically remain in a company for a few years at most before moving on to another job or returning to inland villages with the savings from their factory earnings. The Chinese workforce is a well-disciplined one, capable of excellent performance on a narrow range of tasks, but lacks the years of experience at making lots of different things and the agility for turning around on a dime to do something new.

If a Japanese company wants to focus on fast-changing digital consumer products, it's clear that it needs to keep a significant part of the manufacturing at home—and because they have held on to skilled workers over the years, they can do just that. When we visited Kenwood in October 2004, we learned how the company's turnaround from crippling debt and collapsing sales had started with severe cuts in the company.[7] The number of employees was slashed; divisions were eliminated. The new president decided to stop making mobile phone handsets, because product life cycles were dropping from six to three months. As President Haruo Kawahara explained, with a product that changed that rapidly, the company's future was at stake every few months. Software-development costs were huge, and when the product was not successful, all of that investment was essentially "thrown in the garbage." This was too heavy a burden to carry, but even while scrapping mobile phones, Kenwood reorganized the rest of its manufacturing in order to be able to compete on products that do have rapid model changes.

HOW WE COMPETE

We Keep Skilled Labor at Home

PRESIDENT KAWAHARA OF KENWOOD, A JAPANESE ELECTRONICS COMPANY, TOLD US HOW THE COMPANY SPEEDED UP ITS PRODUCTION CYCLE BY BRINGING MINI-DISK PLAYERS BACK FROM THEIR MALAYSIA PLANT TO JAPAN.

"Our Yamagata, Japan, factory has women workers who live nearby and who have been with the company for years. They are very skilled. In Malaysia, though, workers move around a lot, so you can't build up skills. As a result, the assembly process for the mini-disk player in Malaysia requires twenty-two people, while in Yamagata we need only four. Labor productivity is 1.5 times higher in Japan. One person in Japan can take over five processes, so costs are lower and quality is higher—the defect ratio has dropped by 73 percent since we moved production back to Japan. This has lowered costs, even though salaries are four to five times higher in Japan than in Malaysia. In fact, labor is only 2 to 3 percent of total costs on this product.

"These are the benefits of manufacturing in Japan. It's still better to make very labor-intensive products overseas, but things like digital cameras that are high-density and small form factor, with many parts being assembled into small cabinets or many small chips being placed on a circuit board—these are best made in Japan."

Kawahara told us that Kenwood has the same philosophy worldwide, but their methods must be adjusted according to skill levels and different mentalities. The Shanghai plant, for example, has more people in each cell, a slower flow of work, longer runs, and less-sophisticated machines. The Yamagata plant has more-complex equipment capable of making machine products with more layers and more density.

Introducing cell production in Kenwood plants and getting rid of the assembly lines was hard, Kawahara explained, because there's a dearth of managers with the old manufacturing experience. The managers in the years of the postwar Japanese economic miracle came from engineering-manufacturing backgrounds, but many of the managers who started work in the 1980s were more interested in finance than in the factory. To reorganize Kenwood's plants, Kawahara had to recruit out of retirement men he had worked with years before at Toshiba. It made him wonder whether innovations like the cell production that Kenwood and Canon are introducing would be sustainable. Could the passion for improving manufacturing performance that had been so vital to the Japanese economic miracle be rekindled? The MIT researchers listening to Kawahara wondered whether any such experiments would even be possible in the United States—do the ingredients still exist?

HOW WE COMPETE

Our Companies Last Longer

OUR TEAM ASKED PRESIDENT KAWAHARA OF KENWOOD WHAT HE THOUGHT ABOUT OUTSOURCING MANUFACTURING AND MODULAR PRODUCTION:

"I know that U.S. companies believe that fabless production plus EMS [electronics manufacturing services contractors] is the best approach. But I have strong doubts about this . . . especially in fast-changing markets. Fabless managers don't know about manufacturing anymore. If the technology or the market changes, they just can't adapt. Start-up companies do need contract manufacturers; this is the best approach for them, because there is low investment and fast ramp-up. But it's not for me. This is the strength of the U.S.: new technologies combined with fabless and EMS. In such a system, the flexible value chain is an asset. For the long run, though, where the manufacturing process has to change because of changes of technology and market, you need in-house manufacturing. That's why in Japan our companies last longer. It is another form of competitiveness. We have to change in our own way to meet the challenges."

The Japanese electronics firms we studied have opted for a strategy that uses the potential of Chinese low-wage assembly production in a division of labor that still leaves significant manufacturing as well as product definition, research and development, design, and distribution at home. This is the case even in industries where there is strong potential for fragmentation of the value chain. Japanese strategies focus on the complementarities between integration at home and networks abroad. The 2004 "Nakagawa Report," a "vision statement" on the future of Japanese industry from the Ministry of Economy, Trade, and Industry, describes this dual strategy as driving innovation along "a chain of integration" in Japan with "a thick concentration of advanced component and materials companies" and building production systems outside Japan through partnerships.[8]

Such a dual approach no longer seems widely available in the United States. American activities that have a strongly nonmodular character are indeed more likely to remain at home. But because of an American preference and talent for strategies built on modularity and contracting in the market, what Americans perceive as nonmodular activity is much more limited than what Japanese managers identify as nonmodular.

Beyond that, what Japanese managers identify as opportunities in digital consumer electronics look very different from an American perspective. While Kenwood's Kawahara uses production of the mini-disk players in his Yamagata plant as a way of accelerating product generations and getting the goods to market fast, Apple managers have been able to build an extraordinary success by designing rapid new generations of an iPod that is assembled from outsourced components and made outside the United States. Here we have, as Kawahara put it, two different forms of competitiveness.

In fact, even if an American manager wanted to follow Kawahara's path and use home-based production to capture market share in electronics products with short product cycles, it would be very difficult to do so. In the industries we studied, the necessary ingredients for this kind of internationalization strategy are no longer present in home territory. The large-scale transfer of manufacturing and of many technical design and design functions to contract manufacturers and ODM companies, both within the United States and offshore, has fractured the production system in ways that appear to be irreversible. This is true in many sectors. Zara may be the King of Speed and the hottest company in retail apparel, but there is no one left who could be Zara in the United States. It is still possible to succeed on a smaller scale, as American Apparel and the Knapps are doing with home-base production that drives speed to the customer and speed in the product cycle. Such companies are very important for local and regional economies, and they provide models for other firms. But for the U.S. electronics, auto and auto parts, and textile and apparel industries, these kinds of companies are not the dominant trend.

Legacies and Location

The story of the recovery of Japanese electronics firms certainly builds upon central elements in the Japanese industrial legacy: the importance of keeping production in-house and the use of closely knit networks. But the reflex at work here—the search in a company's treasure chest for past experience that can now be drawn upon to solve new problems—is not a peculiarly Japanese one. Our team saw it at work in all the companies we studied. What does differ from case to case, however, is the legacy itself, and the human, technological, and ideological resources it provides for tackling new problems.

As I described in Chapter 2, a company's legacy—the resources it inherits from its previous experiences—is the product of having grown up in a particular country at a particular point in history. And these resources are also shaped by the unique story of each company as it has defined its goals and overcome hurdles over its lifetime. To return to the example I used in Chapter 2, the Hong Kong apparel manufacturers were mainly industrialists who fled Shanghai when the Communists came to power in 1949. They continued in Hong Kong the family businesses they had owned in China, and they also continued their traditions of setting up each son in the family with his own business, so that over time even the largest and richest companies continued to split into new generations of medium-sized enterprises. More or less by chance, some of them started working as contractor manufacturers for American brands and retailers; others for Europeans. Because the requirements of the European and American lead firms have been very different over time, the capabilities of the Hong Kong firms working with them have been shaped in rather different ways.

The opening of China from 1979 created new opportunities, and Hong Kong businesses had to consider which of the resources they had accumulated over the past could be redeployed to profitable use in the new situation. Fang Brothers, an apparel maker I introduced in Chapter 8, decided to move most of its production to mainland China, keep just enough manufacturing at home to be able to sell goods under the Hong Kong quota, and leave design and marketing in Hong Kong—a city foreign buyers prefer over going to the mainland. Fang continued to focus heavily on U.S. customers, adding a retail business and a designer label (Pringle) aimed mainly at Western countries. Another Hong Kong entrepreneur, Silas Ho, developed a major U.S. brand, Tommy Hilfiger. In contrast, Esquel, which for family reasons had broken ties with its old Hong Kong factories, established itself as a highly integrated company in mainland China, developed a brand in China, and opened retail stores—and even grows some of its own cotton in China. Others, who had prior experience with European brands, are starting to work for large

European retailers and supermarkets like the Centres Leclerc in France and the United Kingdom's Marks & Spencer. These strategies were the outcome of Hong Kong companies' dynamic legacies—each strategy mobilizing assets that were at hand and that were part of its old business repertoire; each strategy utilizing resources from a firm's own reserves as well as new resources the company could access around the world.

For the Italian industrial districts that had reached high levels of profitability and employment growth in the 1980s and 1990s in sectors such as clothing, textiles, shoes, furniture, ceramic tiles, and packaging machines, the opening of Central Eastern Europe in 1989 presented both a threat and an opportunity on the same scale as the one the Hong Kong firms faced in 1979 when they opted for a massive transfer of most of their productive capabilities to mainland China. As the capabilities of their Chinese managers and technicians have risen and as their customers have become more willing to meet them in China than they were in the 1980s and the 1990s, the functions remaining in the electronics and textile and apparel industries in Hong Kong are rapidly disappearing into the mainland.

There is an altogether different picture in the Italian industrial districts. Companies like Sàfilo, Luxottica, Tie Rack, Ermenegildo Zegna, and Max Mara make goods in the same industries that were moved from Hong Kong to mainland China; that's where the Italian trajectory diverges—not only from Hong Kong's but also from those of other Western European economies. Given that Italy's companies compete within the European Union against firms with the same currency (the euro), high wages, expensive social benefit systems, and unionized workforce as Italy's, you might have expected they would follow a similar path, but that's not what we found.

While Italy's district landscape has seen great changes over the past twenty years, its traditional industries remain prosperous and embedded at home. The larger companies in the districts have grown and become more integrated, and some of the smallest firms have disappeared. Still, the average firm size is very small, about four workers. There has been a fall in the number of workers employed in these consumer product industries, but the fall has been less significant than in Italy's neighbors or in the United States. In 2001, Italian employment in the textile and garment industry was still at the 1995 level, while France and the United Kingdom have lost more than 30 percent of their jobs, and Germany more than 20 percent.[9] Even within Italy, the changes in employment patterns are different in the regions with industrial districts from those elsewhere. More new jobs were created in 1991–2001 in the districts than in other areas, and manufacturing declined less in the districts than in Italy overall.[10] And whether measured by worker productivity, or exports, or high-tech exports, the district firms do better.

When compared to the rest of Italy, the district firms are far more likely to enter the international economy by exporting goods they make in Italy, as Luxottica and Max Mara do, than by investing abroad.[11] This may have to do with the small size of the district firms, which makes running overseas operations prohibitively expensive, or with the absence abroad of substitutes for resources like highly skilled labor and very experienced suppliers that they find available in the cluster at home. But even more intriguing: When the Italian district companies do invest abroad, they use their offshored operations in Eastern Europe in ways that are very different from the strategies of other European managers. In the textile and apparel industry in the United Kingdom, 59 percent of the managers we interviewed said they had gotten rid of all manufacturing at home, in contrast to 8 percent of the Italians and 11 percent of the Germans. Why offshore production? The answers of the Italians were again in striking contrast to the others. For the British firms, 71 percent mentioned costs as the main driver, as did 56 percent of the Americans and 52 percent of the Germans. Among the Italians we interviewed, only 36 percent mentioned costs.

Expansion and Diversification

We tried to understand concretely what Italians are striving to get out of offshoring and what Americans are seeking. For Italian firms that are offshoring production, lowering costs certainly counts, but it's not the only reason. Their motivation for going abroad is part of the logic of expansion. Most of the district businesses seemed to be investing in foreign countries mainly to enlarge capacity, and they are not transferring or shrinking local production.[12] As the general manager at Emilia Maglia, the wholly Italian-owned subsidiary of a knitwear factory in Timisoara, Romania, that I introduced earlier in the book, explained to us, they just could not find enough workers in the Emilia-Romagna region of Italy who were willing to sew and knit. The company had soaked up the labor force in its own home district (which has very low unemployment). It had outsourced to Tunisia but found the skill level there inadequate for Emilia Maglia's high-quality work. They also tried using Chinese contract workers who, more or less legally, have established their operations in the heart of the Italian clothing districts. But none of these tactics worked well enough. Establishing a new facility in a country like Romania was Emilia Maglia's only hope of expanding the business.

The manager's explanation of Emilia Maglia's investment in Romania has been confirmed on a larger scale by a survey of Italian companies in Romania.[13] The 2003 study found 12,000 Italian-owned companies in Romania. Of these, 2,000 came from the Venice region industrial districts, which are geographically the closest to Romania. (Overall, 60 percent of all district firm foreign investments are to Romania.[14]) Additionally, Italian lawyers, accountants, IT specialists, and banks have followed the production operations by opening up shop in Romania. The Venice employers association set up an office, Antenna Veneto, in Timisoara, Romania, to assist Italian entrepreneurs in locating sites, finding local suppliers, and maneuvering through the Romanian bureaucracy for all the licenses and authorizations to get started. Antenna Veneto's Italian director told us that the main reason companies seeking his help want to relocate production is that there are no more workers and no more space in Italy. He observed that while employment levels at home have been maintained, firms have to move in order to grow. What they send to Romania is "the poor part of production, while in Italy they're doing mar-

keting and the quality end production." He listed other factors that pre-
dispose Italian firms to offshore—wages that are ten times lower than in
Italy and lower corporate taxes. These serve to counterbalance the many
headaches: corruption at all levels, taxes, customs duties, labor laws that
change all the time, power outages, and less-skilled workers.

The foreign operations of Italian district firms in Central Eastern
Europe are complementary to those that remain in Italy. Parts are made at
a lower cost and will eventually be incorporated into a product finished in
Italy (this is sometimes called "outward processing trade"). A ski boot
maker with operations in the Veneto, in Romania, and in China told us
that the hard plastic shell of the boot is made in Italy because plastic mold-
ing and die-making techniques are tricky and involve trade secrets they
want to protect. Yet these steps take a mere ten minutes of labor. Making
the soft liner of the boot takes twice as long, and so they moved that step to
Romania. Lead time for boots made in Italy with inputs from Romania is
a month, compared to three months in China, so they use China only for
large, standard orders. China and Romania thus serve different objectives
in this firm's globalization strategies: Romania allows them to lower the
cost of a high-end boot that is still mostly produced in Italy; China allows
them to start a new, lower-priced boot business.

We heard many similar stories of expansion and diversification—for
example, that of a mill in Biella, a famous Italian center of fine woolens.
The business spins cashmere and silk yarns in Italy and makes "regener-
ated cotton" yarn (i.e., made from reprocessed rags) in Poland. Because
there are few customers in Italy these days for this cheap yarn and the
operation is relatively simple and labor-intensive, it made sense to locate
such a function not in Italy but in Poland, where wages are one-eleventh
those in Italy. In their Italian operations, labor amounts to 30 percent of
the costs; in Poland, 3 percent. By starting this low-end business, the company broadened its range and buffered itself against bad years in its core
activity.

For most of the Italian district companies, producing in China is still
a very distant prospect. But there were a few among those we interviewed

who were pursuing this route. Even in these cases, production in China has been organized as a complement rather than as a flat-out replacement for activity in Italy. One such initiative, in fact, resulted in a near-disaster. A company I will call Seta Brothers had been buying raw silk yarn from the Chinese, weaving it into greige (plain) fabric in Italy, and selling the cloth to Italian companies that finished and printed the silk.[15] At the end of the eighties, the company discovered that their Chinese supplier (a state silk company with a virtual monopoly on the raw material) had also started making greige fabric and was selling it directly to Seta Brothers' customers in Italy. When Seta Brothers' senior executive protested to his Chinese supplier, he was sharply rebuked: "Don't tell us what to sell. Just be glad we're still willing to sell you the yarn." The executive told us he realized immediately that his greige silk business was finished. He decided the only solution was to move farther up the value chain by weaving silk with other fibers—a very difficult and delicate process—and into dyeing and printing. This move to more sophisticated complex products made in Italy turned into a great commercial success for the company.

Walter Mieli Spa is a company that now has operations both in Italy and in China. Founded in 1935, the company specializes in making silk yarn. It employs about 100 people in Milan, Como, and Brescia, Italy, and 320 at Jiaxing Idea, a joint-venture factory in Zhejiang, China. Having seen a number of its Italian competitors go out of business, Walter Mieli faces fierce competition in China from domestic Chinese producers of silk thread. Walter Mieli's advantage is technology that allows them to make higher-quality yarns that can be woven in China on jet looms originally intended to work with cotton or polyester. The hope is to eventually launch a brand and build a publicly held business in the Chinese market. The Zhejiang plant represents a $15 million investment. The Web site explains they intend to use the trademark "Jiaxilk" in the future when they are satisfied that the quality level is up to their expectations. They admit it has not yet gotten there, but they continue to try.

The Proximity Advantage

Why are textiles and apparel still doing rather well in Italy? It is not that wages are lower there than in the United States or in the rest of Europe. In fact, in 2000, hourly wages in the textile industry were $14.20 in the United States and $14.70 in Italy.[16] And given the decline of the U.S. dollar relative to the euro over the past five years, this gap has widened. The explanation for the stickiness is that the strategies of the Italian district businesses are built on proximity to valuable and quite immobile assets. It is only by remaining in Italy that companies can maintain close and continuous access to local suppliers with highly specialized capabilities; to brand-name firms like Giorgio Armani, Gucci, and Prada whose designers frequently visit the manufacturers and work with them in developing new products; and to customers whose taste for fashion and quality makes them willing to pay more for clothes than Americans will. Italian consumer preferences are an important reason why Italians succeed in product lines where an American business like L. W. Packard, which I introduced in Chapter 1, has failed.

By keeping production in Italy, firms are sticking to valuable assets like design, brands, and skills. They are also staying close to a retail distribution system that sets great stock by selling goods of Italian and, more generally, European provenance. A survey carried out in 2002 found that 43 percent of the clothing sold by Italian retailers had been produced in Europe, in contrast to 18 percent of the clothes sold in Britain, 8 percent in Germany, and 21 percent in France.[17] (Most of the rest was made in Central Eastern Europe, Asia, Turkey, or North Africa.) The apparel sold under Italian brands was also much more likely to have been made in Europe than that proposed by British or French or German labels. These numbers are certainly rough approximations, since there's no systematic monitoring of country-of-origin labels and clothing marketed as "Made in

Italy" undoubtedly contains some offshored components. Even allowing for inflation of the facts, though, Italian retailers and brands (and presumably Italian consumers) still stand out for their preferences for home-made goods. This factor, too, acts as a magnet to attach the high end of domestic production.

The desire to stick close to valuable resources also explains the choices of many of the German textile and apparel companies we visited. Like the United States, Germany has lost many jobs in this industry as firms have moved production abroad to lower-cost sites in Central Eastern Europe and Asia. But German managers regard their skilled workers as hard-to-replace resources. Of the managers in the textile and garment business we interviewed, only 6 percent of the Americans mentioned skills as a reason for keeping some or all of production at home, while 52 percent of the Germans (and 50 percent of the Italians) raised this point. In order to use these talents, German industry tends to keep jobs that require technical education and experience at home—for example, employees in logistics or those who develop new products and prototypes, or who work with expensive materials, or who deal face-to-face with customers.

Boos Textile Elastics in Wupperthal, Germany, makes elastics and elastic knitwear for lingerie, medical, and industrial uses.[18] The fabric is shipped from Germany by air to customers in Asia, sewn, and sold in the United States and European markets. Bernd-Michael Kader, the fourth generation in his family to run this firm of 250 workers, figures he'll have to open a plant somewhere in Asia eventually, after the impact of the 2005 end of quotas shows whether China or Vietnam or Sri Lanka or Thailand would be the best choice. But, he told us, his German skilled workers are his greatest asset. A producer in China can buy the same machines, but without Boos workers, can't match their quality. Locating production in Asia would cost Boos three times as much for technicians—taking home leave, airfares, and boarding school fees into account. Even if Kader opens an Asian production site, he plans to expand medical and technical textile production in his two German plants. He thinks that increasing production on those lines will offset the relocation of lingerie fabric, and he hopes not to have to lay off workers.

Although the total numbers in the German textile and apparel industry are falling, the firms we met with are not transferring all their activities abroad and are keeping skilled (and better-paid) jobs at home. As a result, even while the sector shrinks, the jobs remaining are increasingly higher-paid. In contrast, in the United States, as employment declines, the percentage of skilled white-collar workers in the apparel industry has risen only from 16 percent in 1993 to 23 percent in 2002; in textiles, it is about the same as in the past: less than 20 percent.[19]

Made All Over

Standing back from the interviews that we carried out in Germany, Japan, Britain, France, Italy, and the United States, we see the great transformation of the past twenty years. Where even two decades ago most international exchanges took place between societies through exports and imports across borders, today national productive structures are tightly connected with those abroad, in developing economies as well as in other advanced nations. The goods of everyday life ought truthfully to be labeled "Made All Over." The New Balance sneaker, the Anagram balloon, the Dell computer, the bra with Boos elastic lace, the Apple iPod—each contains parts made in multiple locations around the world. Each reflects a strategy that works by combining the strengths of very diverse societies, economies, and human beings into a single final product.

Our team wondered at the outset of our study whether these changes would mean a convergence toward a uniformity of practice and strategy across countries. Wouldn't the same pressures and the same competitors force everyone to run the same race? Yet however closely in we focused our lens on the same industries, the same sectors, and the same products, we saw that companies were building radically different structures. In part we could explain this by the building materials at hand. The resources created in different national capitalist economies do provide diverse assets—for example, strong institutions for on-the-job training in Germany and Japan; legal traditions that facilitate market-based contracting in the United States and Britain; university-industry linkages that speed transfers from basic research to start-ups in the United States. These factors have all shaped the capabilities that are now incorporated into the strategies with which companies confront the new global challenges. But simply having a legacy to draw from does not guarantee success. In the next and final chapters of the book, I'll discuss what it takes to use these dynamic legacies for today's purposes.

PART SIX

How to Succeed in the Global Economy

CHAPTER 11

Lessons from the Field

Many Models of Success, No Silver Bullets

The MIT team has not unearthed any crystal balls that allow us to see farther than anyone else into the future of the global economy. But we have studied 500 firms under intense pressure from competitors around the world and learned a lot about how companies operate in a time of great uncertainty. We saw the best of them cultivate, extend, and exploit capabilities they had developed based on their legacies — fending off competition that would have destroyed the value of their assets and seizing new ground before challengers could get a foothold. The businesses we studied included firms in slow-tech industries like textile and apparel, where technologies and processes evolve incrementally, and fast-tech industries like electronics, where disruptive innovations regularly but unpredictably wipe out the advantages of yesterday's front-runner. Yet in all of them we were struck by the diversity of the strategies and capabilities that companies employed to build profitable and innovative businesses.

There were winners (and losers) in every sector in every country, but in none of them did a single best model emerge. Rather, we found a variety of successful models that built on different resources—those that were already part of a company's repertoire, as well as those that could be acquired through suppliers and partners. In the U.S. electronic components and telecom equipment industry, for example, there are companies like Cisco (whose 2004 profit/revenue ratio was 20 percent) that outsource all their manufacturing, and others like Intel (whose 2004 profit/revenue ratio was 22 percent) that do it mostly under their own roof. Even for those making the same products, there is no single formula: Dell's personal computers are the heart of a company that is growing by $6 billion to $7 billion a year, while IBM, once the world leader in personal computing, decided that PCs have become a commodity business with low margins and in 2004 sold off its personal computer division after years of losses. As I discussed in Part Four, IBM chose to focus on its services businesses and on the fast-tech segment of electronics, where its innovative capabilities give it an edge.[1]

In the apparel industry, where virtually all large U.S. retailers and brand-name firms outsource and offshore their production, we were surprised to learn that the fastest-growing European clothing retailer is Zara, which, though it makes more than half its garments at home in Spain, *tripled* its net profits over a period (1999–2004) that was extremely difficult for textile and clothing manufacturers in all high-wage countries. We thought it was impossible to make T-shirts in the United States until we interviewed American Apparel in Los Angeles. In an industry where most manufacturing takes place in low-wage countries like Bangladesh, American Apparel has doubled its workforce in the year after our 2004 meeting with them. We see the viability of these different ways of building successful companies in the "same" industries as evidence that no one strategy rules in any of these sectors, even when we examine the industry, product by product, in very fine-grained detail. Diversity is continuously re-created.

The technological and organizational changes of the past fifteen years that made modular production possible across a wide range of industries have contributed to this multiplication of successful models. It's a lot easier for a company to get started if it does not have to build a fully integrated operation but can focus instead on its own particular strong point—whether in product definition or design or distribution or sales—and buy the other services. A business nowadays can purchase from other companies the goods and services it might once have had to produce itself (or, depending on the case, it can sell to others what they might previously have made for themselves). Because Apple was able to build an iPod using components already being made by many other companies and assemble it using contract manufacturers, it could bring its digital music player to market very rapidly.

Fragmentation of the value chain has not only increased the opportunities for innovation by established companies like Apple. It has also opened points of access into the economy for newcomers. The story I relate in Chapter 1 about SMaL—a new digital camera firm that grew out of ideas dreamed up by MIT engineers, who outsourced chip fabrication to Taiwan and detailed technical design to Hong Kong, then sold its "kits" to brand-name companies that assembled the cameras in China—illustrates a process by which thousands of start-ups make their way into the world today.

Modularity, which plays so large a role in the way that globalization is transforming production, opens more opportunities for the birth of new activities. But through the same mechanisms, it also creates more competition at each point along the value chain. Fragmentation into networks means that for each function or mix of functions that a company keeps in-house, it now faces rivals who are concentrating their resources on doing that same thing better than anyone else. It follows that each activity that remains in-house has to be tested against the performance of best-in-class competitors from around the world. Given that innovation rapidly and unpredictably changes products and processes, there is certainly a case to be made for most American firms to keep a wider range of functions in-house than they do now, so that they can swiftly advance in new areas. We have seen the powerful competitive advantages of more integrated companies, like Samsung, Zara, and Sharp, at work in the speed with which these businesses can identify and respond to new opportunities.

But there are dangers in clinging to old models. When we found companies relying on an old faith in the synergies of integration instead of questioning—activity by activity, product by product, process by process—what they do best and what suppliers at home or abroad could do better, we knew we were seeing companies in trouble. Sony in 2005 is one such example. The company has been betting that blockbuster innovations like the Cell chip can save the Sony model and catapult the company back onto a winning streak. Even if this happens, we think the model would work better if it challenged the entrenched belief that all its components play best together when they are all "Made in Sony" parts. Someone in Sony should be asking whether Sony digital music players should play more than just Sony music. Someone should be asking if a Taiwanese ODM might be able to make the high-end Vaios at lower cost, with or without the black lacquer finishes that today can be produced only in Japan. Today, even integrated companies like Sony that choose to operate across a wide range of functions need to challenge which ones should stay in-house and which they should buy from others.

Select on Unique Capabilities, Not Industries

Because companies in the same industries are succeeding with vastly *different* combinations of focus and capabilities, we were often hard put to decide if we were looking at the "same" business. Functions we would once have labeled as manufacturing are now fused with activities we think of as services. The phone companies, for example, increasingly bundle phone service together with the purchase of a cell phone. The set may have the mobile operator's name on it, but in fact it has been designed and manufactured by an ODM or a lead firm like Sharp or Motorola—or maybe Bird or TCL, new Chinese brands. Vodafone, the world's biggest mobile operator, now sells phones specially made for it by Sharp. It raises this question: Is Vodafone competing in the same business as Nokia—which makes most phones in-house and sells them under its own brand?[2] Or take the eyeglass industry. Are eyeglass producers in Italy who sell frames with designer labels in the same business as the no-brand frame maker from Hong Kong? Is Zoff, the Japanese eyeglass retailer that outsources frames to China and lenses to Korea? Dell, Sony, IBM, Hewlett-Packard, Liz Claiborne, Benetton, Zara, Kellwood, and Ralph Lauren are all combining different competencies on different points of the value chain. However we label the industries that include these companies—along with the hundreds of lesser-known firms we looked at—it is clear that successful companies can be built at virtually every point along the value chain.

No Sunset Industries

It's not industry or sector that's important, it's a firm's *capabilities*. In other words, there are no "sunset" industries condemned to disappear in high-wage economies, although there are certainly sunset and condemned strategies, among them building a business on the advantages to be gained by cheap labor. The number of jobs and firms in slow-tech, labor-intensive production of traded goods and services in rich countries will continue to fall—because of technological advances that make it possible to produce more goods with fewer workers, and because of competition from tough and seasoned foreign competitors. While the numbers of workers employed in slow-tech, labor-intensive industries is going down in high-wage countries, the speed at which they are dropping varies greatly from country to country. This matters for one reason—because these workers usually do not find jobs at equivalent wages and benefits when they are laid off.

In Italy, for example, employment in textile and apparel has fallen only gradually—6.5 percent between 2001 and 2003, compared with the drop of 33 percent in apparel employment in the United States in the same years. Even for silk products, where the Italians face fierce competition from China, employment has held up fairly well. The Como silk industry workforce, for example, has gone down 12.5 percent over the past five years, but firms in this region are keeping local operations even as they use offshoring in China to expand their businesses.[3] As I described in Parts Four and Five, the Italians do well not because of protection or low costs, but because of the strategies that weave new and valuable properties into their goods. Though Italy these days also imports more textiles and clothing than in the past, the increases have come mainly in low-end goods like cotton underwear. Domestic firms have already moved up and away from making such products.[4]

Countries like China and India are certain to increase their shares of the clothing market in advanced countries. But this does not mean that there's no room for domestic firms to grow if they develop highly valued products and services—as Lucky Jeans and Juicy Couture do in Los Angeles. Even though the apparel industry is shrinking in the United States, the firms that remain can be very profitable. In the Fortune 500 list of the most profitable industries, apparel ranked in the top ten both for return on assets and return on shareholders' equity over the past ten years (1994–2004) and above the Fortune 500 median on return on revenues over the same decade.[5] "Go figure," *Fortune* concludes in puzzlement. I think it's a mystery only if you believe the economy is divided into sunrise and sunset sectors.

Even in sectors like textile and apparel, there are companies that seize upon distinctive strengths to move themselves out of the reach of the bottom-feeding competitor. Such firms can offer good jobs to their workers. (By "good jobs" I have in mind an undemanding standard: a job paying above the minimum wage and providing health insurance and benefits. Our society can do a lot better than this—but we are still very far from achieving any such minimal level.) Companies like Anagram, the Minnesota metallic balloon company; American Apparel, the Los Angeles T-shirt manufacturer; Solstiss, the French lace weaver; Italian eyeglass makers; Kenwood, the Japanese consumer electronics firm — to mention only a few of those I have presented in the book — do offer such good jobs. If they prosper despite competition from foreign companies with very low-paid workers, it is because they bundle into the products they sell other desirable features, like speed, fashion, uniqueness, and image. These features are hard to imitate, and so the companies can keep the competition at bay at least for a while. No advantage lasts forever, and these companies will have to continue to develop new capabilities if they are to remain ahead of competitors from China and India and Vietnam who are also honing resources beyond simple low-wage labor.

Beyond survival and resilience, there are opportunities for building very profitable businesses in these supposedly sunset sectors. One of the outstanding successes in Italian industry in the past few years is Geox, a shoe company founded in 1995 in Montebelluna (Treviso Province), a region traditionally strong in shoes and sportswear.[6] Geox started with ten people and today employs 5,000 people worldwide. It entered the Italian stock exchange in December 2004 and is now valued at $1.5 billion. Its return on equity (ROE) in 2003 was calculated at 45 percent. It has become the world's fourth-largest shoe brand, and sold 9 million pairs of shoes in 2004. Geox has opened 233 of its own stores in Europe and the United States, and about 46 percent of its sales are outside Italy.

How was it possible to create a dynamic new business in a sector dominated by low-cost producers in countries like China, Vietnam, and Indonesia? Geox's founder, Dr. Mario Moretti Polegato, had his inspiration one hot day while walking around in Reno, Nevada. His feet were burning and painful, and Polegato cut holes in the soles of his shoes to vent the trapped perspiration. He struck on the idea of making a shoe sole with a membrane that would allow moisture to flow out in one direction but prevent water from entering. Geox now holds thirty patents on this basic concept, and so far competitors have not caught up. Geox ads for "the shoe that breathes" show perspiration pouring out of the soles like vapor out of a steam iron. Polegato sees the company's mission as tackling the mysteries of miserable, sweaty, smelly feet. He told us: "Millions of people around the world are wearing rubber-soled shoes—80 percent of humanity! And all of them are suffering from their shoes!" Along with the shoes, Geox stores sell clothing that's also geared to keeping its wearer cool and dry.

Without the years of experience in shoemaking, design expertise, and skilled labor that Polegato found in Montebelluna, Geox would never have gotten off the ground. But once the company started to grow, it rapidly discovered that there were not enough workers in the region, since there is very little unemployment in the district. Today, while Geox research and development of the shoes, design, logistics, and management all take place in Italy, manufacturing is located outside the country. Polegato calls this "intelligent offshoring": All the high-skilled parts stay home; the rest is done in low-wage labor markets.[7] By combining new technology with a legacy of craftsmanship, design, and networked production from the shoe district of Montebelluna, Geox has created a stylish product with original technical features and a very profitable business. At the time of Geox's founding, it would have been hard to imagine a less promising sector for a new venture in an advanced economy like Italy's than a footwear company. Today, while most of the "cutting-edge" dotcoms founded in more or less the same period have disappeared, Geox continues to soar.

Geox shows the strengths of a strategy that builds on new combinations of legacy resources. The legacy in Geox's case was the region—with its highly developed skills in shoemaking. Like longer-established Italian firms in the footwear industry, Geox makes shoes that are attractive and well-crafted. By joining to these qualities technical innovations to the sole and organizational innovations that networked production in the Montebelluna district to manufacturing in Romania and China, Geox created a wholly new shoe business. By continuing to invest in technology, Geox has thus far kept out of the reach of the old players in the industry.

But this is only one example of the kind of legacy a company can build upon. For Dell, the core legacy strengths come from its experience in learning how to track and respond to customers' preferences over the Internet and its ability to coordinate seamless and rapid production involving a myriad of independent suppliers. Dell first developed these skills for making personal computers; now it is building on this knowledge to extend beyond the PC to printers, MP3 music players, monitors, and more. Successes like Dell and Geox have little relation to the inherent characteristics of the industries in which they find themselves—if anything, the industry in either case is unpromising—and everything to do with building unique capabilities that widen the distance between the company and its nearest competitors.

Cheap Labor Is Not a Winning Strategy

Several conclusions follow. First, there are possibilities in all sectors, including traditional or slow-tech ones, for innovative and dynamic enterprises. In fact, the book draws many of its cases from the textile and apparel industries, because we sought to put to the test the common presumption that these sectors are doomed in advanced countries. This bias, I argued at the beginning of the book, comes from a macro approach to understanding the international economy. According to standard trade theories, countries achieve comparative advantages by exploiting the most abundant factors present in their society—so by this reasoning, China and India have an advantage in making and selling goods and services that incorporate high proportions of labor, and the United States, Europe, and Japan have an advantage in making and selling goods and services that require a lot of capital. In fact, most trade takes place between countries with more or less the same factor endowments, like the United States and the European Union, so these theories have trouble explaining even aggregate trade flows in the real world. Nonetheless, what seems intuitively plausible about them is the idea that industries that use lots of unskilled or semi-skilled labor should locate in countries with low-wage workers.

In theory, it might work that way. But as we have observed at the shop-floor level in plants in both advanced and developing countries, it does not. It's true that Chinese factory wages are a fraction of U.S. average hourly compensation for factory workers, and the earnings of Indian software engineers are low compared with those of American counterparts.[8] But even in China and India, with their enormous populations, the wages of experienced technicians and managers are rising rapidly. The CEO of a very successful Hong Kong business with tens of thousands of workers in factories in China explained it to us this way: "If you pay peanuts, you get monkeys." She pays far above the average wages in China in order to be able to hire people with the right kind of education, motivation, and willingness to stay with the company. We heard this point—though in less blunt terms—in many other interviews in Taiwan and China.

A chart of comparative wage rates of workers in countries around the world cannot tell you how much you can lower your costs by moving a factory to one of these places. Absolute labor costs matter, but other factors in the equation—political risk, intellectual-property-loss risk, the price of materials and equipment, transportation, interest rates, the cost of energy, taxes, licenses—are far more important than we ordinarily reckon, as companies like Anagram told us. When companies consider the true landed costs of goods that are coming from offshore production, and not just the manufacturing costs abroad, they find that the advantage over at-home production is greatly reduced. A recent McKinsey set of case studies of California businesses found that once these variables were taken into account, and when the onshore plants were operating efficiently, the high-tech firm would save 0.6 percent by offshoring, the plastics firm would save 6 percent, and the apparel firm would save 13 percent.[9] These savings are so small that gains from satisfying customers with faster lead times of production can often outweigh them.

Even looking narrowly at labor costs, what matters are unit labor costs—how much labor is needed to produce a given value of production. And as the example in Chapter 6 of the higher cost of Emilia

Maglia's fine white wool sleeves knitted in its Romanian plant illustrates, unit labor costs are often higher in less-developed countries. In recently established factories, with inexperienced employees using machinery that they barely know how to set up, maintain, or repair, valuable imported materials are wasted. Time is lost as workers struggle to arrive at work at the same hour traveling on desperately overstressed public transportation. When the workers live in dormitories, as they do around most of the factories in southern China, they tend to arrive on time. But these are populations destined to spend very few years in the factory before heading back to their own hometowns and leaving the managers with the task of bringing another cohort of workers up to standard. Almost every senior executive in a company with operations in China described these difficulties to us in the interviews. This task is all the more daunting since the local Chinese managers are themselves on the move between companies quite frequently.

Even when such low-wage factories are stabilized and when the political difficulties in the environment (arbitrary application of regulations, corruption, grasping local "partners") are dealt with, the other costs in the total chain of production far outweigh labor—the cost of imported materials and equipment, taxes, transportation, insurance, interest rates, risks to intellectual property, and so forth, as I have detailed in Chapter 6. This is why a company like Minnesota's Anagram keeps its main metallic balloon plant at home, even as it leverages some components (decorative trim from China) and services (the attaching of trim to the balloon in Mexico) from low-cost offshore facilities. A business that needs to employ a large semiskilled workforce will probably do better in a low-wage country, all other things being equal—but they very rarely are. The enormous accomplishment of successful foreign investors' factories (and of a limited number of domestic industries) in regions of China like Guangdong is their control over the negative drag weight of "all other things," which makes it possible to realize the advantages of low-cost labor.

Don't Build a Competitor

Among the toughest judgment calls a company faces today is deciding how much to outsource and how deeply to collaborate with its suppliers. Each time they transfer technologies and skills to a partner, they risk creating a new competitor. In several cases we analyzed, contractors did develop their own brands (see the discussion of Acer, Giant Bicycle, and Fang Brothers in Chapter 8), and this led to serious conflicts and breakups with the lead firms. Contract manufacturers we interviewed said that even a hint that they might be developing their own brand would be ruinous to their current relationships with lead firms. Though every senior manager in the OEMs and ODMs we interviewed professed eternal commitment to a creed of never competing with customers, this division of labor seems to us to be a rapidly changing game.

On one side, lead firms need to share information with their suppliers, customers, and alliances in order to support collaboration across corporate boundaries. This is a frequent refrain in recent business-strategy literature. John Hagel III and John Seely Brown, leading management experts, emphasize that in a world of fragmented production where firms keep in-house only their best-in-class activities and outsource the rest, it's a "strategic imperative" for companies to innovate and grow by mobilizing and enhancing the capabilities of the companies with which they partner.[10] IBM, which leads all other companies in patenting (3,248 registered in the U.S. Patent Office in 2004), recently declared a major shift toward sharing technology.[11] It announced in January 2005 that it would start by making 500 patents, mostly for software, available for use without charge, and would continue to add to this pool. The idea is to promote information exchange by developing open technical standards. In this way, others would be encouraged to build on and with IBM technology. John E. Kelly, IBM senior vice president in charge of the initiative, emphasized that patents would still be an important part of IBM's business. "The layer of technology that is open is going to steadily increase," he said, "but in going through this transition we're not going to be crazy. This is like disarmament. You're not going to give away all your missiles as a first step." In dealing with services, though, Kelly pointed out, "When you are co-inventing with a customer, you have to take a lighter hand on intellectual property. It's very different from our proprietary tradition of 'it's ours and we'll license it.'"

On the downside of the balance from the advantages of sharing are deep concerns companies have about dependence and about competition. As lead firms shift more development and design functions to ODMs, it's likely that the technologies the lead firms have to share in order to help their suppliers advance are technologies the contract manufacturers will reuse in products they provide to other brand-name businesses. In assisting your supplier to upgrade his capabilities, you are also helping him to develop skills that will be available to your competitors. Sharp, for example, found that because its suppliers also work for Taiwanese flat-panel-display companies, its newest technologies were rapidly passing to the competition. Now it's reported that Sharp tries to repair machinery in-house to keep their suppliers from learning about malfunctions in equipment that suppliers may have sold to other manufacturers.[12]

Another risk is that the products that lead firms get from their contract manufacturers are bound to show a growing sameness with products the contractors are making for others—thus eroding the brand name's competitive edge in yet another way. Finally, as a lead firm grows more dependent on the OEM and the ODM suppliers, it will usually result in a reduction in the numbers and in the range of experience of the engineering staff back home. I heard from Joe Wrinn, vice president for manufacturing at Teradyne, a Boston-based firm that specializes in making test equipment for semiconductor manufacturing as well as for electronics, automotive, and network systems companies, why it's important for the company's future innovative capabilities to keep hiring entry-level engineers and not to outsource all these jobs, even if salaries might be lower abroad.

We Grow Our Own

JOE WRINN, VICE PRESIDENT FOR MANUFACTURING AT TERADYNE, A BOSTON-BASED COMPANY THAT MAKES TEST EQUIPMENT FOR SEMICONDUCTOR MANUFACTURING

"The way we educate systems architects is by training engineers from the entry level up with specialized knowledge of the company and the experience they need to understand how the whole system interrelates, what its quirks are, how all the pieces play together. If we don't have the entry-level jobs here in the U.S., we're not going to have the higher-level jobs, either. We hire engineers with bachelor's or master's degrees in electrical engineering or computer science from schools like MIT, Cornell, Stanford, and Cal Tech. At school they've studied theory—and here they learn by apprenticeship. A person starts by creating one piece of, say, an operating system for controlling the hardware in a tester. The entry-level engineer might work on the user interface, or on the digital signal processing part of the system.

"They have to learn to make it faster, better, cheaper, more differentiated, better for the customer, and the only way to learn is by starting with a part of the system and over time doing more and more complex jobs under the mentorship of the system architects. Even when we hire midcareer engineers, they take three or four years to learn the system.

"If someone's good, we give them experience all across the company. They'll do a rotation in applications—so they get experience working with customers and learn how they work with the system. Then we bring them back into design engineering. About seven years after they join us, there's a fork in the road, and some go on to architectural work. We have about twelve to fifteen systems architects. The others go on to a 'people' track where they manage the system architects and work on getting the vision implemented, or on hiring and firing, figuring out what gets outsourced, and so forth."

The Facts: Teradyne was founded in 1960 by Alex d'Arbeloff and Nick DeWolfe, two MIT classmates. Their first workshop was one floor up from Joe & Nemo's hot dog stand in downtown Boston. In 2004, Teradyne had $1.79 billion sales; its ratio of net income to net sales was 9.2 percent. It had 6,100 employees worldwide.

What's at stake in growing the next generation of system architects is the very future of the company. When the window of opportunity for big advances in technology and products opens up, it's unlikely that lead firms will be able to see the change coming and move fast enough to exploit these possibilities unless they have maintained a broad range of capabilities in their own workforce. Unless they do, it will not only be too late to hire these specialists; it may also be impossible to do so, since the necessary skills are so tightly connected to knowledge of the firm's internal processes and experiences that they cannot be codified or picked up on the quick.

Beyond the dangers of dependence, there's the risk that suppliers will move to become full-fledged competitors. It was in the interviews with Japanese senior executives that we heard this concern voiced most often. The Japanese managers told us that joint ventures with Koreans and Taiwanese in the 1990s in fields like LCD production had allowed their partners to advance to the frontiers of knowledge and industry more rapidly than they ever would have been capable without Japanese transfers of technologies and know-how. The Japanese believe these technology-sharing decisions have had disastrous consequences, as one after another of the Korean and Taiwanese firms have emerged as competitors in key areas. (The reason why the Japanese had entered into these arrangements was that in the 1990s, big Japanese companies were strapped for capital. New fabs were just too heavy an investment to contemplate alone. The

Japanese are still making alliances for these big projects—but with other Japanese companies.) In the team's most recent interviews in Japan, managers told us they believe that being able to "black-box" intellectual property in the work they do with contract manufacturers is critical. By "black-box" they mean incorporate their new technologies in products and processes in ways that make it impossible for suppliers and competitors to reverse-engineer the technology and to decipher the proprietary secrets embedded in it. When they think they cannot "black-box" a technology, they do not outsource.

As we weighed the benefits gained from sharing technologies against the risks of giving away the store, we saw some clear lessons emerge from our research. Each company needs to adapt these lessons to fit its own circumstances, but still, two points seem to apply across the board. First, the pace of change in advanced technologies is so rapid, the learning capacities of firms around the world so great, and the speed with which ideas circulate so accelerated that no company can count on patents or other forms of legal protection of proprietary knowledge as the sole guarantors of its competitive edge. At best, secrets provide a temporary window of opportunity. The only lasting sources of advantage are the strengths that allow a company to detect new opportunities and develop its capabilities in a constant forward march toward novel products and processes. The space between a company and its rivals that allows it to command premium prices depends ultimately on this forward movement and not on defensive blocking.

Second, maintaining this space and the capabilities for differentiation requires companies to invest in a kind of "excess capacity" that will allow them to advance rapidly in the future in areas that today are on the margins of the firms' current operations.[13] There are many forms of this necessary excess capacity: doing more research than might be needed for evolving today's products along their current trajectory; keeping more engineers and scientists working in functions that have been outsourced (or that might one day be outsourced); paying more managerial attention to the fringes of the business than might be warranted by the amount of revenue that currently flows from these activities; building more skills in the workforce than are fully utilized at present. There is a double rationale for what might appear to be wasteful capacity-building. It gives the company radar to detect early signals of promising new developments close enough to the company's core activities to be real possibilities for future expansion; and it positions the company to move quickly into these areas before competitors have established themselves on the terrain. A company like Teradyne cannot really predict how many system architects it is going to need seven years from now or what they are going to be doing, but it does understand that if it does not employ entry-level engineers today—if it outsources all these jobs—it will not be possible to generate these talents instantly or hire them in the market when the need for the higher-level skills does become a sure thing.

Meeting the China Challenge

While no sector is condemned in advanced economies, no activities—no matter how cutting-edge—belong to us for keeps. India and China and other less-developed countries have vast reserves of individuals as intelligent, hardworking, and motivated as we are. Centers of excellence are rapidly emerging at world-class institutions like Tsinghua, Peking, and Zhejiang Universities in China and the Indian Institutes of Technology in Kanpur, Chennai, and Mombai. Public and private research laboratories attract outstanding talents, and governments support them generously.[14] When we visited the classrooms and laboratories in these universities, we could see that an institution like MIT still has a substantial edge, if only because of the material and human resources accumulated over the centuries from private and public funding. But we smelled the excitement in the air, we recognized good equipment in the laboratories, we saw interdisciplinary groups at work, and we knew we were in familiar territory. We are entering a time in which the graduates of a few top universities from China and India now meet their counterparts from the West as equals.

These examples are reason enough for developing countries to believe that they will not be stuck forever on the bottom rungs of the international economy. They are not, however, evidence for the kind of case that Thomas Friedman made in his recent bestseller, *The World Is Flat: A Brief History of the Twenty-first Century*, when he claimed that talented individuals from all over the world are now competing on a level playing field. His arguments join a loud chorus of public alarm about rising numbers of engineers in low-wage countries and the technological upgrading of companies abroad. Even if the policies that Friedman and others advocate—improvements in education, higher levels of investment in research—are good ideas in and of themselves, the rationale of clear and present national danger from competitors all over a "flat earth" is far off the mark. In most of the world, including Africa, Latin America, and large swaths of the Middle East and Asia, there are no clusters of capabilities or opportunities or educational institutions or companies that come close to resembling the Bangalores and Shanghais that are always presented as examples in articles about the "China menace" or the "India threat" to the American standard of living. In fact, Bangalore and Shanghai are islands playing catch-up, and the societies of which they are a part remain very poor and underdeveloped.

Even in hot spots like Bangalore and Shanghai, there is still a long road ahead for domestic businesses before they will arrive at the performance of companies from advanced industrial countries. The reason is not absence of intelligence and talent. It's that innovation and productivity growth are not a story of individual prowess alone, but of individuals combining their talents with societal capital—the stock of infrastructure in a society, its financial institutions, its legal system, its business practices, its bureaucracy, its research institutions, and its public culture. Societal capital is very difficult to transform rapidly. It's a remarkable achievement that certain areas in the developing world are coming to look more like the advanced industrial countries, but it's far from the same landscape. The world is still round, and the question is how to make the best of it. For companies this means developing strategies that exploit the resources they find in their own home societies and abroad. This means, in the first instance, finding businesses elsewhere that can do what you do at lesser cost. But more important, the best companies find capabilities that are different from those that their own home-based innovation systems generate; for example, a company like 3Com located activities in Israel to capture Israeli skills in local area network switches and in optical networks.

Companies can build on and enhance capabilities at home while also using "intelligent outsourcing"—in the words of Geox president Polegato—to access the growing strength of firms abroad in countries like China. Not all these combinations will be win-win, and for some American companies and workers they clearly will be flat-out losses. But I have provided examples throughout this book of U.S., Japanese, and European company strategies that build at home, even as they also use the new capacities of firms in the developing world. Beyond the company, for a country like the United States, it means addressing the real threats—many of them of our own making—to sustaining the strengths we derive from an innovative economy and an open society.

The leap of China and India into high-tech areas has been sudden and unexpected. Poor countries with large populations and low levels of technological advancement seem to have such a powerful incentive to concentrate on developing low-tech, labor-intensive activities that it has been hard to grasp that they might also be successful on the frontiers of technology. The Chinese government's insistence on supporting national-champion firms with high-tech projects does look like an expensive and futile exercise in promoting image and prestige, as these state strategies have not yet created much of value. But despite the perverse effects of many of the government policies, today we are seeing companies making high-tech products that appear across a wide swath of industries in countries like China and India.

Our team started tracking Chinese high technology in 1996–1997, in the course of our research on the shift of Hong Kong industries into mainland China. The electrical engineers on our team, who are specialists in semiconductor design and fabrication, visited a number of state-owned semiconductor-fabrication plants near Shanghai and Beijing that were said to be trying to produce chips commercially. In a Hua Jing plant in Wuxi, engineers from U.S.-owned Lucent were working alongside the Chinese to transfer Lucent chipmaking technology. Lucent was involved because the government had told the company that if it wanted to sell telecommunications equipment in China, it would have to transfer advanced technology to a Chinese enterprise. In fact, the technology Lucent was transferring was already an old one. Moreover, the Chinese plant could not figure out what to do with the chips they ultimately were able to produce. The factories seemed hopeless and the high-tech plans of the Chinese government looked as if they were heading in the wrong direction. The state's "908" and "909" projects to develop high-tech industries in China emphasized DRAM (memory chip) technologies, but this was hardly a promising field. Making DRAM requires enormous capital investments, and the market was already dominated by the Koreans and the Japanese.

The reports from our colleagues were clear: The facilities they saw were not capable of producing chips at the levels of quality or with the yields that could possibly make viable businesses. The engineers guessed that working Chinese fabs were at least a decade off. They were right about the plants they saw, which have not taken off. But starting in 2001, there has been massive new investment in mainland China fabs like Semiconductor Manufacturing International Corporation (SMIC) and Grace from Taiwanese and other foreign investors. When the researchers returned in August 2002 and visited SMIC and Grace, they reported that these were near state-of-the-art fabs. By 2005, there were six others at this level operating in the Shanghai region and another two scheduled to open. Integrated-circuit design companies like IDT Newave and Vimicro are demonstrating China's absorptive and learning capabilities—if not yet major innovative achievements. The team concluded that China was moving along a much faster trajectory of technological catch-up than we had ever imagined at the outset of our work.

Today, nearly 85 percent of the value of Chinese high-tech exports still comes from foreign-owned companies, virtually all of which rely on some division of labor between R & D and design centers in Taiwan, Hong Kong, Japan, or some Western country, and manufacturing in China.[15] But the progression of Chinese domestic firms into high-tech industries is advancing across a broad front. Chinese domestic cell phone makers like Bird and TCL have emerged as major competitors to Nokia and Motorola in the Chinese market. Alliances with foreign partners are bringing Chinese companies into Western markets. Lenovo (a personal computer producer) bought IBM's personal computer division in December 2004; an alliance of TCL with Thomson, a French company, in 2003 created a global television manufacturer. Chinese companies are now trying to move into flat-screen displays and are using alliances with the Japanese (NEC), Koreans (Hynix), and Taiwanese to acquire the complex capabilities needed for these products.

Huawei Technologies, a telecommunications equipment maker, is one of China's biggest and fastest-growing domestic companies and one that American and European rivals watch with great apprehension.[16] In 2004, its sales in the Chinese domestic market were $3 billion and its international sales were $2.28 billion.[17] Huawei has 40 percent of the Chinese market in fixed-line switchers and about half the transmission equipment business.[18] It recruits hundreds of design engineers from all over China for its Shenzhen research-and-development center. Huawei is investing heavily in third-generation mobile phone services, where it will be up against foreign companies like Alcatel, Lucent, Nokia, Siemens, and Ericsson, which are also trying to capture the market in China for infrastructure and cell phone sets. It has started making inroads into foreign networking markets, and Huawei joint ventures with 3Com and with Siemens are bringing it into new product lines in which it competes with technology leaders like Cisco. A survey of telecom operators around the world rated Huawei eighth among wireline equipment makers (Cisco was first) and fourth for service.[19]

Alongside the giants that, like Huawei, have grown out of state-linked or state-owned enterprises, there are now new private high-tech start-ups that attract venture capital from Silicon Valley, Taiwan, Hong Kong, and Japan. Hangzhou, a pleasant city of 6.5 million people around a lake and parks, is about a two-hour train ride south of Shanghai. It is a hotbed of small and medium-sized technology companies. They recruit graduates from local Zhejiang University's top-ranking engineering departments. Many of these start-ups focus on Chinese localization of technologies created elsewhere, such as one we visited that specializes in products for banks and securities firms. Hangzhou Sunyard System Engineering Company, a software firm, started in 1996 as a breakaway from a Hong Kong company. Its initial funding ($121,000) came from fourteen share-holders (overseas and mainland Chinese) and from short-term bank loans. By 2002, Sunyard had been listed on the Shanghai stock exchange.

We were introduced to Hangzhou Sunyard by one of its directors, David Pan. Pan spent 1990–1997 in the United States studying engi-neering at Stanford University and working with companies in Silicon Valley. When high-tech companies began to emerge in China, Pan decided the time had come to return, and he began to commute between Silicon Valley, Beijing, and Hangzhou. Pan had once been a student at Tsinghua University in Beijing, the foremost technology university in China, and he remained in contact with his old teachers. One of his engi-neering professors, Dean Zhao Chunjun, now heads the powerful Tsinghua School of Management, which places its graduates in the most important posts in the state and industry, and Tsinghua networks under-pin many of the connections between the burgeoning world of high-tech companies and government.

As we listened in on the conversations among Dean Zhao, David Pan, and Hangzhou Sunyard's managers, we were reminded of the tight links in our own MIT world between university research and industry. A 1997 BankBoston study, *MIT: The Impact of Innovation*, had found that MIT discoveries and MIT graduates and faculty were at the origin of 4,000 companies, creating 1.1 million jobs and $232 billion sales rev-enues.[20] These jobs were 80 percent manufacturing (in contrast to the

16 percent of manufacturing jobs in the economy at large). While those of us on the IPC research team were inclined to take the local boosterism with a grain of salt, it did make us more alert to what we were seeing in China. The web of relationships among Silicon Valley, Tsinghua, and Hangzhou was hardly a familiar one, but it did seem to be weaving innovation, commercialization, and entrepreneurial talents together with big spillovers of benefits for the surrounding economy.

At the time of our visit in 2003, Sunyard had about 300 employees in the Hangzhou area and seven in Silicon Valley. Because Chinese checks do not have machine-scannable numbers (the "magic ink" line on U.S. checks), Sunyard saw an opportunity to integrate Chinese optical-character-recognition technology with document-scanning technology. It sells software and a handheld scanner to banks to verify checks. President Guo Huaqiang explained to us that this is a very large market in China, since banks verify checks for more than $12 (100 yuan), in contrast to U.S. banks, which usually verify only checks for more than $50,000. Sunyard also sells payment encryption and image-processing software, and it is a distributor for companies like IBM and Cisco. Most of Sunyard's customers are state-owned enterprises, like banks and securities firms, and relationships are key in getting this business. Sunyard's senior officers were men with long-standing connections in the world of the state bureaucracy. By 2005, Sunyard had widened its product range, and it now sells offshore outsourcing software services as well as its own software products and products it distributes for foreign companies. It has 900 employees, its 2004 revenues were $48.3 million, and its net profits were $7 million.

Exactly how innovative these Chinese high-technology companies are is debatable. There are some extravagant claims about cutting-edge research in China with bargain-basement salaries for top-notch engineers and scientists. On the other side of the debate, a recent study identified only three or four domestic Chinese high-tech successes.[21] Many foreign businesses assert that Chinese high-tech companies are succeeding mainly by reverse engineering and outright intellectual-property theft.

Cisco sued Huawei (2003) for infringing on its patents and copying its source code; the suit was withdrawn a year later when Huawei agreed to change parts of its router and software. A major Japanese electronics firm found Chinese engineers dismantling one of its exhibits at a trade fair to examine the components. Taiwan Semiconductor Manufacturing Company (TSMC) pursued its complaints in court about the role of former senior TSMC managers in using TSMC technology to set up fabs in mainland China, and won a $175 million settlement and cross-patenting rights from SMIC.[22] These are just the tip of an iceberg of charges of this kind, but even leaving such allegations aside, there's a question about whether *any* of the Chinese domestic firms are likely to emerge as real contenders on the frontiers of industry in the near future.

Douglas B. Fuller, one of the members of our team, spent three years tracking down electronics companies in China and assessing their innovative abilities.[23] He concluded that the large domestic companies were still highly dependent on foreign technologies and not likely to be seedbeds of innovation anytime soon. But he did find striking examples of original high-tech capabilities in "global hybrids," companies funded by foreign investment and run by returnees—overseas Chinese relocating to the mainland, or Chinese returning from studies abroad. The capital for these companies comes from abroad (mainly from Taiwan and Hong Kong), but operations are almost entirely carried out in China. For these companies, China is home base. The core strategy of the successful hybrids builds on the research, development, and production capabilities they can mobilize in China.

Fuller looked, for example, at integrated-circuit design houses that are trying to develop new products in China rather than dividing up their activities between "recognized centers of innovation, such as Silicon Valley, and recognized centers of sweat, such as China." These hybrid IC design houses are staking their future on using brilliant talents they find in China, rather than on combining low-end work in China with high-end functions abroad. Among the promising set of global hybrids, fabless design companies like Verisilicon, Newave, Comlent, and Vimicro stand out for the complexity of the problems their engineers are solving and their success in identifying promising market niches.

No Birthrights

However striking the advance today of American businesses in high-technology areas, they cannot assume that the lead in innovative activities is theirs to keep by birthright. The frontiers of knowledge are becoming ever more contested territories. For example, between 1988 and 2001, the number of patents filed in the United States by Asian companies from China, South Korea, Singapore, and Taiwan (and excluding Japan) rose from less than 2 percent to 12 percent.[24] In software, Israel and Ireland, very small economies that were still technological backwaters in the 1980s, have moved into the front ranks of patenting, exports, and new-company formation. The speed with which they covered this road demonstrates the extraordinary opportunities that globalization offers to newcomers.

Dan Breznitz, a member of our team, studied technological "leapfrogging" in information technology industries in Ireland, Israel, and Taiwan.[25] In all three cases, government played a vital role in enabling backward and poor economies to move to the technological frontier. The Irish government over the past twenty years focused on job creation and devised tax incentives, training programs, and land-use policies to attract multinational companies like Dell to locate plants in Ireland. Over the same two decades, Taiwan emphasized policies that favored domestic high-technology firms, and out of these policies came firms like Taiwan Semiconductor Manufacturing Company (TSMC). Israel concentrated on building science-based industries and encouraged linkages between its own nationals, leading technology firms abroad, and cutting-edge companies like Checkpoint and Aladdin (data-security software businesses). All three states provided tax benefits for foreign firms — a practice continued around the world today by governments seeking multinational investment. (Paul S. Otellini, president of Intel, recently stated that building a fab in the United States rather than abroad costs $1 billion more over the fab's first ten years—not because of capital costs or wages but because of what foreign countries offer in tax breaks.[26]) All three governments invested heavily in public education, research, and early-stage development, and were able to create hothouse environments in which previously dormant entrepreneurial talents came to life and flourished.

Without the changes in the international economy that allowed companies to access and combine resources from multiple locations around the world, however, it is unlikely that any of these government policies would have succeeded. By leveraging capital, expertise, partners, and customers outside their own small domestic markets, these newcomer firms in Ireland, Israel, and Taiwan were able to grow into new industries. Companies could plug themselves into the international economy as suppliers in open global networks. They did not have to reinvent the whole wheel; they could focus on particular niches, and by exploiting the new modularity, they could advance into high-technology areas rapidly. Their dynamism spilled over into the surrounding economy, so that while some of their partners were foreign-based businesses, others were local suppliers and customers. Of course, the state politics and policies that fuel technological advance in China and India today are quite different from those of the small economies that surged to the frontier in the nineties.[27] But the main mechanism at work in these giant economies is the same as that in Ireland, Taiwan, and Israel: Companies are ready to use all the opportunities now available for partnering with investors and innovators outside their own borders to develop their own capabilities.

These information technology companies are heading for terrain on which Americans are not accustomed to having much company. The distance between the front-runners and those catching up is still great, but there's nothing in the DNA of American entrepreneurs that assures their lead into the future. If U.S. firms wish to remain out on the far edge of the technological frontier, there is still much they can do with the assets in their own rich legacies to enhance their strengths. But to maintain the momentum of the great leaps forward in information technology that grew out of places like Bell Laboratories, Xerox PARC, and IBM Yorktown Heights—research centers that today have been reorganized to yield shorter-term results—Americans must look beyond the boundaries of individual companies. We need to consider how the innovative and dynamic capabilities of the American economy can be sustained in an environment in which businesses focus on their next quarterly earnings. This is the subject to which I turn next.

CHAPTER 12

Beyond the Company

Legacies: A Renewable Resource

When we started our journey through the hundreds of companies we would study over five years, we wanted to learn what it would take to make globalization work for our society. As products and services and capital stream in across borders, will dynamic and innovative industries continue to grow in our own country? When businesses are able to hire workers with more or less comparable skills at lower wages abroad, what will induce them to stay at home? We tried to puzzle out which new industries are emerging in the United States and whether they will all have to be fast-tech. What kinds of jobs will they create, and for whom? How, in an open international economy, can the United States build a good society with opportunities for all Americans to do well?

While national institutions and policies were not on our research agenda, we were certainly aware of the fact that companies need many public goods that they cannot generate by themselves. Rule of law, a competent system of public administration, and an environment free of violence, for example, are mostly taken for granted by American corporations operating in the United States. When they locate abroad in societies without these conditions, businesses have to resort to very imperfect substitutes, like private security guards, worker dormitories surrounded by high barbed-wire fences, and "special arrangements" with police, judges, and local mafias. There are many other macro-political and macro-economic factors, like law and order and the stability of the currency, that will affect individual companies that decide to locate abroad. The list of the background conditions that American institutions provide—if a complete one could be drawn up—would be very long indeed. They would be essentially the same foundations that in all advanced industrial democracies undergird a good terrain for business.

But beyond these foundations, national public policy and institutions shape specific company strengths in some countries and not others. Workforce skills, know-how about building supplier networks, close relationships with banks, and collaboration with others in the same industry are firm-level assets that have been created with a heavy input of public resources. The skills of the Japanese manufacturing workforce, for example, have been formed by public schools that excel in bringing almost every student to a high uniform standard and then by private companies, which invest heavily in continuous on-the-job training and retraining. National regulation of the banks, corporate governance codes, standard accounting rules, and competition legislation are all conditioning factors that shape distinct national systems of corporate finance. The resources in a company's legacy are in part, at least, a product of the nation in which that business emerged and first operated.

The historical differences in the ways capitalism developed in Japan, the United States, the United Kingdom, Italy, and Germany are perpetuated, because resources these systems generate get used in new combinations for new objectives. The skilled Japanese workers, whose talents are the product of institutions and policies designed to educate the workers of the postwar mass-manufacturing industries, today are resources that keep high-value-added production in Japan, even as many of the jobs that Japanese workers used to do move out to China. The availability of these highly trained workers (as well as the social stigma against firing them) is an incentive for firms to select one technology over another, one new stream of future products over another. Any firm's legacy is a fund of such assets and capabilities, and the business picks and chooses among them as it works out new directions. Through the legacy, past choices influence current strategies.

The legacies on which companies build are vulnerable, as they get worn down by age and the friction of poorness of fit. Institutions and norms created in one kind of world continue to operate in circumstances very different from their original situation, and often adaptation runs into resistance. But interests that emerged around old ways of doing business are not so easy to displace. Legacies are not like DNA that goes on indefinitely reproducing familial traits. While legacies have deep roots in the decisions of the past and in the thicket of institutions and interests that grows up around the pathways from these prior experiences, they need to be nurtured by new choices today. We should think about legacies not as destiny but as an ever-expanding reservoir of choices. Our actions in the present are required to keep it full and deep.

Is There a Role for Government?

Though we did not analyze institutions and policies at the national level, we saw their impact everywhere—embedded in the resources that companies have available to deploy. At the end of the project, then, when we debated among ourselves what it would take to preserve and renew the strengths of American firms, we had to think about national policies, too. Our conclusions are tentative—after all, we did not study the U.S. national government and its role in the economy. But we realize that to maintain the openness and dynamism of the American economy, there are decisions and investments to be made that go well beyond what any one company can do. We do not simply inherit the capabilities for an innovative economy rich in opportunities for employment and expansion. We have to re-create them through decisions about new investments today, decisions made by government as well as by the private sector.

There are critics and advocates of globalization—analysts like William Grieder and Kenichi Ohmae—who, despite their differences, are equally skeptical that government can play much of a role in an economy as integrated into the global system as the U.S. economy is today.[1] The claim is that in a world of global production networks and capital mobility, companies have lost their nationality. Multinationals can move anywhere in the world, so why need they bother about policies and institutions of any particular country? What leverage could any one government's actions have on the footloose and free multinational? But we have discovered that the reality is very different from this image of the rootless corporation.

Even when a company has spun off pieces of production and moved them abroad, home base still matters. Home is where companies have their headquarters. The largest share of corporate assets is held in home territory.[2] Home markets are usually the MNC's largest customer base, and the goods and services a company makes bend toward the tastes and needs of its compatriots. (The situation is different, of course, for multinationals from very small countries, like Philips in the Netherlands, or Nokia in Finland.) On the whole, physical proximity to customers allows product developers and designers to grasp far better and sooner than others what people want. It's the interactions with customers and the ability to interpret their reactions that Dell's vice president, Dick Hunter, emphasized to us as Dell's principal competitive advantage. A foreign company like Samsung that depends heavily on U.S. consumers is likely to send design teams to work in the United States. But this is still a distant second best to being a member of the society your products are sold in, where you can watch your aunts using their cell phones or your cousins choosing their jeans. Most R & D remains at home, too. In 2000, U.S. multinationals carried out R & D expenditures of $131.6 billion (87 percent of the total) in the United States while doing $19.8 billion of R & D in their overseas affiliates.[3]

Because of the preponderance of resources that remain at home—even under globalization—home-country institutions and policies do continue to have an important shaping role in the way companies compete. To renew the resources that companies draw on from their national environments means, then, devising and re-forming policies that contribute to the future productivity and innovative capacity of the home society. Some of these necessary steps are policies governments need to initiate, as they are measures beyond the ability of any private person or company to implement. They fall into three areas that our group came to see as critical for renewal: policies to sustain openness, policies to improve education, and policies to support innovation across the economy.

A Legacy of Openness: Ours to Keep if We Can

The dynamism of the U.S. economy requires that Americans accept a world in which every year many firms will disappear and their human and material resources will be absorbed and recombined in new activities. The openness of such a society—without built-in protection against domestic or foreign competition—creates tremendous uncertainties about what will happen to any particular individual and about what becomes of the economy. No one can foresee with precision the shape of new industries or the jobs of the future. Even the forecasting experts usually err by extrapolating current patterns and making assumptions that are too conservative about the industries of the future. Their mistakes cut in both directions. For example, in 1988 the Bureau of Labor Statistics (BLS) predicted a rise in the number of jobs for gas station attendants, but it did not catch the trend to self-service stations, and by 2000 the number of gas station jobs had fallen by half.[4] Of the twenty sectors that the BLS thought would lose most jobs, half of them actually gained over the period (1988–2000). In addition to the rate of growth or decline of existing activities, we cannot know what kinds of jobs will be created by industries that do not exist now. Yet new ones are bound to spring up, if the past is any guide. William Nordhaus, a Yale economics professor, estimated that fewer than a third of the goods and services we use today are related in any way to products that were around 100 years ago, so it is reasonable to anticipate innovations even if we cannot exactly predict them.[5]

But someone who has lost a job and cannot find a new one that pays as much is not likely to be reassured to learn that somehow, historically, this has always worked out and new jobs have appeared from somewhere. After all, today we seem stuck in a "jobless" economic recovery. This is only the second time since World War II that a revival in output after a recession (that "officially" ended in November 2001) has not been accompanied by a marked increase in employment.[6] The other episode was the recovery after the 1990–1991 recession. That time, starting eighteen months after the official end of the downturn, employment opportunities did eventually rise rapidly. Then there was a boom—a wave of new jobs in information technology industries, and a surge of employment and earnings growth that raised all boats in the economy.

Although so many predictions since the Industrial Revolution about productivity gains and automation reducing the stock of jobs have been proven wrong, it's natural to wonder whether now they might be right. In fact, this recovery does look different from the one after the 1990–1991 recession, because then it was the rate of job destruction that held employment levels down; this time, it's the slow rate of job creation that seems to be the problem.[7] After crying wolf so often, perhaps this time the pessimists about technological advance and employment have really spotted one. We can only hope that once again the dynamic recomposition of old activities and the emergence of innovative new businesses will generate new job opportunities across the economy, as we have seen many times in the past. Of course, we cannot know exactly what these will be.

As researchers who work and breathe in one of the most dynamic local economies in the country, we line up with the optimists. We see the strength and depth of the innovative capabilities of the United States—and hence the favorable prospects for a powerful wave of new activities and employment—if only we can maintain the openness and dynamism of our society. Even from our privileged vantage point, though, we observe a disturbing division in the country over the costs and gains and the distribution of the benefits of globalization. Fears about globalization and uncertainties about the future are building into demands for protection. There is a loud and rising clamor for maintaining "critical" industries at home, for "leveling playing fields," for forcing equal access to foreign markets, for making the Chinese revalue the yuan, and other such solutions that point the finger of blame abroad. It's not that the policies of others are blameless—nor are ours, for that matter, to take as an example the heavy toll wreaked on farmers in poor countries by the agricultural subsidies of the United States, the European Union, and Japan. It's that focusing on these disorders of the trade regime distracts us from looking at what we need to do within our own country. Equally dangerous, seeking solutions in protectionism works against our own basic strengths as a society open to recombining resources in ever more productive uses.

Worries about globalization reflect a real problem. Some of the fears grow out of confusion about why jobs disappear. The lion's share of job losses in the United States in recent years has to do with productivity growth, not trade and outsourcing. Still and all, globalization benefits some of us a lot more than others. Even if, as economists assure us, there would be enormous overall gains from a further opening of trade and an increase in global integration, there is no reason to think that these benefits would raise the well-being of everyone equally.[8] On the contrary. The losses from globalization are borne disproportionately by some groups in society, and this will be true in the future, too. In a climate of economic and political uncertainty, the ripples of anxiety spread from those directly impacted by trade and offshoring to many other parts of society. Today practically everyone feels in one way or another vulnerable to changes outside the domestic economy and outside the reach of our own democratic institutions.

What makes this mood dangerous is that openness to change is vital for renewal in the economy. We think the greatest strengths in the legacy of American companies are the result of an open environment in which different innovators, technologies, organizational forms, and ideas about how to succeed can emerge and contend. In this setting, stagnant activities are more likely to disappear and new, more productive ones to take their place. While we can admire and to some extent learn from the ways in which the Italian districts and the Japanese big companies turn their old assets to new uses, we cannot import these patterns, nor should we. We need to recognize that American firms' distinctive advantages lie in different capabilities, and we must identify them, maintain them, and enhance them.

The spur to dynamic transformation of industries and markets in the United States often comes from new actors and new activities that spring up outside existing businesses. American public policies and institutions encourage this. Venture capital, equity funding of industry, tight connections between centers of research and end users, flexible labor markets, market-based contracting, and the other institutional features of "liberal market capitalism"—to return to the distinctions of Chapter 2— create a system with many opportunities for players who can innovate across the boundaries of existing businesses—in contrast to the Japanese and German systems, where resources are concentrated in the hands of established insiders and innovation on the margins has little chance. Above and beyond the incentives for innovation that policy and institutions provide in the United States, there is the tremendous advantage of proximity to a vast market of rich consumers interested in buying new products. Powerful advertising, marketing, and retail businesses all work to build this customer base for emergent goods and services.

Along with the liberal market institutions that favor rapid acceptance of new ways of doing things, there are widely shared norms of efficiency, transparency, and standardization, and they, too, facilitate change. A number of the foreign managers admiringly raised this point in the interviews when comparing their companies to American firms. A China-based manager of a large Japanese corporation told us that because of the diversity of the American population, the United States has had to develop standard rules, and not too many of them.[9] Then, he said, the Americans simply apply abroad what they do at home.

In contrast, he related his experiences in a joint venture in a Singaporean semiconductor plant. He tried to translate Japanese job descriptions into English, but the translation read something like: "Do this-and-that in an appropriate way to some extent." This kind of ambiguity was intelligible to Japanese, who share the same cultural context and know how to fill in the blanks, but it did not work for other employees. An Italian entrepreneur who had opened a plant to make lining fabric in China made the same point with a backhanded compliment: "I watched how Americans operate in China. They make very, very detailed lists of tasks. Their experience in working in the United States with low-skill, unqualified workers prepared them for China. They're organized for dealing with uneducated people. It's like making fast food. It's all spelled out."

Because of these institutions and norms and the climate of openness in which they function, American entrepreneurs have been able to rapidly develop new organizational types. The country's propensity to grow new players has made American businesses particularly successful in seizing the opportunities offered by radical leaps in technologies, at a moment when the advantages of established firms are exploded by a burst of innovation outside the turf they control.[10] Companies like Cisco and Dell have grown up around the Internet and the potentialities of fragmented production networks. The ability to jump on technological discontinuities and to build new companies to exploit them is one of the great strengths of the system. Modularity has been one of the key enabling processes of this organizational transformation over the past twenty years. But even for those technologies and for those parts of the economy that require greater integration within the four walls of a company, it is vital to maintain an open space for the emergence of new players.

There is no way of eliminating the uncertainties and risks that derive from a competitive economy and from the free flow of goods, services, and capital across borders except by eliminating openness. But if we are to preserve this openness, we need to address the deepest and most legitimate fears about its consequences. These anxieties have to do with losing the chance of earning enough through one's best efforts and hard work to support a family's needs for food, shelter, education, medical care, and provision in old age. There are already a large number of working families in the United States that live on the brink of economic disaster.[11] Two and a half million families with working parents are officially below the poverty line ($18,392). Another 6.7 million working families have incomes low enough to make them very vulnerable to a single economic blow.[12] As the recent report of the Working Poor Families Project summarized it: "Twenty-eight million jobs in the United States, almost a quarter of all jobs, cannot keep a family of four above the poverty level and provide few or no benefits."

Given this picture, it's no wonder that people worry about losing their jobs. Middle-aged employees who lose work today in the United States are not likely to be reemployed at the same wages and benefits they enjoyed in the positions they once held. Too many of the new jobs in the economy pay incomes that do not move families over the federal poverty line.[13] There are already many proposals on the table that address these issues—for universal access to health care, portable pensions, wage insurance, negative income tax credits, unionization, and educational reform.[14] Such policies that would cushion the risks of change for individuals can be compatible with an economic openness that allows for the rise and fall of companies and industries and the emergence of new activities. While our team has no special competence for choosing among these social policy options, we do see them as the realistic alternatives to economic protection, which by closing doors and protecting the status quo would handicap the greatest strengths in this country.

We believe that the future prosperity of the United States depends on maintaining broad public support for openness and for the rapid redeployment of resources from one activity to another so that the new can emerge. To prevent this consensus from unraveling, people need the assurance that losing a job and looking for another one does not mean losing everything. When the risks are too great for too many people—who have too little control over their future livelihoods—the chances of a backlash are high. There is real urgency, then, in coming up with social policies that provide insurance for individuals against the risks of globalization—even as society remains open to the challenges of competition from abroad and to the transformation by new ideas and new technologies from within.

Educating All of Us

One of the greatest boons that public institutions provide to private enterprises is a flow of educated people into the workforce. Over the years, America's colleges, universities, and community colleges have done reasonably well at preparing students for rapidly changing occupations and industries. The number of Americans who benefit from these institutions has grown, with the percentage of high school graduates entering postsecondary school increasing from 47 percent in 1973 to 62 percent in 2001.[15] The problem is that all the others are left with whatever they have acquired in high schools as their stock of learning for life. There is a lot of evidence that tells us that America's high schools are not doing a good enough job for most students. In international mathematics, science, and reading examinations, American fifteen-year-olds do far worse than children from countries like Finland, Korea, and the Netherlands, and less well even than students from post-Communist countries like the Czech Republic, Poland, and Hungary.[16]

Bill Gates, Microsoft's founder, summed up the dismal picture in a February 26, 2005, speech to a state governors' conference on high school education:[17]

When I compare our high schools to what I see when I'm traveling abroad, I am terrified for our workforce of tomorrow. In math and science, our fourth-graders are among the top students in the world. By eighth grade, they're in the middle of the pack. By twelfth grade, U.S. students are scoring near the bottom of all industrialized nations.

We have one of the highest high school dropout rates in the industrialized world. Many who graduate do not go on to college. And many who do go on to college are not well-prepared—and end up dropping out. That is one reason why the U.S. college dropout rate is also one of the highest in the industrialized world. The poor performance of our high schools in preparing students for college is a major reason why the United States has now dropped from first to fifth in the percentage of young adults with a college degree.

The percentage of a population with a college degree is important, but so are sheer numbers. In 2001, India graduated almost a million more students from college than the United States did. China graduates twice as many students with bachelor's degrees as the U.S., and they have six times as many graduates majoring in engineering.

In the international competition to have the biggest and best supply of knowledge workers, America is falling behind. That is the heart of the economic argument for better high schools. It essentially says: "We'd better do something about these kids not getting an education, because it's hurting us." But there's also a moral argument for better high schools, and it says: "We'd better do something about these kids not getting an education, because it's hurting them."

Today, most jobs that allow you to support a family require some postsecondary education. This could mean a four-year college, a community college, or technical school. Unfortunately, only half of all students who enter high school ever enroll in a postsecondary institution.

. . .

If we keep the system as it is, millions of children will never get a chance to fulfill their promise because of their zip code, their skin color, or the income of their parents. That is offensive to our values, and it's an insult to who we are. Every kid can graduate ready for college. Every kid should have the chance.

The scene Gates describes has not improved much over the past twenty years. In writing *How We Compete*, I went back to *Made in America*, the study in which MIT researchers diagnosed the sources of the faltering economic performance of American companies in the 1980s in order to see how the problems that we had highlighted at the time had been addressed. I saw how the world of production has been transformed since the 1980s. Many of the recommendations that the MIT group put forward then have become the basic operating code of American companies ("focus on the effective use of technology in manufacturing"; "embrace product customization and production flexibility"; "shop internationally"; "innovate in production processes," and so forth).[18] But one of the main weaknesses identified in *Made in America* still stands virtually unimproved. The authors wrote: "Basic schooling from kindergarten through high school is seriously deficient to the extent that it leaves large numbers of its graduates without basic skills in reading, writing, and mathematics. Only a tiny fraction of young Americans are technologically literate and have some knowledge of foreign societies. Unless the nation begins to remedy these inadequacies, it can make no real progress on all the rest."[19]

There have been some modest improvements in secondary education since the 1970s—most of them made twenty years ago.[20] But American children's performance compared with that of students in other countries continues to look mediocre, with older children doing even worse than students in lower grades. The efforts at improving the country's schools, including the changes introduced by the 2001 No Child Left Behind Act, have not measured up to this challenge. In some places, they have made matters worse by pushing out of the schools those students whose test scores would have dragged down the numbers by which the system now measures performance.

On-the-job training and retraining of workers has also not advanced over this twenty-year period. For workers with only secondary school education, "following Joe around" remains the main form of acquiring new skills on the job. Whatever resources American companies devote to training are lavished on employees who have university degrees. Companies everywhere are more likely to invest in better-educated workers, but the skew is much steeper in the United States than in other advanced economies (four times more participation of the university graduates in career- or job-related training, compared with 1.96 times more participation of the university-educated in Germany, or 1.58 times more in Sweden).[21] There's a serious neglect of the potential for learning and lifetime employability of people of average intelligence and academic attainment.

In a way, the weaknesses of the American training system are the opposite side of the coin of some of the strengths of its labor market flexibility. Exactly because workers move around quite freely between jobs, allowing employers to hire the skills they need in the labor market instead of nurturing them in-house in the workers they already employ, there is a disincentive for employers to invest in human resources. The kind of continuous on-the-job upgrading of skills that would build lifetime employability is "too expensive" for companies who can get rid of the workers they have and find others in the labor market—or else move the jobs out of the country and use a workforce educated by someone else's taxes. The spiral here is downward.

Among our greatest concerns today is one that was not on the list in the 1980s—how to make good companies and good jobs stick in the United States. Then, our challenge seemed to be import penetration. Today, the fragmentation of the system of production has changed the problem. Now it's the prospect that the resources available to companies abroad—and well-educated and lower-cost workers are one of the main attractions—will induce businesses to shift their activities abroad. Unless the skills of the American workforce at all levels provide a compelling reason for locating activities at home, the appeal of foreign labor markets with educated workers at lower wages is likely to induce the very race to the bottom that we fear the most under globalization. Even though many of our concerns have evolved since the eighties, the conclusion of *Made in America* still stands: "[W]ithout major changes in the ways schools and firms train workers over the course of a lifetime, no amount of macro-

economic fine-tuning or technological innovation will be able to produce significantly improved economic performance and a rising standard of living."[22]

Investment for Innovation
in a World of Modularity

The American faith that a new surge of growth and employment lies just
ahead depends above all on the belief in our ability to stimulate new
innovation. The boom at the end of the 1990s was a transformative economic moment for many Americans. Its clear message was that increases
in prosperity grow out of increases in the scientific and technological
capabilities of society. Profits and wages soared as waves of discovery in
information technology and communication poured into new products
and services. A renaissance of entrepreneurial spirits and creativity lifted
a broad swath of the American economy. Powerful new companies like
Cisco, Broadcom, Dell, Amazon, and eBay emerged, while old-style corporations struggled to escape the fate of the dinosaurs. For the first time
since the early seventies, median wages rose and even the lower tier of the
labor market saw increases in earnings.

It's not at all clear that we can anticipate a repetition of this virtuous
cycle from innovation to boom in the future. The great technological
leaps that made the nineties glorious grew out of institutions that have
now been destroyed, or at least very much altered. The question arises of
whether we can expect any such future miracles from the organizations
that replaced them. The radical shrinking of the great central research
laboratories, like AT&T's Bell Laboratories, Xerox's Palo Alto Research
Center (PARC), and those at IBM and DuPont, has fundamentally
shifted the balance in the kinds of research being carried out in private
industry. Richard K. Lester and Michael J. Piore, professors of engineering and economics, respectively, at MIT, have analyzed the dynamics of
interaction among researchers in the settings in which some of the big

new products and services of the nineties were born.[23] They trace out a pattern of change in which clusters of scientists and engineers who were once relatively free to pursue open-ended research agendas across disciplinary boundaries have now been disbanded and regrouped, and the laboratories in which they worked have now been attached to particular product divisions within the companies.

AT&T's Bell Laboratories was once the premier corporate research facility in the country. Founded in 1925, Bell Labs gave birth to revolutionary innovations, including the first transistor, Touch-Tone phones, stereo recording, telephone switches, the fax, and Unix software.[24] There was path-blazing basic research in areas like information theory. Bell researchers won eleven Nobel Prizes. It was in AT&T's Bell Laboratories in the sixties and seventies that cellular technology developed. Within the four walls of the laboratory, radio and telephone engineers coming from a wide range of specialties engaged in an open-ended exploration of new technologies. The result was an outpouring of new products—with benefits, however, that were not always captured by AT&T.

This world began to unravel at the end of the 1990s. First, under the pressure of telecommunication deregulation, AT&T spun off Bell Labs along with its equipment manufacturing to a new company, Lucent Technology. For cost cutting, some facilities were closed (for example, the Silicon Valley branch in 2001) and the research activities overall were refocused on nearer-term results. When Bill O'Shea was appointed president of Bell Labs in 2001, Lucent described his mission: "to couple our marketing and sales efforts with our innovating engine." In the other telecommunications firms that Lester and Piore studied, like Nokia and Motorola, research expenditures on cell phones had originally been spread over large and diversified corporate structures. These companies, too, have been restructuring, and in them as well, research has been attached to "profit centers." The downsizing of large, vertically integrated companies reduced the possibilities for "cross-subsidizing" the work of central research and development labs.

The dismantling of these great corporate research-and-development engines was a response, in part, to the new competitive pressures the companies were experiencing. By harnessing R & D ever more tightly to commercializable products and bringing the scientists closer to developers and marketers, the companies hoped to get a bigger bang from their research bucks. They also wanted, simply, to cut their overall budgets. After a surge in R & D spending in the late nineties, this economizing impulse has resumed. Companies that were prime movers in the information technology boom of the late nineties are now cutting back on their R & D expenditures. Cisco, Dell, HP, Lucent, Motorola, Ericsson, and Nortel, for example, all spent a smaller percentage of sales on R & D in 2004 compared with 2003, and for most of them, the trend has been downward since 2000.[25]

Beyond these cost-trimming moves, however, there was another dynamic at work. As modularity and fragmentation began to transform the corporate landscape, the range of innovation that companies were interested in supporting shrank and the research agenda became more focused. Once the rationale for building vertically integrated companies, with their "excess capacity" of functions and a willingness to cross-subsidize less-profitable activities within the company, disappeared—the corporate support for broad-based blue-sky research diminished.[26] Modularity, with its multiple opportunities for newcomer firms, has many advantages but, on the other hand, looks to have some worrisome effects. Fragmentation of production seems to discourage wide-ranging research by any one company, with no compensating mechanism kicking in to build public support for the activities that firms are shedding.

Modularity may dry up the well of innovation at home in yet another way. It provides far more possibilities than ever existed in the past for outsourcing and offshoring R & D. A March 21, 2005, BusinessWeek article tracks the shrinkage of corporate research expenditures as design and development projects are transferred to contractors in developing countries.[27] Initially, the electronics contract manufacturers (the OEMs and the ODMs discussed in Part Four) worked to specifications and designs provided by the lead brand firms. But when the IPC team interviewed Taiwanese original design manufacturers like Quanta, Compal, and ASUSTeK in 1999–2000, we found them taking on major parts of the detailed design and design work for notebook PCs and other PC products.

Today, brand-name companies are using the ODMs to design more and more products, including parts or all of new digital cameras, mobile phones, and PDAs. *BusinessWeek* quotes Quanta's founder and chairman, Barry Lam, saying: "What has changed is that more customers need us to design the whole product. It's now difficult to get good ideas from our customers. We have to innovate ourselves."[28] Quanta is expanding its research facilities in Taiwan; it also announced (April 2005) a $20 million research collaboration with MIT's Laboratory for Computer Science and Artificial Intelligence (CSAIL). Now big global suppliers like Flextronics are also getting in on the design act. Some of the same shifts are reported in industries like pharmaceuticals and aircraft. If such trends continue, lead firms' incentive to invest in R & D would be even further diminished. It's possible that the *BusinessWeek* article is too alarmist. The managers we talked with in brand-name companies (American, European, and Japanese) were keenly aware of the dangers of losing intellectual property when they moved design work overseas. They understood that their edge depends on differentiating technology that carves out new market niches. And the gap between their innovational capabilities and those of their suppliers still seems to be a very wide one in most sectors. Still, the new data reinforce our concern that anchoring advanced technologies at home can no longer be taken for granted.

Private industry is by far the largest provider (and performer) of R & D in the United States, funding 65.5 percent of the total in 2002.[29] Twenty years ago, the rising curve of private industry's investments in R & D crossed over and started to exceed the federal government's declining curve.[30] During the same twenty-year period, federal expenditures for defense R & D have always exceeded nondefense expenditures, with a steep rise in the former after 2001. Federal government funding for civilian R & D does, however, remain very important (28.3 percent of the total in 2002), especially in health areas. Increasingly, this federal money goes to universities. U.S. biotech and pharmaceutical companies fish for discoveries in what I think of as a rushing stream of basic biological and medical research pouring out of university laboratories that are massively supported by public funds. In 2004, for example, the U.S. federal government sponsored $411.9 million of research at MIT—78 percent of the institution's total research budget. The lion's share of this came from the U.S. Department of Health and Human Services ($159 million). It's not only U.S.-owned companies that are fishing in this stream. To take our local Cambridge, Massachusetts, pond as evidence: The names on the refurbished factory buildings around Kendall Square, MIT, are often those of German, French, Japanese, and Swiss pharmaceutical firms, who are here because they find their own national research waters too poorly stocked.

Whether a company can make a product it can sell out of the discoveries it catches in the stream depends mainly on how it deploys its own internal resources. But without access to the stream, or if the stream dries up, nothing in the legacy of the company is likely to sustain its ability to produce innovative products. Not all industries are as dependent as biotech and pharmaceuticals are on the spillovers from public investments in basic research. But across a wide range of products and services like the Internet, which grew out of grants by the Defense Department's Advanced Research Projects Agency (DARPA), government funding has contributed to the emergence of new industries and the transformation of old ones. There's reason to be concerned, then, about the fact that the federal spending on R & D has been slowing at the same time that company-funded R & D spending has plateaued. Within the Department of Defense budget, funding for basic and applied research fell sharply in 2004, and within DARPA, resources were shifted from more open and basic research in academic institutions to more focused short-term research.[31]

The institutions that nourish research and development, like those that support education and those that sustain the public's commitment to the openness of the economy, are foundations of a productive and innovative society. These foundations need to be able to bear the weight of adjustment to earth-shattering movement in the international economy. Powerful new competitors have arisen in regions of the world that only yesterday were marginalized peripheries; new technologies are undermining the advantages of established players; new politics have cast down the boundaries that once demarcated and protected national territories of competition. Each one of these shifts unsettles the previous generation's solutions for dealing with the distributional consequences of economic growth, educating the workforce, and providing incentives for innovation. How to adjust and reinforce these public foundations is too large a task for private initiatives alone to undertake. We recognize that our research at the ground level of the firm does not provide the answers. We know only that even the best of the companies that we have seen in the United States will suffer if there is a failure to renew the stock of public resources on which they continue to draw in building their own capabilities.

How We Compete

In the course of the research, the team met people with remarkable flair, energy, and passion. When interviewing Richard Clareman, the founder of Self-Esteem, a $125-million-a-year Los Angeles company that makes hot fashion for "tween"-aged girls, I asked him what he thought about the future of his business. He said that maybe a company like Liz Claiborne or Jones New York or Kellwood would try to buy him out. "But," he said, "I don't want to [be bought out]. Why can't we be the next Jones or Liz or Kellwood?" The interview was in March 2004. Self-Esteem was shifting its manufacturing from domestic to Asian suppliers. I asked him if he was worried about being squeezed by Chinese competition after January 2005, when quotas would disappear. Clareman joked: "It's like dancing with the wolves! We know that China is gaining, and some people feel—'They're coming! Get out!'" Clareman clearly relished the challenge. He said he thought that Self-Esteem could stand up to the competition by catching fashion that young women want, by quick turn, and by building a label.

The optimism and entrepreneurial spirit of men and women like Clareman and Geox's Polegato, Michael Dell, and Quanta's Barry Lam drive the search for responses to tough new competition. However much our team looked for patterns and for institutional and technological explanations of the evolution of the economy over the past twenty years, the interviews never let us forget that human actions and determination drive these processes of transformation. The diversity of models of success that we found in each sector we studied leaves open space for strategy and selection; to make it is to choose. In slow-tech and high-tech industries, in downtown Los Angeles, Kyoto, Japan, and in Timisoara, Romania, we found no single globalization imperative—only men and women discovering how to combine the assets and experiences of their own companies with outside resources in ways that opened new possibilities for competition across the entire range of the economy. Succeeding in a world of global competition is a matter of choices, not a matter of searching for the one best way—we discovered no misconception about globalization more dangerous than this illusion of certainty.

Notes

PART ONE: A World of Opportunity and Danger

CHAPTER 1: Who's Afraid of Globalization?

1. In a poll done by the Chicago Council on Foreign Relations, June 1–June 31, 2002, 51% thought globalization was good for their standard of living, 28% thought it was bad; 51% thought it was bad for job security, 32% thought it good. When the polls were repeated two years later, support for globalization had fallen slightly. Declining support for globalization in U.S. opinion over the years 1999–2004 shows up in the "Americans and the World" IPoll Database, Roper Center for Public Opinion Research, University of Connecticut. For the views of Europeans, see the survey carried out for the European Commission in the member countries of the European Union, October 2003 and reported November 2003, by Eurobarometer, EOS Gallup Poll.

2. The monthly story count is based on our analysis of newspapers and magazines in Lexis-Nexis over the period from January 2003 to September 2004.

3. Janco Associates, *The Coming Commoditization of Compensation*, http://common. ziffdavisinternet.com/download/o/02216/Baseline0901-p28-29.pdf, September 2003.

4. Diana Farrell, "Offshoring: Is It a Win-Win Game?" San Francisco: McKinsey Global Institute, August 2003. *The Economist* also had an optimistic read of the situation, in Ben Edwards, "A World of Work," November 11, 2004. http://www.economist. com/printededition/PrinterFriendly.cfm?Story_ID=3351416.

5. Cited in "Outsourcing 101," *Wall Street Journal*, May 27, 2004. http://global.factiva. com/en/arch/print_results.asp.

6. Michael M. Phillips, "More Work Is Outsourced to U.S. Than Away from It, Data Show," *Wall Street Journal*, March 15, 2004, p. A2.

7. Laura Abramovsky, Rachel Griffith, and Mari Sako, "Offshoring of Business Ser-

vices and Its Impact on the UK Economy," Oxford: Advanced Institute of Management Research, 2004.

8. N. Gregory Mankiw, "Remarks at the National Association of Business Economists 2004 Washington Economic Policy Conference," March 25, 2004. www.whitehouse.gov/cea/nabe-20040325.html.

9. Paul Samuelson, "Where Ricardo and Mill Rebut and Confirm Arguments of Mainstream Economists Supporting Globalization," *Journal of Economic Perspectives*, 18, (3) (2004): 135–46. See also Ralph E. Gomory and William J. Baumol, *Global Trade and Conflicting National Interests*, Cambridge: MIT Press, 2000.

10. Kenichi Ohmae, *The Borderless World*, New York: HarperCollins, 1990, p. x.

11. Thomas L. Friedman, *The Lexus and the Olive Tree*, New York: Farrar, Straus and Giroux, 1999, pp. 373–74.

12. William Greider, *One World, Ready Or Not*, New York: Simon & Schuster, 1997, p. 12.

13. The tool kit image and the ideas behind it are from Ann Swidler, *Talk of Love: How Culture Matters*, Chicago: University of Chicago Press, 2001.

14. This definition leaves out values, lifestyles, religion, music, cinema, in all of which the spread of ideas across national borders suggests a wider meaning for globalization. Here I stick with a narrower and more "economistic" definition in order to understand more concretely, even if less broadly, what kinds of responses are possible.

15. There is a good discussion of how to measure globalization as compared with internationalization in Paul Hirst and Grahame Thompson, *Globalization in Question*, second edition, Cambridge: Polity Press, 1999. This book, along with Martin Wolf, *Why Globalization Works*, New Haven: Yale University Press, 2004, are the best all-around introductions to theories and evidence about globalization.

16. Kevin H. O'Rourke and Jeffrey G. Williamson, *Globalization and History*, Cambridge: MIT Press, 1999. Michael D. Bordo, Barry Eichengreen, and Douglas A. Irwin, "Is Globalization Today Really Different than Globalization a Hundred Years Ago?" National Bureau of Economic Research, 1999; Richard E. Baldwin and Philippe Martin, "Two Waves of Globalization: Superficial Similarities, Fundamental Differences," in H. Siebert, ed., *Globalization and Labor*, Tuebingen: Mohr Siebeck, 1999; Lee A. Craig and Douglas Fisher, *The Integration of the European Economy, 1850–1913*, New York: St. Martin's Press, 1997.

17. T. J. Hatton and Jeffrey G. Williamson, *The Age of Mass Migration*, Oxford: Oxford University Press, 1998.

18. O'Rourke and Williamson, pp. 43–53.

19. Edmond Théry, *Le Péril Jaune*, Paris: Félix Juven, 1901, p. 308.

20. Harley Withers, *War and Lombard Street*, London: Smith, Elder & Co., 1915.

21. Interview, November 3, 2003. See also Zane's comments in Alexandra Harney and Richard McGregor, "China Gets Set to Clothe America When Quotas End," *Financial Times*, July 20, 2004, p. 9.

22. According to J. P. Crametz, a director at a California telecom procurement business, cited in Jesse Drucker, "Global Talk Gets Cheaper—Outsourcing Abroad Becomes Even More Attractive as Cost of Fiber-Optic Links Drops," *Wall Street Journal*, March 11, 2004, p. B1.

23. There's a veritable mountain of data, scholarly analysis, and journalistic accounts of each of these crises. For an extraordinary guide to it all, see the Web site of Nouriel Roubini at www.rgemonitor.com.

24. Thanks to MIT professor Jing Wang for the reference to the Yunnan survey and to the Procter & Gamble story, as well as for the chance to read draft chapters of her manuscript on building brands in China.

25. The 1989 movie *Field of Dreams* starred Kevin Costner. On the many failures of those who tried to pursue their dreams in China, see Joe Studwell, *The China Dream: The Quest for the Last Great Untapped Market on Earth,* London: Profile Books, 2002, and Tim Clissold, *Mr. China,* New York: HarperBusiness, 2005.

26. One analysis prepared for a congressional committee estimated that the deficit amounted to a displacement of 1.5 million actual or potential jobs, 1989–2003, that could have been supported had a volume of production corresponding to the excess of imports over exports taken place in the U.S. instead of China. Robert Scott, "US-China Trade, 1989–2003, Impact on Jobs and Industries, Nationally and State by State," prepared for U.S.–China Economic and Security Review Commission, Economic Policy Institute working paper, #270, January 2005.

27. See the analysis in Michael L. Dertouzos, Robert M. Solow, Richard K. Lester, *Made in America: Regaining the Productive Edge,* Cambridge, MA: MIT Press, 1989.

28. Richard Darman, Director of the Office of Management and Budget in the first Bush administration, said: "Potato chips or silicon chips—who cares? They are both chips." This triggered a massive reaction from high-tech industry executives, like Andrew Grove, CEO of Intel, who denounced it as "not a sign of ignorance but of the laissez-faire attitude that sought no national policy for high technology outside of defense." Speech to Commonwealth Club, May 17, 1993. http://www.commonwealthclub.org/archive/93/93-05grove-speech.html.

29. Samuel P. Huntington, "America's Changing Strategic Interests," *Survival* 33 (1) (1991): 3–17.

30. www.wto.org/english/news_e/pres05__e/pr401_e.html.

31. These calculations are from Raphael Kaplinsky, "How Does It All Add Up? Caught Between a Rock and a Hard Place," chapter 6 of unpublished mss.

32. There are major debates over exactly what combination of these elements explain the "East Asian Miracle." See: World Bank, *The East Asian Miracle: Economic Growth and Public Policy,* New York: Oxford University Press, 1993; on Taiwan in particular, Chi Schive, *The Foreign Factor: The Multinational Corporation's Contribution to the Economic Modernization of the Republic of China,* Stanford: Stanford University Press, 1990; John A. Mathews and Dong-Sung Cho, *Tiger Technology: The Creation of a Semiconductor Industry in East Asia,* Cambridge: Cambridge University Press, 2000; Alice H. Amsden and Wan-wen Chu, *Beyond Late Development,* Cambridge, MA: MIT Press, 2003; Suzanne Berger and Richard K. Lester, editors, *Global Taiwan,* Armonk, NY: M. E. Sharpe, 2005.

33. Bram J. Bout, "Keeping Taiwan's High-Tech Edge," *The McKinsey Quarterly,* no. 2 (2003), pp. 1–3.

34. For the new mantras on rebuilding companies by learning to identify and leverage innovation around the world, see Yves Doz, José Santos, and Peter Williamson, *From Global to Metanational,* Cambridge: Harvard Business School Press, 2001.

35. Bureau of Labor Statistics payroll survey, cited in Edmund L. Andrews, "In the Latest Numbers, Economists See the Cold, Hard Truth About Jobs," *New York Times*, March 6, 2004, p. B3.

36. Elka Koehler and Sara Hagigh, "Offshore Outsourcing and America's Competitive Edge: Losing Out in the High Technology R & D and Services Sectors," Washington, D.C.: Office of Senator Joseph Lieberman, May 11, 2004.

37. From the start of the March 2001 recession to mid-2003, 15 percent of factory jobs held by blacks were terminated, in contrast to about 10 percent of factory jobs held by whites. Louis Uchitelle, "Blacks Lose Better Jobs Faster as Middle-Class Work Drops," *New York Times*, July 12, 2003, pp. 1, B14.

38. James Glassman, quoted in Louis Uchitelle, "Layoff Rate at 8.7%, Highest Since 80's," *New York Times*, August 2, 2004, p. C2.

39. For direct quotations from the L. W. Packard interview, as with other persons interviewed and cited in the text, I sought authorization from the interviewee. When such authorization was refused—or when the comments were such that they might damage a company—I mask the identity of the person interviewed and the business and sometimes use a pseudonym for the company name. In the case of large companies, we have used publicly available data and material that has appeared in print as well as data collected in the interviews.

40. Louis Uchitelle, "As Factories Move Abroad, So Does U.S. Power," *New York Times*, August 17, 2003, p. B4.

41. Cited in Eduardo Porter, "Job Growth Picks Up But Misses Forecasts," *New York Times*, February 7, 2004, pp. B1, B3.

42. The early years of SMaL have been chronicled in a Harvard Business School case, Clayton M. Christensen and Scott D. Anthony, *Making SMaL Big: SMaL Camera Technologies*, N-603-116, March 17, 2003. Sodini has provided additional information about the company.

43. Ibid., p. 5.

44. Press release, "Cypress Acquires SMaL Camera Technologies," February 14, 2005.

45. PricewaterhouseCoopers, the management firm, and *USA Today* reported that close to 40 percent of U.S. start-ups employ staff abroad from the beginning. Chris Nuttall, "Straight from Mountain View to Mumbai: Offshoring: Silicon Valley technology start-ups are finding that it is more efficient to go global from day one," *Financial Times*, February 23, 2005, p.17.

CHAPTER 2: A Preview of the MIT Globalization Study

1. For more facts and figures on the Globalization Study, as well as working papers that explore methodology and definition in greater detail, see the Web site for the project: http://www.howwecompete.com.

2. Andy Serwer, "The Education of Michael Dell," *Fortune*, March 2, 2005, pp. 73–81. The magazine cover proclaims: "Dude! Dell's No. 1. America's Most Admired Companies."

3. The interviews were conducted by teams of researchers, using an "interview guide." A copy of the interview guide is at http://www.howwecompete.com.

4. Ohmae, 1990, p. 18.

5. Cited in *The Economist*, October 7, 1995, p. 15.

6. Dani Rodrik, *Has Globalization Gone Too Far?*, Washington, DC: Institute for International Economics, 1997, pp. 16–27. Matthew J. Slaughter and Philip Swagel, "The Effect of Globalization on Wages in the Advanced Economies," Washington: International Monetary Fund, 1997.

7. Adrian Wood, *North-South Trade, Employment, and Inequality: Changing Fortunes in a Skill-Driven World*, Oxford: Oxford University Press, 1994; G. Burtless, "International Trade and the Rise in Earnings Inequality," *Journal of Economic Literature* XXXIII (June 1995): 800–816; Robert C. Feenstra, "Integration of Trade and Disintegration of Production in the Global Economy," *Journal of Economic Perspectives* 12 (4) (1998): 31–50.

8. Michel Albert, *Capitalism vs. Capitalism*, New York: Four Wall Eight Windows, 1993 [1991].

9. Peter A. Hall and David Soskice, eds., *Varieties of Capitalism*, Oxford: Oxford University Press, 2001.

10. Our approach draws on that of Edith Penrose, *The Theory of the Growth of the Firm*, Oxford: Oxford University Press, 1995 (1959). Penrose's resource-based approach to firm strategy continues to inspire a variety of researchers today—e.g., Florence Palpacuer, "Competence-Based Strategies and Global Production Networks. A Discussion of Current Changes and Their Implications for Employment," *Competition & Change*, 4 (2000): 353–400.

11. Paul A. David, "Clio and the Economics of QWERTY," *American Economic Review* 75 (2) (1985): 332–37.

12. For a clear and sophisticated presentation of the choices about organization and strategy that face firms today, see John Roberts, *The Modern Firm: Organizational Design for Performance and Growth*, Oxford: Oxford University Press, 2004.

13. Figures are from "The Best Performers: 2005," *BusinessWeek*, April 4, 2005, pp. 66–144; "The Forbes 2000," *Forbes*, April 12, 2004; and Daniel Akst, "Welcome to Sherwood Forest, Er, Wal-Mart," *New York Times*, March 4, 2005, News of the Week in Review, p. 6.

14. "iPod Impact," *Technology Review*, March 2005, p. 25.

PART TWO: The "Lego" Model of Production

1. W. H. Miller, "John Young's Mission: HP's CEO Becomes the Point Man for Competitiveness," *Industry Week*, February 9, 1987, p. 53, cited in Geoffrey G. Parker and Edward G. Anderson, Jr., "From Buyer to Integrator: The Transformation of the Supply-Chain Manager in the Vertically Disintegrating Firm," *Production and Operations Management* 11 (1) (2002): 75–91. I draw on their account of Hewlett-Packard here.

CHAPTER 3: Breaking Up the Corporation

1. Takahiro Fujimoto, "Architecture, Capability, and Competitiveness of Firms and Industries," Paper prepared for Saint-Gobain Centre for Economic Research, 5th Conference on "Organizational Innovation within Firms," Paris, November 7–8, 2002.

2. "Insight from Standard & Poor's," Scoring the World's Carmakers, March 25, 2005. http://yahoo.businessweek.com/investor/content/mar2005/pi20050330_4086_PG2_pi036.htm.

3. Iain Carson, "Perpetual Motion: A Survey of the Car Industry," *The Economist*, September 4, 2004, p. 15.

4. James Surowiecki, "The Financial Page: All Together Now," *The New Yorker*, April 11, 2005, p. 26.

5. The parallels between fragmentation today and fragmentation before the rise of large vertically integrated companies are drawn and debated in Richard N. Langlois and Paul L. Robertson, *Firms, Markets, and Economic Change*, London: Routledge, 1995; Richard N. Langlois, "The Vanishing Hand: The Changing Dynamics of Industrial Capitalism," *Industrial and Corporate Change* 12 (2) (2003):351–85; Naomi R. Lamoreaux, Daniel M. G. Raff, and Peter Temin, "Beyond Markets and Hierarchies: Toward a New Synthesis of American Business History," *American Historical Review* 108 (2) (2004); Charles F. Sabel and Jonathan Zeitlin, "Neither Modularity Nor Relational Contracting: Inter-Firm Collaboration in the New Economy. A Critique of Langlois and Lamoreaux, Raff, and Temin," *Enterprise and Society* 5 (3) (2004); and Timothy Sturgeon, "Modular Production Networks: A New American Model of Industrial Organization," *Industrial and Corporate Change* 11 (3): 451–96.

6. Alfred D. Chandler, Jr., *The Visible Hand: The Managerial Revolution in American Business*, Cambridge: Belknap/Harvard University Press, 1977; and *Scale and Scope: The Dynamics of Industrial Capitalism*, Cambridge: Harvard University Press, 1990.

7. Lamoreaux et al., citing research by Richard Edwards, "Stages in Corporate Stability and the Risks of Corporate Failure," *Journal of Economic History* 35 (June 1975): 428–57.

8. Niall Ferguson, "Survival of the Biggest," *Forbes 2000*, April 12, 2004, p. 140.

9. Gary Fields, *Territories of Profit: Communications, Capitalist Development, and the Innovative Enterprises of G. F. Swift and Dell Computer*, Stanford: Stanford University Press, 2004. The Singer case is sketched out in Lamoreaux, Raff, Temin, Swift, in Langlois (1995). Each of these authors draws on a large body of similar cases.

10. Fields, op. cit., 94.

11. *Encyclopaedia Britannica*, volume 9, University of Chicago, 1949, pp. 490–92, 493–94.

12. Michael Piore and Charles Sabel, *The Second Industrial Divide*, New York: Basic Books, 1984.

13. Sebastian Brusco and Sergio Paba define the Italian districts as local labor markets with higher-than-average manufacturing employment in small and medium firms

specialized in one sector. By this reckoning, in 1991 in northern and central Italy there were 238 districts. Brusco and Paba, "Per una storia dei distretti industriali italiani dal secondo dopoguerra agli anni novanta," in Fabrizio Barca, ed., *Storia del Capitalismo Italiano*, Rome: Donzelli, 1997, 265–333; Sebastiano Brusco, "The Emilian Model: Productive Decentralisation and Social Integration," *Cambridge Journal of Economics* 1982(6): 167–84; Vittorio Capecchi, "A History of Flexible Specialisation and Industrial Districts in Emilia-Romagna," *Industrial Districts and Local Economic Regeneration*, Geneva: ILO, 1990; Giacomo Becattini, *Distretti Industriali e Made in Italy*, Turin: Bollati Boringhieri, 1998; Suzanne Berger and Richard Locke, "*Il Caso Italiano* and Globalization," *Daedalus*, July 2001.

14. Banca d'Italia, *Relazione del Governatore*, Assemblea Generale Ordinaria dei Partecipanti, Rome, 1997, p. 83; L. Federico Signorini, ed., *Lo sviluppo locale. Un'indagine della Banca d'Italia sui distretti industriali*, Rome: Donzelli, 2000.

15. See the industry studies reported in Michael L. Dertouzos, Richard K. Lester, and Robert M. Solow, *Made in America*, Cambridge: MIT Press, 1989.

16. "Lean manufacturing" was used by James P. Womack, Daniel Jones, and Daniel Roos, *The Machine That Changed the World*, New York: HarperPerennial, 1991, to describe the superior performance of Japanese auto companies.

17. Ronald Dore, *British Factory, Japanese Factory*, Berkeley: University of California, 1973. Other influential accounts of Japanese industrial experience were James C. Abegglen and George Stalk, Jr., *Kaisha: the Japanese Corporation*, New York: Basic Books, 1985; Ramchandran Jaikumar, "Postindustrial Manufacturing," *Harvard Business Review*, November–December 1986; Kim B. Clark and Takahiro Fujimoto, *Product Development Performance: Strategy, Organization, and Management in the World Auto Industry*, Cambridge: Harvard Business School Press, 1991.

CHAPTER 4: The New American Model

1. The term is Timothy J. Sturgeon's, in "Modular Production Networks: A New American Model of Industrial Organization," *Industrial and Corporate Change*, 11 (3): 451–96.

2. Tushar Dhayagude, Manesh Jayagopal, T.J. Manayathara, Sanjeev Suri, Aditya Yaga, "Is the IDM Model Doomed . . . Emergence of the Fabless-Foundry Model in the Semiconductor Industry," Evanston, Illinois: Kellogg Graduate School of Management (2001), p. 28.

3. Modularity in design and modularity in production are two separate matters, but an increase in the possibility of either one is likely to produce incentives for advancing the other. See the discussion of these reciprocal influences in Richard Langlois, "Modularity in Technology and Organization," *Journal of Economic Behavior and Organization* 49 (1): 19–37; and Arnaldo Camuffo, "Turning Out a 'World Car': Globalization, Outsourcing, and Modularity in the Auto Industry," *Korean Journal of Political Economy*, vol. 2, 2004, pp. 183–224.

4. Carliss Y. Baldwin and Kim B. Clark, *Design Rules. The Power of Modularity*,

Cambridge: MIT Press, 2000, p. 171. Baldwin and Clark provide a theory of modular design and a history of the impact of IBM's System/360 on the emergence of the modern modular computer industry.

5. Modularity as a response to growing complexity and uncertainty is emphasized in several other "classic" studies of this phenomenon: Raghu Garud, Arun Kumaraswamy, and Richard Langlois, *Managing in the Modular Age: Architectures, Networks, and Organizations*, Oxford: Basil Blackwell, 2003; S. Arndt and H. Kierzlowski, eds., *Fragmentation: New Production Patterns in the World Economy*, Oxford: Oxford University Press, 2001; Gary Gereffi, John Humphrey, Timothy Sturgeon, "The Governance of Global Value Chains: An Analytic Framework," *Review of International Political Economy* 12 (1) (2005): 78–104.

6. See Baldwin and Clark, Chapter 7, "Creating System/360, the First Modular Computer Family," pp. 169–94.

7. Carliss Y. Baldwin and Kim B. Clark, "Where Do Transactions Come From? A Perspective from Engineering Design," in Paper Prepared for the Saint-Gobain Centre for Economic Research, 5th Conference, "Organizational Innovation Within Firms," Paris, November 7–8, 2002.

8. Ibid., p. 7.

9. Patrick Porter, "Deciphering RosettaNet," *CIO Insight*, Ziff Davis Publishing, July 1, 2001.

10. This discussion of electronics was prepared by Tayo Akinwande, Douglas Fuller, and Charles Sodini and presented in their paper "Digitization and the Rise of the Modular Model: Reorganization and Relocation in the Global Electronics Industry," as well as many presentations to our team seminars.

11. Geoffrey G. Parker and Edward G. Anderson, Jr., "From Buyer to Integrator: The Transformation of the Supply-Chain Manager in the Vertically Disintegrating Firm," *Production and Operations Management* 11 (1) (2002): 75–91.

12. See Parker and Anderson, op. cit., and Jason Dedrick and Kenneth L. Kraemer, "Knowledge Management Across Firm and National Boundaries: Notebook PC Design and Development." Report, Alfred P. Sloan Foundation Center for the Personal Computing Industry, University of California, Irvine, 2003.

13. For a good discussion of these issues in electronics, see Dieter Ernst, "Limits to Modularity: A Review of the Literature and Evidence from Chip Design," Working Paper no. 71, East-West Center, 2004.

14. Laurie J. Flynn, "Apple's 4th-Quarter Profit More Than Doubled," *New York Times*, October 14, 2004, p. C1.

15. The paragraph draws on Rob Walker, "The Guts of a New Machine," *New York Times Magazine*, November 30, 2003, pp. 78–84.

16. David Carey, "Popular iPod Gets a Makeover," *EE Times*, January 5, 2004, http://www.eetimes.com/article/showArticle.jhtml?articleId=18310767.

17. Richard N. Langlois and Paul L. Robertson, *Firms, Markets, and Economic Change*, London: Routledge, 1995.

18. AnnaLee Saxenian, "Taiwan's Hsinchu Region: Imitator and Partner for Silicon Valley," in *SIEPR Discussion Paper No. 00-44*. Stanford, CA, 2001; John A. Mathews

and Dong-Sung Cho, *Tiger Technology. The Creation of a Semiconductor Industry in East Asia*, Cambridge: Cambridge University Press, 2000.

19. Interviews with Dr. Chikara Hayashi, former president and CEO, Ulvac.

20. TSMC does not make public—and we did not request in interviews—the names of its customers. The information in the text comes from Faith Hung, "Taiwan's Foundry Giants Prepare for China Investment," *Electronic Business News*, January 22, 2002; and Grigoriy Gubankov, "X-bit Watch: ATI vs. NVIDIA Fight Continues," *Electronic Business News*, May 31, 2003.

21. "Special Report: Creating a New IBM," *Think*, no. 5, 1992.

22. Parker and Anderson, op. cit., p. 81.

23. "The Info Tech 100," *BusinessWeek*, June 21, 2004, p. 93.

24. This term is the most confusing of all, since OEM is often used in the U.S. in exactly the opposite sense—to designate a brand-name multinational corporation whose "original equipment" is being made by others.

25. For the fiscal year ending March 31, 2004. http://www.flextronics.com/Investors/EarningsReleases/shareholder_letter_04.asp.

26. See his "Modular Production Networks: A New American Model of Industrial Organization," *Industrial and Corporate Change*, 11(3): 451–96.

27. On the dynamic quality of relationships between lead firms and suppliers and the diversity in these arrangements even in the same industries, see Gary Herrigel and Volker Wittke, "Varieties of Vertical Disintegration: The Global Trend Toward Heterogeneous Supply Relations and the Reproduction of Difference in US and German Manufacturing," in Glenn Morgan, Eli Moen, and Richard Whitely, eds., *Changing Capitalisms? Internationalisation, Institutional Change, and Systems of Economic Organisation*, Oxford: Oxford University Press, 2005.

28. We carried out 84 interviews in auto and auto-parts companies in the U.S., Canada, Mexico, Japan, Taiwan, China, Thailand, Germany, and Romania. We tried particularly to see the same companies operating in different markets—so, for example, we talked to Bosch managers in the U.S., Mexico, China, and Germany. We also visited companies making more or less identical products in different countries—so, for example, we saw wire harness makers in Mexico, China, and Romania, as well as all the major U.S. assemblers operating in different regions.

29. Takahiro Fujimoto, "Architecture, Capability, and Competitiveness of Firms and Industries," Saint-Gobain Centre for Economic Research 5th Conference, "Organizational Innovation Within Firms," November 7–8, 2002, p. 10.

30. Timothy Sturgeon and Richard Florida, "Globalization and Jobs in the Automotive Industry," Final Report to the Alfred P. Sloan Foundation, Cambridge: International Motor Vehicle Program, MIT, 2000.

31. Interview, November 7, 2000.

32. Interview, January 1, 2002.

33. Kathleen Kerwin, "How Would You Like Your Ford?" *BusinessWeek*, August 9, 2004, p. 34.

34. Shoinn Freeman, "Chrysler to Expand Ohio Plant, in Novel Venture with Suppliers," *Wall Street Journal*, August 4, 2004, online Factiva Dow Jones & Reuters.

35. Timothy Sturgeon and Richard Florida, "Globalization, Deverticalization, and Employment in the Motor Vehicle Industry," in *Locating Global Advantage. Industry Dynamics in the International Economy*, edited by M. Kenney with R. Florida, Stanford: Stanford University Press, 2004.

36. This discussion draws heavily on Sturgeon and Florida.

37. Op. cit., p. 55.

38. Teresa Lynch, "Internationalization in the Automotive Industry: Motivations, Methods, and Effects," Globalization and Jobs Project Research Note #2, Cambridge: International Motor Vehicle Program, MIT, 1998.

39. Shoinn Freeman, "Chrysler to Expand Ohio Plant, in Novel Venture with Suppliers," *Wall Street Journal*, August 4, 2004, online Factiva Dow Jones & Reuters.

PART THREE: Made All Over

CHAPTER 5: The Dilemma: Should You Stay or Should You Go?

1. Interview, July 11, 2000, and January 5, 2005, fax.

2. Claudia H. Deutsch, "Outsourcing Design," *New York Times*, December 20, 2004, pp. C1, C9.

3. William M. Bulkeley, "IBM's Palmisano Sees Huge Gains in Outsourcing," *Wall Street Journal*, May 20, 2004, p. B5 (online).

4. "Time to Bring It Back Home?" *The Economist*, March 5, 2005, p. 63.

5. Since suppliers and subcontractors are less unionized and have lower wages than big, vertically integrated firms, there might have been a fall in wages even if all the jobs had remained in the U.S.

6. J. Steven Landefeld and Ralph Kozlow, "Globalization and Multinational Companies: What Are the Questions, and How Well Are We Doing in Answering Them?" Paper read at Conference of European Statisticians (2003), at Geneva, pp. 5–6. See also Raymond J. Mataloni, Jr., "Survey of Current Business: U.S. Multinational Companies," Washington, D.C.: U.S. Bureau of Economic Analysis, 2004.

7. See Mataloni, 2004; also see United States Government Accountability Office (GAO), "International Trade. Current Government Data Provide Limited Insight into Offshoring of Services," Washington, D.C.: GAO, 2004, p. 24.

8. Dani Rodrik argues that even imports from high-wage companies make demand for domestic workers more elastic, hence makes their wages and jobs less secure. Dani Rodrik, *Has Globalization Gone Too Far?* Washington, D.C.: Institute for International Economics, 1997.

9. United States Government Accountability Office (GAO), "International Trade. Current Government Data Provide Limited Insight into Offshoring of Services," Washington, D.C.: GAO, 2004.

10. Ibid., p. 67.

11. Ibid., p. 3.

12. The statistics collected by the Bureau of Labor Statistics of the U.S. Department of Labor concern job losses reported by "companies employing at least 50 work-

ers where at least 50 people filed for unemployment insurance during a five-week period and the layoff lasted more than 30 days." Bureau of Labor Statistics, "Extended Mass Layoffs Associated with Domestic and Overseas Relocations, First Quarter 2004," June 10, 2004. http://www.bls.gov/mls.

13. Kate Bronfenbrenner and Stephanie Luce, "The Changing Nature of Corporate Global Restructuring: The Impact of Production Shifts on Jobs in the US, China, and Around the Globe." Submitted to the U.S.-China Economic and Security Review Commission, October 14, 2004, p. 79. Other analyses that conclude for much higher rates of job loss due to offshoring are cited in Louis Uchitelle, "A Missing Statistic: U.S. Jobs That Went Overseas," *New York Times,* October 5, 2003. http://www.nytimes.com/2003/20/05/business/05ECON.html?ex=1066362701&ei=1&en=4d7ac7290c9fb434.

14. Lori G. Kletzer and Howard Rosen, "Easing the Adjustment Burden on US Workers," in *The United States and the World Economy: Foreign Economic Policy for the Next Decade,* edited by Fred Bergsten, Washington, D.C.: Institute for International Economics, 2005, pp. 313–42.

15. Bronfenbrenner and Luce, op. cit., p. 32.

16. The picture that emerges of training under the TAA does not vary much from earlier studies of training of disadvantaged workers. A 1994 OECD study found little support for the effectiveness of government training programs. James Heckman, professor at the University of Chicago, concluded that "zero is not a bad number" when summarizing the results of his research on the effects of the Jobs Training Partnership Act, which involved large-scale training for disadvantaged workers. Cited in "Training and Jobs: What Works?" *The Economist,* April 6, 1996, pp. 19–21.

17. On the service jobs that can be moved offshore, see Frank Levy and Richard J. Murnane, *The New Division of Labor: How Computers Are Creating the Next Job Market,* Russell Sage Foundation, Princeton: Princeton University, 2004.

18. Charles L. Schultze, "Offshoring, Import Competition, and the Jobless Recovery." The Brookings Institution Policy Brief #136, Washington, D.C., August 2004.

19. Mary Amiti and Shang-Jin Wei, "Fear of Service Outsourcing: Is It Justified?" IMF Working Paper WP/04/186, Washington, D.C.: International Monetary Fund, October 2004.

20. John McCarthy, Forrester Research, "3.3 Million U.S. Services Jobs to Go Offshore," November 11, 2002, cited in GAO, pp. 44–45.

21. Cited in Paul Blustein, "Implored to 'Offshore' More; U.S. Firms Are Too Reluctant to Outsource Jobs, Report Says," *Washington Post,* July 2, 2004.

22. The bus driver example is drawn by Martin Wolf, *Why Globalization Works,* New Haven: Yale University Press, 2004, p. 85, from the World Bank; *World Development Report 1995: Workers in an Integrating World,* Oxford: Oxford University Press, pp. 10–14.

23. Bureau of Labor Statistics, *Current Economic Survey,* reported on BLS Web site, August 24, 2004.

24. The figures come from the OECD STAN database for Industrial Analysis. The ILO figures are somewhat different, but the picture is more or less the same. See Hilde-

gunn Kyvik Nordås, "The Global Textile and Clothing Industry post the Agreement on Textiles and Clothing." Geneva: World Trade Organization, 2004, p. 10.

25. The archives of Gratry and others are held in Lille, France, at the Centre des archives du monde du travail. I have described the French foreign-investment experience in Suzanne Berger, *Notre Première Mondialisation*, Paris: Seuil, 2003.

26. There is a large literature on the subject. For excellent overviews, see Paul Q. Hirst and Grahame Thompson, *Globalization in Question. The International Economy and the Possibility of Governance*, Cambridge, UK: Polity Press, second revised edition 1999; Peter Dicken, *Global Shift*, New York: Guilford Press, 4th edition, 2003; John H. Dunning, *Multinational Enterprises and the Global Economy*, Wokingham, UK: Addison-Wesley, 1993; Edward M. Graham, *Global Corporations and National Governments*, Washington, D.C.: International Institute of Economics, 1995.

27. D.C. Coleman, *Courtaulds. An Economic and Social History*, 3 vols., Oxford: Oxford University Press, 1969.

28. Ibid., II: 106.

29. Ibid., II: 110.

30. Ibid., II: 116–19.

31. Jim Mann, *Beijing Jeep: How Western Business Stalled in China*. New York: Simon and Schuster, 1989; Eric Thun, *Changing Lanes in China. Foreign Direct Investment and Auto Sector Development*. New York: Cambridge University Press, 2005.

32. On the history of U.S. textile protection, see Ellen Israel Rosen, *Making Sweatshops: The Globalization of the U.S. Apparel Industry*, Berkeley: University of California Press, 2002.

33. On Hong Kong textile and clothing industry, see Suzanne Berger with David Gartner and Kevin Karty, "Textiles and Clothing in Hong Kong," in S. Berger and R. K. Lester, *Made by Hong Kong*, Hong Kong: Oxford University Press, 1997.

34. Two-thirds of Mauritius exports go to the European Union. Starting in 2001, the U.S. also extended duty- and quota-free access to Mauritius-made goods, under the African Growth and Opportunity Act (AGOA).

35. The ramie and the vest with zip-on sleeves examples come from James Lardner, "Annals of Business: The Sweater Trade, Parts I and II," *The New Yorker*, January 11, 1988, pp. 39–73, and January 18, 1988, pp. 57–73.

36. Yilu Zhao, "When Jobs Move Overseas (to South Carolina)," *New York Times*, October 26, 2003, p. B4.

37. Keith Bradsher, "China Protests U.S. Limits on Textiles," *New York Times*, November 20, 2003, pp. W1, W7.

38. See the discussion of such gravity-type models in Carolyn L. Evans, "The Economic Significance of National Border Effects," Federal Reserve Bank of New York, October 15, 1999, pp. 4ff; and James E. Anderson and Eric van Wincoop, "Trade Costs," *Journal of Economic Literature* XLII (September 2004): 691–751.

39. John McCallum, "National Borders Matter: Canada-U.S. Regional Trade Patterns," *American Economic Review* 85 (June 1995): 615–23; John F. Helliwell, *How Much Do National Borders Matter?* Washington, D.C.: Brookings Institution, 1998; and Michael A. Anderson and Stephen S. Smith, "Do National Borders Really Matter?

Canada-U.S. Regional Trade Reconsidered," *Review of International Economics* 7, 2 (1999): 219–27.

40. Françoise Maurel, Rapport du Plan, *Scénario pour une Nouvelle Géographie Économique de l'Europe*, Paris: Economica, 1999, Rapport du Groupe "Géographie économique," p. 62.

CHAPTER 6: Making It Cheaper

1. Witold J. Henisz and Andrew Delios, "Uncertainty, Imitation, and Plant Location: Japanese Multinational Corporations, 1990–1996," *Administrative Science Quarterly* 46 (2001): 443–75.

2. Ron Hira, "U.S. Immigration Regulations and India's Information Technology Industry," *Technological Forecasting and Social Change* (in press).

3. Op. cit., p. 10.

4. Wilbur Chung and Juan Alcacer, "Knowledge Seeking and Location Choice of Foreign Direct Investment in the United States," unpublished paper, p. 24.

5. Cited in Alan B. Krueger, "Economic Scene," *New York Times*, August 19, 2004, p. C2.

6. David G. McKendrick, "Leveraging Locations. Hard Disk Drive Producers in International Competition," in Martin Kenney with Richard Florida, editors, *Locating Global Advantage*, Stanford: Stanford University Press, 2004.

7. See Pete Engardio, Aaron Bernstein, and Manjeet Kripalani, "Is Your Job Next?" *BusinessWeek*, February 3, 2003, pp. 50–60.

8. William M. Bulkeley, "IBM to Export Highly Paid Jobs to India, China," *Wall Street Journal*, December 15, 2003, p. B1.

9. My discussion here draws on Martin Wolf, *Why Globalization Works*, New Haven: Yale University Press, 2004, pp. 175–77.

10. McKinsey estimate in Bout (2003), p. 2.

11. The name of the company has been changed in this text.

12. Financial data are from 2003 annual reports. Our team carried out interviews at Luxottica on October 12, 1999. See also Arnaldo Camuffo, "Transforming Industrial Districts: Large Firms and Small Business Networks in the Italian Eyewear Industry," *Industry and Innovation*, 10 (4) (2003): 377–401.

13. David Birnbaum, *Birnbaum's Global Guide to Winning the Great Garment War*, Hong Kong: Third Horizon Press, 2000, p. xix.

14. Ibid., p. xx.

15. Ibid., p. 26.

16. Mike Flanagan, "The Ground Rules for Sourcing After 2005," Management Briefing, Bromsgrove, UK: Just-style.com, 2004, p. 22.

17. The study by supply-chain consultants Technology Forecasters is reported in Barbara Jorgensen, "Where the Costs Are," *Electronic Business*, July 2004.

18. Elizabeth Becker, "U.S. Loses Final Ruling on Subsidies for Cotton," *New York Times*, March 4, 2005, p. C2.

19. David Barboza, "Stream of Chinese Textile Imports Is Becoming a Flood," *New York Times*, April 4, 2005.

20. "The Great Stitch-Up," *The Economist*, May 28, 2005.

21. American Apparel and Footwear Association, *Trends*, http://www.appareland-footwear.org/data/trends2003Q2.pdf, Table 2.

22. The discussion of location in Mexico here and in the following paragraphs draws on Marcos Ancelovici and Sara Jane McCaffrey, "From NAFTA to China? Production Shifts and Their Implications for Taiwanese Firms," in S. Berger and R. K. Lester, *Global Taiwan: Building Competitive Strengths in a Global Economy*, Armonk, NY: M. E. Sharpe, 2005.

23. Frederick H. Abernathy, John T. Dunlop, Janice H. Hammond, and David Weil, A *Stitch in Time: Lean Retailing and the Transformation of Manufacturing—Lessons from the Apparel and Textile Industries*, New York: Oxford University Press, 1999; and Frederick H. Abernathy, John T. Dunlop, Janice H. Hammond, and David Weil, "Globalization in the Apparel and Textile Industries: What Is New and What Is Not?" in *Locating Global Advantage: Industry Dynamics in the International Economy*, edited by M. Kenney with R. Florida, Stanford: Stanford University Press, 2004.

24. Clothing imported into the United States from China, Hong Kong, Taiwan, and Korea fell from 63 percent of imports by volume in 1984 to 19 percent in 2000, while imports from Mexico and CBI rose over the same period from 7 percent to 39 percent.

25. Ibid., p. 44.

26. Marcos Ancelovici and Sara Jane McCaffrey, "From NAFTA to China? Production Shifts and Their Implications for Taiwanese Firms," in S. Berger and R. K. Lester, *Global Taiwan*, Armonk, NY: M. E. Sharpe, 2005, p. 166.

27. EIU, "Mexico Economy—Foreign Direct Investment Overview," London: Economist Intelligence Unit, October 20, 1999; Josephine Bow, "Made in Merida: The Next Hot Mexican Label," *Women's Wear Daily*, August 17, 1999.

28. *Taiwan Economic News*, "Hong Ho to Set Up Textile Plants in Mainland China," July 18, 2003.

29. *Just-Style*, "Mexico: An Action Plan for Yucatan," April 26, 2004.

30. Quoted in David Barboza, "Stream of Chinese Textile Imports Is Becoming a Flood," *New York Times*, April 4, 2005.

31. "The China Threat," Unified Industry Briefing, September 3, 2003.

32. U.S. International Trade Commission, "Textiles and Apparel: Assessment of the Competitiveness of Certain Foreign Suppliers to the US Market," Washington, D.C., Abstract, 2004.

33. American Manufacturing Trade Action Coalition (AMTAC) Executive Director Auggie Tantillo, quoted in National Council of Textile Organizations press release, June 16, 2004.

34. Guy de Jonquières, "Clothes on the Line: The Garment Industry Faces a Global Shake-Up as Quotas End," *Financial Times*, July 19, 2004, p. 11.

35. Bob Begg, John Pickles, and Adrian Smith, "Cutting It: European Integration, Trade Regimes, and the Reconfiguration of East-Central European Apparel Regimes,"

Environment and Planning 35 (2003): 2191–2207. See also Hildegunn Kyvik Nordås, "The Global Textile and Clothing Industry post the Agreement on Textiles and Clothing," Geneva: World Trade Organization, 2004.

36. *Crain's New York Business*, "Garment Makers Find the Right Fit," May 17–23, 2004, p. 2.

37. Sistema Moda Italia–Associazione Tessile Italiana on revised ISTAT data and 2001 census.

38. Elizabeth Becker, "Textile Quotas to End, Punishing Carolina Towns," *New York Times*, November 2, 2004, pp. 1, C10.

39. In 1998, for example, unemployment rates in leading textile and garment districts were 4.3 percent in Biella (woolen fabric), 3.4 percent in Belluno (shoes), 3.4 percent in Reggio Emilia and Treviso (garments), and 4.7 percent in Modena (garments).

40. Barbara Fiammeri, "Il distretto di Carpi, la città proibita delle imprese cinesi," *Il Sole-24 Ore*, June 18, 2002, pp. 1, 15.

PART FOUR: Competing in a Modular World

1. Interviewed in October 2004. We also met with Takashima in 2001 and 2002.

CHAPTER 7: Tracking Strategies from the Grass Roots Up

1. *BusinessWeek*, April 4, 2005, p. 134.

2. This account is based on information publicly available on the Web and on company interviews in 2001 and 2003.

3. Janice Revell, "Up, Up, and Away," *Fortune*, April 18, 2005, p. 232.

4. "An Unknown Giant Flexes Its Muscles," *New York Times*, December 4, 2004, http://www.nytimes.com. The sources cited by the article are IDC, Portelligent Inc., and Stanford University.

5. Companies do not usually break down their profits in ways that allow us to know how much they make on particular product lines, but in December 2004, IBM did detail its losses on PCs. *New York Times*, December 31, 2004, p. C4.

6. Cited in Steve Lohr, "IBM Sought a China Partnership, Not Just a Sale," *New York Times*, December 13, 2004.

7. Interview with Pou Chen managers, July 2, 2001. Also: Richard Dobson, "Pou Chen Corp: Shoe-in for Success," *Topics* (American Chamber of Commerce, Taipei), vol. 33, no. 8, pp. 52–54.

8. Gary Rivlin, "Who's Afraid of China? Not Super-Efficient Dell," *New York Times*, December 19, 2004, section 3, pp. 1, 4.

9. "Q & A: How Dell Keeps from Stumbling," *BusinessWeekonline*, May 14, 2001. In 2004, in an interview with ASCET (Achieving Supply Chain Excellence through Technology) publisher Barry Jacobs, Hunter estimated that of their P&L (profits and losses), 75–80 percent is in inventory and manufacturing and "Much of that overall

cost is the supply chain." June 15, 2004, ASCET, vol. 6, www.ascet.com/documents. asp?grlD=134&d_ID=2512.

10. Interview with Dick Hunter, January 12, 2005.

11. Interview with Dick Hunter, January 12, 2005.

12. Andy Server, "The Education of Michael Dell," *Fortune*, March 7, 2005, p. 76.

13. Karen Southwick, *The Pragmatic Radical*, November 21, 2004, http:news.com. com/The+pragmatic+radical/2008-1001 3-5110303.html.

14. "Shareholder Scoreboard. The Best and Worst Performers of the WSJ 1000," *Wall Street Journal*, February 28, 2005, p. R4.

15. Scott McNealy, "The Advantages of the Global Village," *Financial Times*, June 8, 2005, p. 15.

16. Quoted in Saul Hansell, "New Man at Top Crossing Oceans to Confront Internal Borders," *New York Times*, March 8, 2005, pp. C1, C8.

17. Quoted in James Brooke, "Sony Plans to Eliminate 20,000 Jobs Over 3 Years," *New York Times*, October 29, 2003, pp. W1, W 7.

18. John Markoff, "Smaller Than a Pushpin, More Powerful Than a PC," *New York Times*, February 7, 2005.

19. As evaluated in 2002 in a study at the University of Mannheim and the University of Tennessee of the world's top 500 supercomputers. Cited in John Markoff, "Smaller Than a Pushpin, More Powerful than a PC," *New York Times*, February 7, 2005, p. C3.

20. David Carey, "Sony PlayStation 2: Got(analog)game?" *PlanetAnalog*, August 26, 2003, http://www.planetanalog.com/showArticle?articleID=13900168.

21. Interviews with Toshiba, 2001, 2002, and 2004.

22. Financial data are from 2003 annual reports. Our team carried out interviews at Luxottica on October 12, 1999. See also Arnaldo Camuffo, "Transforming Industrial Districts: Large Firms and Small Business Networks in the Italian Eyewear Industry," *Industry and Innovation*, 10 (4) (2003): 377–401.

23. Operating margin is the ratio of net income to net sales.

24. On the ranking of technology companies, see *BusinessWeek*, June 21, 2004, pp. 93–101. On operating margins in the technology industry, see *BusinessWeek*, December 13, 2004, p. 104.

25. Luxottica, 2003 Annual Report, Part VI, "Luxottica Group-History and Overview," p. 3. www.luxottica.com/english/investor-relation/index-datifinazieri.html.

26. Interview at Zoff, June 18, 2003, and e-mail from Takashi Ueno, February 3, 2005.

CHAPTER 8: Brand-Name Firms, No-Name Manufacturers, and Everything in Between

1. The auto and auto-parts industries are discussed in Chapter 2.

2. Bruce Einhorn, David Rocks, Andy Reinhardt, "How Sharp Stays on the Cutting Edge," *BusinessWeek*, October 18, 2004, pp. 28–29. Our account draws also on an

interview in 2004 with senior managers at Sharp and on its 2004 Annual Report (for the year ending March 31, 2004). Sharp's ratio of operating income to net sales was 5.4% in 2004; of net income to net sales: 2.5%.

3. Yoshiko Hara, "Sharp Preps 8th Generation LCD Fab," *EE Times*, January 7, 2005, http://www.eet.com/article/showArticle.jhtml?articleId=57300426.

4. http://www.conway.com/ssinsider/bbdeal/bd020218.htm.

5. http://english.chosun.com/w21data/html/news/200501/200501160007.html; James Brooke and Saul Hansell, "Samsung Is Now What Sony Once Was," *New York Times*, March 10, 2005, pp. C1, C9.

6. Pete Engardio and Moon Ihlwan, "The Samsung Way," June 16, 2003, *BusinessWeekonline*, www.businessweek.com/print/magazine/content/03_24/b3837.

7. www.businessweek.com/magazine/content/04_48/b3910003.htm.

8. The parent firm is Inditex SA. This account draws on Kasra Ferdows, José A. D. Machuca, and Michael Lewis, "Zara," European Case Clearing House, No. 603-002-1, 2002; Nicolas Harlé, Michael Pich, and Ludo Van der Hayden, "Marks & Spencer and Zara: Process Competition in the Textile Apparel Industry," INSEAD No. 602-010-1, 2002; and Arnaldo Camuffo, Pietro Romano, and Andrea Vinelli, "Back to the Future: Benetton Transforms Its Global Network," *MIT Sloan Management Review*, vol. 43, no. 1 (fall 2001), pp. 46–52, and publicly available sources.

9. Interviews at Benetton, October 13, 1999, and January 18, 2002.

10. Kasra Ferdows, Michael A. Lewis, and Jose A.D. Machuca, "Rapid-Fire Fulfillment," *Harvard Business Review*, November 2004, pp. 104–10.

11. Robert Gavin, "It's Like Printing Money," *Boston Globe*, November 1, 2004, pp. C1, C4.

12. Ben Elgin, "Carly's Challenge," *BusinessWeek*, December 13, 2004, pp. 101–08. See also Ben Elgin, "Can Anyone Save HP?" *BusinessWeek*, February 21, 2005, pp. 28–35.

13. Reported in Elgin, December 13, 2004, p. 100.

14. Scott Morison, "New HP Chief Rules Out Radical Steps," *Financial Times*, March 31, 2005, p. 21.

15. Interview, April 12, 2002, and e-mail, February 17, 2005.

16. This account draws on an interview with HP's Joan Canigueral, Director of Supply Chain Operations, IPG Consumer HW-EMEA, May 19, 2003. We are grateful to him for one of the most detailed and valuable interviews in our study.

17. IPC interview, January 21, 2002. See also Yves Doz, José Santos, and Peter Williamson, *From Global to Metanational*, Cambridge: Harvard Business School Press, 2001.

18. Over the years, Intel has entertained projects to develop consumer electronic products—but has backed out, in part at least because of the resistance of customers like Dell to finding its supplier as a competitor. Cliff Edwards, "Intel," *BusinessWeek*, March 8, 2004, pp. 56–64.

19. Interviews, January 22, 2004. Also, Anne-Laure Quilleriet, "Dentelles en Mutation," *Le Monde*, January 7, 2004, p. 25.

20. Shigenobu Nagamori, interview, October 8, 2004. Nidec also makes small pre-

cision motors for automotives, home applicances, and other digital consumer goods, like cell phones, iPods, and DVDs. It has 80,000 employees and had more than U.S. $3 billion sales in 2004. Peter Marsh, "Investing in China: Nidec Assembles a Small Empire: An Advanced Manufacturing Complex Is Being Constructed in Pinghu City," *Financial Times*, July 28, 2004.

21. Peter Clarke, "SanDisk, Silicon Labs Leap in 2003 Fabless Rankings," *Silicon Strategies*, March 18, 2004. Eight of the ten largest fabless integrated-circuit suppliers are U.S. companies.

22. "The Info Tech 100," *BusinessWeek*, June 21, 2004, p. 93.

23. 2003 data provided by Eric Miscoll, Technology Forecasters, phone interview, October 7, 2004.

24. Flextronics is incorporated in Singapore, but its top management and key functions are located in San José, California. Tax breaks make it likely that Flextronics' headquarters will remain in Singapore.

25. Timothy J. Sturgeon and Ji-Ren Lee, "Industry Co-Evolution: A Comparison of Taiwan and North American Electronics Contract Manufacturers," in Suzanne Berger and Richard K. Lester, *Global Taiwan*, Armonk: M. E. Sharpe, 2005, Figure 2.3, p. 56.

26. Interview at Foxconn, July 29, 2002; and Dennis Normile, "Why Is Hon Hai So Shy," April 1, 2004, http://www.reed-electronics.com/eb-mag/index.asp?layout=articlePrint&articleID=CA405740.

27. Timothy J. Sturgeon and Ji-Ren Lee, "Industry Co-Evolution: A Comparison of Taiwan and North American Electronics Contract Manufacturers," in Suzanne Berger and Richard K. Lester, *Global Taiwan*, Armonk: M. E. Sharpe, 2005, Table 2.3, p. 51.

28. Interview, April 15, 2003, and newspaper accounts in *Jingji Ribao* (*Economic Daily*), May 21, June 24, September 30, October 13, November 6, 2002.

29. Interview with Aling Lai, January 20, 2000, and e-mail, January 20, 2005.

30. Interview with BenQ managers at their Suzhou, China, plant, July 30, 2002; Jason Dean, "BenQ Builds a Brand," *Far Eastern Economic Review*, October 23, 2003, pp. 38–40; James Miles, "Dancing with the Enemy," *The Economist*, Survey of Taiwan, January 15, 2005, pp. 9–10. BenQ has started selling low-cost LCD TVs in the U.S. and has 1 percent of the market. Eric Taub, "Flat Screens at Rock-Bottom Prices," *New York Times*, February 14, 2005.

31. Interview, January 12, 2005.

32. Interview, January 12, 2005.

33. For the best account of this, see Frederick H. Abernathy, John T. Dunlop, Janice H. Hammond, and David Weil, *A Stitch in Time: Lean Retailing and the Transformation of Manufacturing—Lessons from the Apparel and Textile Industries*, New York: Oxford University Press, 1999.

34. To borrow Simon Head's expression in "Inside the Leviathan," *New York Review of Books*, December 16, 2004, pp. 80–90.

35. The information on Wal-Mart is drawn from Gunnar Trumbull and Louisa Gay, *Wal-Mart into Europe*, Boston: Harvard Business School, 2004; Jeff Madrick, "Economic Scene: Wal-Mart May Be the New Model of Productivity, But It Isn't Always Wowing Workers," *New York Times*, September 2, 2004, p. C2.

36. Virginia Postrel, "Economic Scene: Lessons in Keeping Business Humming, Courtesy of Wal-Mart U," *New York Times*, February 28, 2002.

37. Masahiro Aoki and Hirokazu Takizawa, "Modularity: Its Relevance to Industrial Architecture." Paper prepared for Saint-Gobain Centre for Economic Research 5th Conference, "Organizational Innovation Within Firms," November 7–8, 2002.

38. For reasons obvious from the material, I am not using the firm's real name. The interview was carried out in June 2003.

39. Rone Tempest, "Barbie and the World Economy," *Los Angeles Times*, September 22, 1996.

40. Reuters, "CLSA Global Emerging Markets, Annual Report 1999," cited in Jean Boillot and Nicolas Michelon, *Chine, Hong Kong, Taiwan. Une nouvelle géographie économique de l'Asie*, Paris: La Documentation Française, 2001, p. 142.

41. Erica L. Plambeck and Terry A. Taylor, "Sell the Plant? The Impact of Contract Manufacturing on Innovation, Capacity and Profitability," unpublished paper, September 2001.

42. McKinsey, cited in Iain Carson, "Perpetual Motion: A Survey of the Car Industry," *The Economist*, September 4, 2004, figure 4, p. 8.

43. Timothy J. Sturgeon, "Exploring the Risks of Value Chain Modularity: Electronics Outsourcing During the Industry Cycle of 1992–2002," Working Paper MIT-IPC-03-003, Industrial Performance Center, 2003, pp. 32–33.

44. Robert Ristelhueber, "CM Firms Don't Want Inventory Ownership," *EBN*, May 3, 2001.

PART FIVE: **Make It at Home? Or Offshore?**

CHAPTER **9: Made in America?**

1. Interview with Marty Bailey, Vice President for Operations, March 25, 2004, and fax, February 16, 2005.

2. Interview with Douglas Fang, July 2, 2001, and newspaper accounts.

3. Interview with Herb Spivak, January 31, 2005; Darien Fonda, "Sole Survivor," *Time*, November 8, 2004, pp. 48–49.

4. Interview, April 5, 2004.

5. Interview, June 16, 2004.

6. Interview with Haruo Kawahara, President and CEO, October 6, 2004. Michiyo Nakamoto, "Made in Japan: Tide of History Is Halted in Search for Quality," *Financial Times*, March 30, 2005, p. 2.

7. Alpha is not the real name of the firm. The interview was carried out on June 10, 2003.

8. The discussion of Liz Claiborne's strategies draws on articles in the press and on an interview with Robert Zane, Senior Vice President, Manufacturing, Sourcing, Distribution, and Logistics, November 5, 2003.

9. Adam is not the real name of the company. The interview was conducted in Los Angeles on March 23, 2004.

10. Interview, January 14, 2002.

11. Michael L. Porter, "Clusters and the New Economics of Competition," *Harvard Business Review*, November-December 1998. See also his ongoing Cluster Mapping Project, Institute for Strategy and Competitiveness, Harvard Business School, http://data.isc.hbs.edu/isc/cmp_overview.jsp.

12. For the first major study of high-tech clusters, see AnnaLee Saxenian, *Regional Advantage: Culture and Competition in Silicon Valley and Route 128*, Cambridge: Harvard University Press, 1994.

13. On organizational structures and the design process, see Richard K. Lester and Michael J. Piore, *Innovation: The Missing Dimension*, Harvard University Press, 2004.

14. Steven K. Vogel, "How Do National Market Systems Evolve? Theoretical Perspectives and the Japanese Case," manuscript, Berkeley, California, 2003.

15. Cited in Vogel, p. 8.

16. See also Dieter Ernst, "Searching for a New Role in East Asian Regionalization: Japanese Production Networks in the Electronics Industry," East-West Center Working Paper No. 68, March, 2004.

17. Chunli Lee, "Strategic Alliances of Chinese, Japanese and U.S. Firms in the Chinese Manufacturing Industry: The Impact of 'China Prices' and Integrated Localization," paper presented at Fairbank Center for East Asian Research, Harvard University, October 4, 2004.

18. Ibid., p. 8.

19. Ian Rowley, "Lessons from Matsushita's Playbook," *BusinessWeek*, March 21, 2005, p. 32.

20. Nippon Keidanren, *Japan 2025. Envisioning a Vibrant, Atttractive Nation in the Twenty-First Century*, n.d.

21. Takashi Marugami, Takeshi Toyoda, Takeshi Kasuga, Mayumi Suzuki, "Survey Report on Overseas Business Operations By Japanese Manufacturing Companies," *JBICI Review* 7 (2003): 1–78. See the preceding year's survey, with quite similar responses: Shinji Kaburagi, Shiro Izuishi, Takeshi Toyoda, Mayumi Suzuki, "JBIC FY 2001 Survey. The Outlook for Japanese Foreign Direct Investment (13th Annual Survey)," *JBICI Review* 6 (2002): 1–57.

22. Marugami et al., pp. 19–20.

23. Thanks to Reo Matsuzaki for pointing out this finding.

24. See Takeshi Inagami and D. Hugh Whittaker, *The New Community Firm. Employment, Governance and Management Reform in Japan*, Cambridge, UK: Cambridge University Press, 2005; and D. Hugh Whittaker, "Hitachi and Emerging 'Japanese-style' MOT," Doshisha University, 2004.

CHAPTER 10: Building on a Legacy at Home

1. Jun Kurihara, "Japan's Industrial Revitalization: Its Origin and Future," *Japan Economic Currents*, Keizai Koho Center, No. 46, July 2004. For Matsushita, in the last quarter of 2004, sales of flat-panel TVs and DVD recorders (under the Panasonic

label) pushed its profits up 47 percent. Todd Zaun, "Digital Cameras and TV's Lift Matsushita Profit 47%," *New York Times*, February 5, 2005, p. B3.

2. Government data cited in Michiyo Nakamoto, "Japan's Electronics Industry Revived," *Financial Times*, August 5, 2004.

3. Elizabeth Becker, " '04 Trade Deficit Sets Record, $617 Billion," *New York Times*, February 11, 2005, C1. Overall U.S. trade deficit was $617.7 billion, equal to more than 5 percent of the U.S. economy. The Commerce Department reported losing ground not only in manufacturing but also in advanced technology goods and in services.

4. Nikkei, *How Canon Got Its Flash Back. The Innovative Turnaround Tactics of Fujio Mitarai* (translated by M. Schreiber and A. M. Cohen), Singapore: John Wiley & Sons (Asia), 2001 (2004).

5. The discussion of Matsushita draws on interviews on March 10, 2004, June 27, 2001, and March 24, 2000, as well as articles in the press and Lee (2004), op. cit.

6. Todd Zaun, "Two Deals in Japan Alter Flat-Panel TV Business," *New York Times*, February 8, 2005, p. C18.

7. The discussion of Kenwood is based on articles in the press and an interview with President Haruo Kawahara, October 6, 2004.

8. The "Nakagawa Report Toward a Sustainable and Competitive Industrial Structure," was produced by the Ministry of Economy, Trade, and Industry (METI), May 2004. Summary in English.

9. Eurostat New Chrono Database, cited in Nicholas Owen and Alan Cannon Jones, "A Comparative Study of the British and Italian Textile and Clothing Industries," 2003, p. 4.

10. L. Federico Signorini, ed., *Economie locali, modelli di agglomerazione e apertura internazionale*, Rome: Banca d'Italia, 2004, pp. 18–21. For a far gloomier account of the future of the Italian districts, see Michael Dunford and Lidia Greco, *After the Three Italies: Industrial Change and Regional Economic Performance* (forthcoming), especially Chapter 10, on textiles and clothing, and the conclusion, which calls the decline in employment in these sectors in the districts a "crisis."

11. Stefano Federico, "L'internazionalizzazione produttiva italiana e i distretti industriali: un'analisi degli investimenti diretti all'estero," in *Economie locali, modelli di agglomerazione e apertura internazionale*, edited by L. F. Signorini, Rome: Banca d'Italia, 2004, p. 407.

12. The following section draws on our study of the impact of globalization on networked district production in Suzanne Berger and Richard M. Locke, "*Il Caso Italiano* and Globalization," in *Daedalus*, vol. I: The European Challenge (spring 2001), pp. 85–104.

13. Interview with Fabio Bordignon, Antenna Veneto Romania, June 18, 2003; Centro Estero Veneto, "Prima Indagine sulla Presenza Veneta in Romania," Mestre, 2003. The Industrial Performance Center team carried out thirteen interviews in Romania.

14. Fabio Farabullini and Giovanni Ferri, "Passagi a Est per le banche italiane e i distretti industriali," in *Economie locali, modelli di agglomerazione e apertura internazionale*, edited by L. F. Signorini, Rome: Banca d'Italia, 2004, p. 466.

15. The name of the company has been changed in this account.

16. Textile Outlook International from Werner International data cited in Robin Anson, "Textiles and Apparel Sourcing Options to 2005 and Beyond: Can Asia Compete with Mexico, Sub-Saharan Africa and the Euro-Periphery?" Paper presented at Interstoff Asia Autumn 2002, Hong Kong, October 3, 2002, www.textilesintelligence.com/til/press.cfm?prid=301.

17. IFM/Eurovet, *Journal du Textile*, no. 1704, April 22, 2002, p. 4.

18. Interview, March 31, 2003.

19. Presentation by Sara Jane McCaffrey, "Textiles and Apparel After NAFTA: The US Story," MIT Industrial Performance Center, February 20, 2003.

PART SIX: **How to Succeed in the Global Economy**

CHAPTER 11: **Lessons from the Field**

1. Dell's 2004 profit-revenue ratio was 6.2 percent; IBM's was 8.8 percent. The figures come from *Fortune* magazine, April 18, 2005. Exactly because the companies encompass different activities in electronics, any particular measure of their returns is of limited value. I use them here only to illustrate the point that different strategies in the same industries can produce more or less equivalent returns.

2. "Special Report: Nokia's Turnaround. The Giant in the Palm of Your Hand," *The Economist*, February 12, 2005, pp. 67–69.

3. Robert Galbraith, "District System Facing Challenge," *International Herald Tribune*, February 22, 2005, p. 12.

4. Paul Brenton and Anna Maria Pinna, "The Declining Use of Unskilled Labour in Italian Manufacturing: Is Trade to Blame?" Working Document No. 178, Centre for European Policy Studies, 2001, p. 18.

5. "Fortune 500: How the Industries Stack Up," April 18, 2005, p. F-28. Of the eleven apparel companies on the Fortune 500 list, our team carried out interviews with senior executives in six of them.

6. Interview with the founder and president, Dr. Mario Moretti Polegato, January 18, 2002; Arnaldo Camuffo, Andrea Furlan, Pietro Romano, and Andrea Vinelli, "Breathing Shoes and Complementarities: How Geox's Strategy Is Rejuvenating the Footwear Industry," December 2004; Jason Horowitz, "Inside Italy's Hottest Shoes, the Coolest Toes," *New York Times*, March 1, 2005. http://www.geox-ir.com/.

7. Geox owns and operates a plant in Timisoara, Romania, and brings Romanians to Montebelluna for training. Turnover rates in Romania are high—20–30 percent a year. As we observed elsewhere, this means a heavier investment on the management side. Geox has fifteen Italians in the Romanian plant. (In 2002, the cost of locating one Italian in the Romanian plant was equivalent to the cost of employing 100 Romanians.) Most of the other Geox shoes are made in Asia by contract manufacturers like Pou Chen.

8. Judith Banister calculated that workers earn $0.64 an hour in China, as contrasted with $21.11 per hour in the U.S. Estimates prepared for the Bureau of Labor

Statistics, cited in Peter Coy, "Just How Cheap Is Chinese Labor?" *BusinessWeek*, December 13, 2004, p. 46. Whether Chinese wages are rising and by how much is a disputed matter.

9. Presentation by Ronald C. Ritter to the Leaders for Manufacturing Workshop (by video), February 11, 2005. The research was reported in Ronald C. Ritter and Robert A. Sternfels, "When Offshore Manufacturing Doesn't Make Sense," *McKinsey Quarterly*, no. 4, 2004, p. 124.

10. John Hagel III and John Seely Brown, *The Only Sustainable Edge. Why Business Strategy Depends on Productive Friction and Dynamic Specialization*, Boston: Harvard Business School Press, 2005.

11. This discussion and the quotes from IBM executives are based on Steve Lohr, "Sharing the Wealth at I.B.M.," *New York Times*, April 11, 2005, pp. 1, 4.

12. "Special Report: Manufacturing in Japan. (Still) Made in Japan," *The Economist*, April 10, 2004, p. 59.

13. This idea is developed in Stefano Brusoni and Keith Pavitt, "Modularity and the Division of Cognitive Labour Within/Across Organizations." Paper prepared for Saint-Gobain Centre for Economic Research, 5th Conference, "Organizational Innovation Within Firms," November 7–8, 2002, Paris.

14. In 2003, China spent $60 billion on research and development, compared with the U.S., which spent $282 billion, and Japan, $104 billion. China graduated 325,000 engineers in 2004—five times as many as in the U.S. Cited in Ted C. Fishman, "The Chinese Century," *New York Times Magazine*, July 4, 2004, pp. 22–51.

15. "Technology in China: The Allure of Low Technology," *The Economist*, December 20, 2003, p. 99.

16. Huawei's links to the government and to the People's Liberation Army are murky; however, the company claims to be a private one.

17. "The Challenger from China: Why Huawei Is Making the Telecoms World Take Notice," *Financial Times*, January 11, 2005, p. 13.

18. On Huawei, see Chris Buckley, "Rapid Growth of China's Huawei Has Its High-Tech Rivals on Guard," *New York Times*, October 6, 2003, pp. C1, C3; and "Special Report: China's Champions: The Struggle of the Champions," *The Economist*, January 8, 2005, pp. 59–61. The IPC interview at Huawei was carried out in July 2002.

19. "See Huawei Run," *The Economist*, March 5, 2005, pp. 60–61.

20. The study claimed that if the companies the graduates and faculty created had formed an independent nation, their revenues would have made it the twenty-fourth-largest economy in the world.

21. Ming Zeng, professor at INSEAD, cited in *The Economist* (December 20, 2003).

22. January 30, 2005.

23. Douglas B. Fuller, "Building Ladders Out of Chains: China's Technological Development in a World of Global Production," PhD dissertation, MIT Department of Political Science, 2005.

24. www.nsf.gov/sbe/srs/seind04/c)/c)s1.htm, Table 0–11.

25. Dan Breznitz, "Innovation and the State. Development Strategies for High-

Technology Industries in a World of Fragmented Production: Israel, Ireland, and Taiwan," PhD dissertation, MIT Department of Political Science, 2005.

26. Quoted in John Markoff, "Intel Officer Says High Taxes Could Send Plant Overseas," *New York Times*, April 1, 2005, p. C12.

27. On the differences between policies in India and China, Simon Long, "The Tiger in Front: A Survey of India and China," *The Economist*, March 5, 2005.

CHAPTER 12: Beyond the Company

1. These arguments are presented in Chapter 1.

2. In 1993, 73 percent of the manufacturing assets and 77 percent of the services assets of U.S. MNC's were located in the U.S., according to Paul Hirst and Grahame Thompson, *Globalization in Question*, second edition, Cambridge, U.K.: Polity Press, 1999. See especially Chapter 3, "The Internationalization of Business Activity," and the data on location of manufacturing affiliates, sales, assets, and profits, pp. 82–83.

3. National Science Board, *Science and Engineering Indicators 2004*, Arlington, VA: National Science Foundation, Division of Science Resources Statistics, http://www.nsf.gov/sbe/srs/seind04/front/nsb.htm. See Chapter 4, "U.S. and International Research and Development: Funds and Technology Linkages," pp. (4) 1–70.

4. Andrew Alpert and Jill Auyer, "Evaluating the BLS 1988–2000 Employment Projections," *Monthly Labor Review*, October 2003, pp. 13–37.

5. Cited in Ben Edwards, "A World of Work. A Survey of Outsourcing," *The Economist*, November 13, 2004, p. 14.

6. Stacey R. Schreft and Aarti Singh, "A Closer Look at Jobless Recoveries," *Economic Review. Second Quarter 2003*, Federal Reserve Bank of Kansas City, pp. 45–66; Erica L. Groshen and Simon Potter, "Has Structural Change Contributed to a Jobless Recovery?" *Current Issues in Economics and Finance*, vol. 9, no. 8, Federal Reserve Bank of New York, August 2003.

7. R. Jason Faberman, "Gross Jobs Flow over the Past Two Business Cycles: Not All 'Recoveries' Are Created Equal," BLS Working Paper 372, Washington, D.C.: U.S. Bureau of Labor Statistics, June 2004.

8. For a recent estimate that emphasizes tremendous increases (from $450 billion to $1.3 trillion a year) in U.S. national income from more free trade, see Scott Bradford, Paul Grieco, and Gary Hufbauer, "The Payoff to America from Global Integration," in Fred Bergsten, editor, *The United States and the World Economy: Foreign Economic Policy for the Next Decade*,Washington, D.C.: International Institute of Economics, 2005.

9. Interview, June 27, 2001.

10. Clayton M. Christensen, *The Innovator's Dilemma: When New Technologies Cause Great Firms to Fail*, Boston: Harvard Business School Press, 1997.

11. Tom Waldron, Brandon Roberts, and Andrew Reamer, *Working Hard, Falling Short. America's Working Families and the Pursuit of Economic Security*, Working Poor Families Project, October 2004. See also David K. Shipler, *The Working Poor: Invisible*

in America, New York: Knopf, 2004; and Michelle Conlin and Aaron Bernstein, "Working . . . And Poor," *BusinessWeekonline*, May 31, 2004. http://www.businessweek.com/print/magazine/content/04_22/b3885001_mz001.htm?chan=mz&.

12. These statistics come from Waldron et al. (2004).

13. In seven of the ten occupations that the Bureau of Labor Statistics predicts will grow the most between now and 2012, jobs are mainly low-wage and annual earnings under $18,000. These include janitors, waiters, food workers, cashiers, hospital workers, and customer service representatives. Cited in Steven Greenhouse, "If You're a Waiter, the Future Is Rosy," in News of the Week in Review, *New York Times*, March 7, 2004.

14. There is a good discussion of many of these options in Lori G. Kletzer and Howard Rosen, "Easing the Adjustment Burden on US Workers," in *The United States and the World Economy: Foreign Economic Policy for the Next Decade*, edited by Fred Bergsten, Washington, D.C.: Institute for International Economics 2005, pp. 313–42.

15. http://www.nsf.gov.sbe/srs/seind04/c1/c1c/htm.

16. The OECD Program for International Student Assessment (PISA) tested 250,000 fifteen-year-olds in forty-one countries. The results are reported in "Learning for Tomorrow's World—First Results from PISA 2003 Executive Summary," www.pisa.oecd.org.document/55/0,2340,en_32252351_32236173_3391. Other surveys comparing U.S. fourth-graders with those abroad are reported in http://nces.ed.gov/pubs2005/timss03/tables/table_06.asp.

17. www.gatesfoundation.org/MediaCenter/Speeches/BillGSpeeches/.

18. Michael L. Dertouzos, Richard K. Lester, and Robert M. Solow, *Made in America*, Cambridge: MIT Press, 1989, Chapter 10: "Imperatives for a More Productive America."

19. Ibid., p. 143.

20. http://www.nsf.gov.sbe/srs/seind04/c1/c1chtm.

21. Lori G. Kletzer and William L. Koch, "International Experience with Job Training: Lessons for the U.S.," in C. O. Leary, R. Straits, and S. Wandner, editors, *Job Training Policy in the U.S.*, W. E. Upjohn Institute for Employment Research, 2004, Table 5.

22. Op. cit., p. 81.

23. See their 2004 *Innovation: The Missing Dimension*, Cambridge: Harvard University Press, on which my account draws heavily (especially Chapter 8).

24. www.bell-labs.com/about/history/timeline.html.

25. Pete Engardio and Bruce Einhorn, "Outsourcing Innovation," *BusinessWeek*, March 21, 2005, p. 87.

26. As these changes in the corporate world unfolded in the early 1990s, university researchers watched with more than a touch of self-interest. But the hope that companies would transfer resources to universities to do the more basic research they no longer did in-house was disappointed. On the contrary, the universities' research agenda was increasingly geared to commercial ends. Derek Bok, *Universities in the Marketplace. The Commercialization of Higher Education*, Princeton: Princeton University Press, 2003.

27. Pete Engardio and Bruce Einhorn, "Outsourcing Innovation," *BusinessWeek*, March 21, 2005, pp. 84–94.

28. Ibid., p. 90.

29. National Science Board, *Science and Engineering Indicators 2004*, Arlington, VA: National Science Foundation, Division of Science Resources Statistics, pp. 4–9. http://www.nsf.gov/sbe/srs/seind/o4/front/nsb.htm.

30. Ibid., Figure 4.9.

31. www.aaas.org.spp.rd.

Index

Abbassi, Yousef (Cisco), 141–42
Accenture, 95
Acer, 182–83, 262
Advanced Micro Devices (AMD), 167–68, 230
Advantest, 233
Aladdin, 275
Albert, Michel, 39–40, 41
Alcatel, 272
ALi, 178
Amazon, 153, 292
American Apparel, 24, 47, 133, 201–3, 205, 252, 256
American Express, 75
Anagram Corporation, 208–9, 247, 256, 261
Analog Devices, 79, 174, 175, 185
Anderson, Edward, 83
Ansolabehere, Paul (Anagram), 208–9
Aoki, Masahiro, 191
Aoki, Teruaki (Sony), 155, 156, 157–58, 159, 166
Apple Computer, 49, 51, 118, 180, 195, 230
  iPod, 62, 77–78, 153, 230, 237–38, 247, 253

Applied Materials, 80
Argentina, 15
ARM, 77, 177
Asia, 15, 83, 84, 117, 128, 133, 214. *See also specific countries.*
ASUSTeK, 84, 90, 295
ATI, 81
Auto and auto parts industry, 33, 38, 85–89, 103–5, 176–77, 193, 220

Bailey, Marty (American Apparel), 201, 202
Baldwin, Carliss Y., 74
Bangladesh, 127, 131, 252
Bell Laboratories, 292–93
Benetton, 35, 68, 169, 170, 255
BenQ, 182–83
Biella, 36, 243
Bird mobile phone, 26–27, 111, 254, 271
Birnbaum, David, 124
BMW, 41, 87, 160
Book publishing, 203, 207–8
Boos Textile Elastics, 246–47
Borderless World, The (Ohmae), 6, 37, 38

Bosch, 85, 86, 88, 176
Bradshaw, Robert C. (MSL), 143
Brand-name firms, 179–83, 185,
    192–94, 222
Brembo, 120, 176
Breznitz, Dan, 275
British Electric, 71
British Factory, Japanese Factory
    (Dore), 71
Broadcom, 30, 79, 81, 177, 292
Bronfenbrenner, Kate, 97, 98
Brown, John Seely, 262
Bulgaria, 132
Burlington, 128, 129
Burma, 118
Burroughs, 80

Cadence, 78, 79
Cambodia, 127
Cambridge Silicon Radio, 81
Canada, 111
Canon, 229, 231, 236
Cap Gemini, 95
Capitalism vs. Capitalism (Albert),
    39–40
Caribbean Basin countries, 20, 21, 110,
    127, 128, 214
Celestica, 83, 84, 143, 179, 195
Chandler, Alfred D., Jr., 65
Chang, Morris, 79, 113
Charney, Dov, 203
Chartered, 79
Checkpoint, 275
Chi Mei Optoelectronics Corp., 148
China, 3, 11, 13, 18, 20, 25, 32, 38,
    109–10, 117, 267–75
  analysis of industry relocation,
    130–35
  auto industry, 88, 103–5
  bribes and corruption, 125–26
  as consumer market, 16, 110–11, 217
  foreign direct investment in, 19, 109,
    156, 178, 221, 225–28, 239–40,
    261, 271, 273

Hangzhou city, 272–73
  high technology in, 269–75
  Japan and, 229–30, 232
  labor cost, 93–94, 97, 117, 123–24,
    174, 208, 237, 260
  manufacturing in, 14, 18–20, 21, 22,
    23, 27, 28, 35, 36, 79–80, 108–10,
    113–14, 117, 120, 123–24, 141,
    146–48, 158, 162, 174, 178,
    179–80, 205, 214–16, 243, 255,
    258, 271
  opening of, 90, 96, 239
  patents filed by, 275
  political stability concerns, 118–19
  productivity and real labor costs, 120,
    122–23, 225
  textiles and apparel, 107–8, 109–10,
    126–35, 243–44, 256, 297–98
  U.S. trade deficit with, 16
  workforce, 219, 234, 267, 279–80
Circuit City, 224
Cirrus Logic, 158
Cisco Systems, 26–27, 30, 141–42, 165,
    179, 195–96, 272, 273, 274, 286,
    292, 294
Clareman, Richard (Self-Esteem),
    297–98
Clark, Kim B., 74
Cluster economy, 30, 177, 178, 216–18
Coca-Cola, 16
Comlent, 274
Commodities, 52, 83, 90, 146–53, 160,
    163, 164, 252
Compal, 84, 295
Contract manufacturing. *See* Original
    design manufacturers (ODMs),
    and Original equipment
    manufacturers (OEMs).
Convergence model, 8, 21, 36, 37, 38,
    39, 42, 43, 44, 49, 145, 247
Coordinated market economies, 41–43
Courtaulds, 103, 104
Crystal Semiconductor, 81
Currency and money supply, 15, 37, 49

Cypress Semiconductor Corporation, 26, 77

DaimlerChrysler, 88, 89
  Jeep, 87, 89, 103
Dana, 89
D'Arbeloff, Alex, 265
Davis, Jim (New Balance), 204
Davos World Economic Forum, 6
DEC (Digital Equipment), 142
Dell, Michael, 152–53, 298
Dell Computer Corporation, 8, 14, 24, 29, 30, 35, 47, 66, 84, 94, 150–53, 155, 159, 160, 164, 171, 173, 180, 183, 185, 211, 230, 247, 252, 255, 258–59, 275, 280, 286, 292, 294
Delphi, 85, 88, 104
Delta Woodside, 128
Denso, 86
DeWolfe, Nick, 265
Dongu-Anam, 79
Dore, Ronald, 71
DuPont, 64, 65

eBay, 292
Economy, U.S., 25, 34, 280–82, 292–94
EDS, 95
Egypt, 131
Eisenhower, Dwight D., 106
Electronics, 33, 35, 51, 52, 54–55, 75–76, 78–82, 100, 101, 120, 140, 144, 148, 166–68, 174–77, 179–81, 182–83, 194, 209–10, 219–20, 252, 271
  Japanese, 229–38
  OEMs, ODMs, and global suppliers, 84–85, 148, 156–58, 194–97. *See also* Semiconductors.
Elpida, 167, 193
Employment, 99, 217. *See also specific countries.*
  employer threats of relocation and wages, 38–39, 116
  high wages and company survival, 8–9, 35, 202, 217, 256–57

innovation and job creation, 25–26, 282–88, 292
labor costs, 74, 88, 89, 96, 115–26, 208, 212–13, 217, 225, 246–47, 260–61
low-cost sites, 20, 25, 93–94, 97
low-wage strategies, 53–54, 259–61
outsourcing/offshoring and, 4–5, 20, 25, 94, 95–96, 97–101, 255–56, 287
productivity, 120, 213, 218, 235
real costs of cheap labor, 118–26, 260–61
retraining, 98–100, 288–92
skilled workforce, 76–77, 98, 218–20, 225, 231, 234–36, 246, 248, 258, 279–80, 288–92, 297
TAA, 98
turnover problems, 234
unions and, 89, 116
working poor, 287
Ericsson, 84, 179, 227, 272, 294
Ermenegildo Zegna, 68, 240
Esquel, 239
Europe, 15, 17, 52, 95, 132
European Union (EU), 20, 101, 110, 111, 127, 240
Eyeglass companies, 26–27, 68, 122–23, 160–64, 240, 255, 256–57

Fabrication plants (fabs), 15, 20, 73, 80–81, 114, 167–68, 175, 270, 274, 276
Fanuc, 233
Fang Brothers, 30, 85, 182, 186–87, 188, 204, 223, 239, 262
Fawkes, Mike (Hewlett-Packard), 172–73
Federated Department Stores, 128, 188
Ferguson, Niall, 65
Fields, Gary, 66
Fiorina, Carleton S. (Carly), 171–72
Flextronics, 27, 30, 84, 95, 158, 165, 174, 179, 195, 224

Ford Motor Company, 64, 65, 66–67, 69, 85, 87–88, 102, 223
Fragmentation. *See* Modularity, Networks.
France, 20, 34, 50, 102, 109, 183–84, 240, 241
Freescale, 166
Friedman, Thomas, 6, 268
FujiFilm AXIA, 26
Fujimoto, Takahiro, 60–61
Fujitsu, 30, 47, 78, 137, 139, 231, 233
Fuller, Douglas B., 274

G. F. Swift & Company, 64, 65–66
Gap, 30, 34, 49, 128, 169, 170, 185, 222
Gates, Bill, 288–90
GATT (General Agreement on Tariffs and Trade), 96, 106
Geox, 68, 257–58, 269, 298
Germany, 17, 20, 35–36, 40, 41–42, 99, 101, 114, 133, 160–61, 183, 191–92, 241, 246–47, 279
GFT, 142
Giant Bicycle, 93, 181, 182, 262
Gifford, Kathy Lee, 203
Glidden, John (L. W. Packard), 21–24, 36, 127
Global hybrids, 274–75
Globalization, 3–9, 14–24, 35–38, 73, 90, 136, 268, 281, 284
    causes and drivers of, 35, 38, 47, 48, 59, 96, 135–36
    convergence model, 36–39, 43–44
    dynamic legacies model, 44–47, 248
    government role in economy and, 6–7, 15, 37
    history of, 9–16, 136
    models of business success, 251–59
    modularity and, 25–26, 51, 52, 75–90, 96, 136, 137, 140–41, 158, 179, 192–94, 218–22, 252–54, 261, 294
    national varieties of capitalism model, 39–44

    unique capabilities and business success, 254–59, 298
    winners and losers in, 142–46, 251–77
Global suppliers, 84–85
General Motors (GM), 8, 65, 69, 85, 88, 102, 103, 223
    NUMMI, 71
Grace Company, 20, 79, 178, 270
Gratry Enterprises, 102
Greenspan, Alan, 5
Grieder, William, 280
Grupo M, 119
Guilford Mills, 128, 129
Guo, Huaqiang, 273

H & M, 169, 170
Hagel, John, III, 262
Haier, 108–9, 111, 227
Haiti, 119
Hall, Peter, 41–42
Hangzhou Sunyard, 272, 273
Hayashi, Chikara, 220
Hewlett-Packard (HP), 35, 57, 76, 78, 82, 83, 84, 94, 95, 118, 153, 166, 167, 171–74, 179, 180, 224, 255, 294
Hitachi, 17, 70, 71, 140, 166, 166, 167, 193, 233
Ho, Silas, 239
Hollington, Patric, 183–84
Honda, 104
Honduras, 127
Honeywell, 95
Hong Ho, 129–30
Hong Kong, 19, 26, 45, 46–47, 106–8, 109, 113, 125, 132, 193, 204, 223, 239–40, 260, 269, 271
Hon Hai, 30, 179–80
Huawei Technologies, 271–72, 274
Hungary, 20, 132, 174, 179
Hunter, Dick L. (Dell), 151, 152, 183, 185, 280
Huntington, Samuel, 18

Hurd, Mark (Hewlett-Packard), 171
Hynix, 271

IBM, 63–64, 74–75, 78, 79, 80, 82–83,
    84, 90, 95, 117, 140, 146–49, 153,
    155, 158, 159, 160, 166, 167, 171,
    180, 182, 223, 252, 262–63, 271,
    273
IDT Newave, 270, 274
Immigration, 10, 11, 13, 37
    guest workers, 114
India, 3, 25, 127, 132, 268
    educating workers in, 219
    foreign direct investment in, 19
    high-tech areas, 269
    outsourcing to, 14, 18, 20, 28, 97,
        114, 117, 120–21, 256, 260
Indonesia, 118, 124, 131
Industrial Performance Center (IPC),
    MIT Globalization Study, 7–9,
    29–55
Infineon, 166, 174, 175
Infosys, 114
Integrated device makers (IDMs), 79
Intel, 30, 35, 79, 84, 153, 165, 173,
    175–76, 230, 276
Internet, business and, 75
International Finance Corporation, 119
International Monetary Fund, 6, 13
Inventec, 77
IP (intellectual property), 81, 157,
    158, 159, 182, 184, 220, 265–66,
    274
Ireland, 143, 275, 276
Israel, 269, 275, 276
Italy, 169, 269
    cluster economies in, 30, 216–17
    expansion and diversification in,
        241–44
    eyeglasses, 68, 122–23, 161–64
    industrial districts, 67–69, 113, 122,
        134, 162, 240–42, 285
    "Made in Italy" label, 204, 245–46
    textiles and apparel, 22, 24, 34, 35,

    36, 101, 120–22, 133–34, 142, 184,
        216–17, 240–45, 255–56
    wages, 245
    worker productivity, 120–21
Itema Group, 216–17

Jabil, 84, 179, 195
Japan, 17–18, 19, 26–27, 35, 38, 43, 47,
    52, 53, 82, 104, 106, 156–57, 166,
    193, 209–10, 220–21, 223, 265–66,
    279, 285. *See also specific companies.*
    China, investments in, and, 225–28,
        271
    domestic production, 224–28,
        229–38, 269
    electronics and revitalization, 229–38
    firms in, varieties of capitalism
        model, 39–43, 53
    "full-set-localization" model, 225–28
    "just in time" model, 70–73
    keiretsu, 18, 70
    labor costs, 35, 40, 43, 116–17
    restructuring industry in, 167
Johnson, Cass, 130–31
Johnson Controls, 88
Jones New York, 185, 297
Jordan, 131
Juicy Couture, 256

Kader, Bernd-Michael (Boos Textile),
    246
Kawahara, Haruo (Kenwood), 234–38
Keidanren, 227
Kellwood, 127, 165, 185, 188, 255, 297
Kelly, John E. (IBM), 262–63
Kenwood, 209–10, 234–38, 257
Keynes, John Maynard, 13
Knapp, Joe and Judy, 206–7, 238
Kutaragi, Ken, 155
Kyocera, 177

L. W. Packard, 21–24, 30, 36, 94, 127,
    128–28, 142, 146, 165
Lai, Aling (Thunder Tiger), 181

Lam, Barry (Quanta), 295, 298
Lear Corporation, 86, 87
Lee Chi Enterprises, 93
Lee, Chunli, 226
Legacies, 44–47, 238–41, 248, 258–59, 278–80
Lenovo, 90, 146–48, 271
Lester, Richard K., 292–93
Levi Strauss, 64, 67, 119
Lewis, Chris, 196
Lexus, 87
Liberal market economies, 41, 42
Limited, The, 185
Lin, Ah-Ping (Lee Chi), 93–94
Liu, King (Giant), 181
Liz Claiborne, 14, 34, 47, 85, 127, 128, 165, 182, 185, 186, 187, 188, 213, 221, 222, 255, 297
  Lucky Jeans, 149–50, 256
Logitech, 26
Los Angeles-based business, 132–33, 149–50, 201–2, 206–7, 256, 295
Luce, Stephanie, 97
Lucent Technology, 270, 272, 293, 294
Luen Tai, 188
Luxottica, 68, 122–23, 161–64, 240, 241

Machine That Changed the World, The (Womack et al.), 71
Made in America, 32–33, 71, 142, 290, 291–92
Magna, 86, 88, 89
Malaysia, 117, 131, 179, 209, 235
Mankiw, N. Gregory, 5
Mann, Catherine, 4
Manufacturing, 57, 124, 165–97
  Barbie dolls, 192–94
  cell or pod production, 224–25, 231, 233
  as a commodity, 83
  controlling production in contract manufacturers, 186–87
  decision to remain at home or go offshore, 201–28, 246–47, 262–67

developing nations, 18–19, 117, 120–21, 125, 127
  domestic products vs. imports, 110–12
  exit, 82–85
  in-house, 52, 60–61, 63–64, 136, 146, 157, 159, 161–62, 175–76, 231–38, 252
  integration in, 221–24
  jobs lost, 100–101, 241, 287
  labor costs, 74, 88, 89, 96, 115–26, 208, 212–13, 217, 225, 246–47, 252
  legacies and, 44–47, 238–41, 278–80
  Lego model of production, 61, 63–64, 94, 136. *See also* modularity.
  location and, 102–12, 114–15, 204–5, 217–18, 245–46
  lowering costs, 113–35
  "Made All Over," 247–48
  semiconductor production, 78–82
  speed and, 207–10, 233–34, 236–37, 253–54
  supply-chain integrator, 76–77
  workforce needs, 114, 130, 132, 218–20, 288–92
  See also ODMs; OEMs; *specific countries.*
Marks & Spencer, 204, 240
Marx, Karl, 37, 117
Matsushita, 30, 47, 52, 70, 78, 154, 166, 167, 226–27, 229, 232–33
Mattel's Barbie, 192–94
Mauritius, 106–7, 131
Max Mara, 68, 240, 241
Maytag, 109
McFeely, Drake (W. W. Norton), 207–8
McNealy, Scott (Sun Microsystems), 153
Mediatek, 178
Mentor Graphics, 78, 79
Mexico, 15, 20, 21, 35, 97, 103–5, 109, 110, 120, 127–30, 147, 179, 213–14, 223
  maquiladora plants, 129, 208

Microsoft, 75, 153, 173, 179, 214
Milliken, 71
MIT (Massachusetts Institute of
  Technology), 264, 265, 267,
  272, 296
MIT: *The Impact of Innovation*
  (BankBoston), 272–73
Mita, 142
Mitsubishi, 70, 193
Mitsui, 70
MNCs (multinational corporations),
  96, 102, 223, 234, 280
Modularity, 25–26, 51, 52, 75–90, 96,
  136, 137, 140–41, 158, 179, 192–94,
  218–22, 252–54, 286, 294–95
Morocco, 131
MOSIS foundry system, 78
Motorola, 30, 72, 78, 118, 166, 179,
  226, 227, 234, 254, 271, 293, 294
MSL (Manufacturers' Services
  Limited), 143–44
Murata, 177

NAFTA (North American Free Trade
  Agreement), 22, 109, 127, 130, 213
Nagamori, Shigenobu, 176
National models. *See* Varieties of
  capitalism model.
NEC, 17, 78, 166, 167, 271
Networks and mutual dependence,
  190–97, 253
New Balance, 85, 204–5, 247
New Economy, 7–8
New York City-based business, 132,
  133, 169
Nidec, 77, 176–77, 229
Nike, 30, 141, 203, 204–5
Nissan, 104
Nokia, 175, 227, 255, 271, 272, 280,
  293
Nordhaus, William, 283
Nordstrom's, 128
Nortel, 294
Nvidia, 81, 177

Ohmae, Kenichi, 6, 37, 38, 280
On Semiconductor, 158
Oregon Scientific, 26
Organization, company, 61–72
  American pyramid, 70
  design-only, 177–78
  from ideas to customers, 63
  Japanese "just in time" model, 70–73
  multiplier effect, 77–82, 113
  network and mutual dependence,
    190–97
  new American model (modularity),
    73–90
  pure-play foundry, 79–80, 81, 141,
    178
  vertical integration, 30, 64–67, 78,
    146, 163, 165, 166–69, 201–10
Original design manufacturers (ODMs)
  and contract manufacturers, 15,
    29–30, 49, 75, 77, 82, 83, 84–85,
    90, 141–42, 156–58, 174, 177,
    179–83, 210–16, 222, 223, 236,
    238, 253, 254, 294–95
  competition from, 262–67, 274–75
  controlling production at, 186–89
  position in the network of, 192–94
Original equipment manufacturers
  (OEMs), 84–85, 148, 156, 157,
    165, 177, 180, 262, 294
O'Shea, Bill (Bell Labs), 293
Otellini, Paul S. (Intel), 276
Outsourcing and offshoring, 7, 15, 47,
    49, 51–53, 57, 59, 64, 84, 88,
    125–26, 179–83, 218–22, 233,
    255, 297
  building a competitor and, 262–67
  business-process operations, 95
  communication technologies and,
    14, 57
  as expansion and diversification,
    241–44
  impact on employment, 4–5, 16–24,
    95–96, 97–101, 255–56, 287–88
  integration increased by, 222–24

"intelligent," 258, 269
labor costs, 115–25, 204, 241
location, 87–89, 94–98, 117–18,
    204–5, 217–18, 245
real costs, 115–26
reasons for, 96, 105, 113–36, 241
strategies for, 139–64
supply chains and, 207, 211–16, 223
transportation costs, 213–15
workforce needs, 114, 130, 132

Palmisano, Samuel J., 147–48, 152
Pan, David (Sunyard), 272
Parker, Geoffrey, 83
Path dependencies, 46
Personal computers. See Dell, IBM,
    Sony, Lenovo, Hewlett-Packard,
    Acer, Apple.
Pharmaceuticals, 114–15
Philippines, 118
Philips, 30, 79, 148, 166, 167, 179,
    280
Piore, Michael J., 292–93
Poland, 20, 132
Polegato, Mario Moretti (Geox),
    257–58, 269, 298
Porter, Michael L., 217
Portugal, 217–18
Pou Chen, 30, 85, 148–49, 205
Pringle, 204, 223
Procter & Gamble, 16
Pure-play foundry, 79–80, 81, 141, 167,
    178

Qualcomm, 177
Quanta, 29, 30, 84, 90, 295, 298

R&D, 24–25, 80, 82, 115, 117, 148,
    152–53, 155, 218, 220, 257–58,
    271, 281
    federally funded, 295–96
    job creation and, 25–28, 282–88, 292
    modular production and, 77–82, 141,
        253
    U.S., 281, 292–97

Ralph Lauren, 128, 185, 186, 188, 222,
    255
RCA, 67
Realtek, 178
Reebok, 205
Relocation, 59, 117–18, 204–5. See also
    Outsourcing and off-shoring
Renesas, 193
Ricardo, David, 36
Roach, Stephen A., 25
Rollins, Kevin D. (Dell), 150
Romania, 20, 87, 121–22, 125, 132,
    191–92, 196, 210–11, 242–43, 258
RosettaNet, 75
Russia, 15, 16, 19, 90, 96, 102, 117

Sàfilo, 68, 161–64, 240
Samsung, 8, 30, 49, 52, 146, 154, 158,
    165, 165, 167–68, 171, 254, 280
Samuelson, Paul, 5–6, 36
Sanders, Jerry, 167–68
SanDisk, 177
Sanmina-SCI, 84, 147, 174, 179, 195
Sanyo, 158, 226–27, 231
Schwinn, 181, 183
Scotland, 147, 204, 223
Self-Esteem, 297–98
Semiconductor production, 78–82,
    113–14, 140, 141, 263–65, 269–75
Sharp, 77, 154, 166–67, 229, 233, 254,
    255, 263
Shimaseiki, 108
Siemens, 30, 41, 78, 84, 88, 95, 166,
    167, 183, 271
    Automotive, 88
Silicon Labs, 81
Singapore, 19, 79, 117, 174, 275
Singer Sewing Machine, 64, 65, 66
Slaughter, Matthew, 4
SMaL, 25–26, 27, 253
SMIC (Semiconductor Manufacturing
    International Corporation), 20, 79,
    178, 270, 274
Sodini, Charles, 25–26
Software

companies, 33–34, 114
technologies and outsourcing,
    211–12, 275
Solectron, 30, 75, 84, 95, 179, 195
Solstiss, 176, 256
Sony, 35, 47, 49–50, 51–52, 62, 78, 94,
    95, 148, 150, 166, 167, 168, 179,
    180, 226, 227, 231, 254, 255
    "Big Bang" strategy, 153–60
Soskice, David, 41–42
South Korea, 19, 74, 79, 117, 124,
    167–68, 221, 227, 255, 265, 271,
    275
Spain, 173–74. *See also* Zara.
Spivak, Herb (New Balance), 204, 217
Sri Lanka, 131
ST Microelectronics, 35, 79, 174–75,
    185
Stringer, Sir Howard (Sony), 154
Sturgeon, Timothy, 85
Sumitomo, 70
Sun Microsystems, 81, 153
Surowiecki, James, 62

Taiwan, 19, 20, 35, 49, 51–52, 75, 77,
    78–79, 81, 84, 113, 114, 117, 120,
    125, 128, 129–30, 132, 141, 148,
    158, 165, 167–68, 178, 179–83,
    192, 193, 221, 223, 230, 233, 260,
    265, 270
    bicycle company in, 93–94, 181, 262
Takashima, Akira (Fujitsu), 137, 231, 233
Target, 187
TCL, 254, 271
Technology Forecasters, 124–25
Technology, 8, 17, 18, 19, 35
    birthrights and U.S. business, 275–77
    modularity in production and, 25–27,
    52, 75–76, 136, 140–41, 158
    See also specific technologies.
Telecommunications, 14, 57, 26–27,
    108, 109, 111, 143, 254–55, 271
Teradyne, 263–65, 267
Texas Instruments, 35, 77, 79, 81, 82,
    158, 166, 175, 175

Textiles and apparel, 8, 19, 21–24, 26,
    33, 34–35, 45, 50, 51, 53, 67–69,
    71–72, 85, 100–101, 105–8,
    109–10, 116–17, 120–24, 126–35,
    142, 168–69, 176, 182, 183–92,
    196–97, 203–7, 210–17, 238,
    239–47, 252, 255–56, 297–98
Thailand, 131
Théry, Edmond, 11
Thomson Company, 271
3Com, 269, 272
Thunder Tiger, 181–82
Tie Rack, 68, 240
Tommy Hilfiger, 239
Toray, 116–17, 167
Toshiba, 17, 77, 78, 155, 159, 160, 166,
    167, 236
Toyota, 8, 43, 60–61, 87, 104, 176
    NUMMI, 71
Toy manufacturing, 192–94, 208
Toys "R" Us, 38, 181, 192–94
TPV Vision, Inc., 148–49
Trade, 16, 20, 38, 104, 110–12
    agreements, 20, 21, 22, 96, 106, 109,
    127
    barriers, 12, 107, 108–12, 118, 173
    end of protection, 126–35
    open borders, current, and, 13–14, 37
    practices, foreign, 17–18
    protectionism, 284
    Structural Impediment Initiative, 38
    tariffs, 11, 12, 13, 14, 20, 102, 103,
    110, 111, 204
    textile/apparel quotas, 38, 105–8,
    110, 126–35, 297
    U.S. exports-imports, 17, 18
    U.S. trade deficit, 16, 38
TRW, 86, 88
Tsinghua School of Management,
    272–73
TSMC (Taiwan Semiconductor
    Manufacturing Company), 35,
    78, 80, 81–82, 113, 274, 275
Tunisia, 131
Turkey, 131, 132

Ukraine, 132, 174
Ulvac Technologies, 80, 141, 220–21
UMC (United Microelectronics Corporation), 79, 167, 178
Uniqlo, 26–27
United Kingdom, 5, 40, 101, 119, 177, 210–11, 240, 241, 279
United States businesses, 23, 24, 132–33, 238
  American pyramid, 70
  domestic production, 201–10, 237, 269
  educating and retraining workers, 288–92, 297
  foreign investors, 102–3, 109
  government role in, 280–97
  high-technology areas, birthright and, 274, 275–77
  innovation, 285, 292–97
  labor costs, 3, 4, 16–24, 43, 74, 88, 89, 245, 247, 256
  legacies and emerging industry, 278–80
  legacy of openness, 282–88
  Los Angeles-based business, 132–33, 149–50, 201–2, 206–7, 256, 295
  "Made in the U.S.A." label, 151–52, 201–9
  MNCs, 96, 97, 223
  modularity in, 73–90, 140–41, 286, 294
  New York City-based business, 132, 133, 169
  vertical integration, 30, 64–67, 78, 166, 201–10

Valeo, 88
Varieties of capitalism model, 36, 39–43, 47, 53, 279, 285

Verisilicon, 274
Vertical companies, 30, 64–67, 78, 146, 163, 165, 166–69, 201–10
  deverticalizing, 88
VIA, 81, 178
Vietnam, 123, 124, 132, 205
Vimicro, 270, 274
Visteon, 88
Vodaphone, 254–55
Vogel, Stephen K., 225
Volkswagen, 62, 67, 87, 103, 104, 105

Wal-Mart, 49, 65, 128, 162, 163, 187, 188–90, 215
Walter Mieli Spa, 244
Warnaco Swimwear, 130, 187, 223
White, Harry Dexter, 13
Williams, Roger, 130
Winser, Kim (Pringle), 204
Womack, James, 71
World Bank, 6, 13, 119, 131
World Is Flat, The (Friedman), 268
Wrinn, Joe (Teradyne), 263–65
WTO (World Trade Organization), 6–7, 14, 96, 105, 106, 109–10, 126

Xilinx, 177

Yasuda, 70
Young, John, 57
Yue Yuen, 148
Yun Jong Yong, 168

Zane, Bob (Liz Claiborne), 14, 213, 214
Zara (Spain), 8, 35, 49, 165, 168–69, 171, 238, 252, 254, 255
Zeiss (Carl Zeiss Group), 160
Zhao, Chunjun, 272
Zoff, 26–27, 163, 255

The MIT Industrial Performance Center Globalization Team

Top row, left to right: Charles Sodini, Douglas Fuller. *Bottom row, left to right:* Richard Lester, Tayo Akinwande, Edward Cunningham, Edward Steinfeld, Suzanne Berger, Dan Breznitz, Teresa Lynch, Sara Jane McCaffrey, Marcos Ancelovici, Timothy Sturgeon.